The New York Times

SEAFOOD COOKBOOK

The New York Times

SEAFOOD
COOKBOOK

250 Recipes for
More Than 70 Kinds of
Fish and Shellfish

Edited by
FLORENCE FABRICANT

St. Martin's Press
New York

www.stmartins.com

Design by Kathryn Parise

LIBRARY OF CONGRESS CATALOGING-IN-PUBLICATION DATA

The New York times seafood cookbook : 250 recipes for more than 70 kinds
    of fish and shellfish / [compiled by] Florence Fabricant.—1st ed.
        p. cm.
    Includes index (p.335).
    ISBN 0-312-31231-8
    1. Cookery (Seafood) I. New York times.
TX747.N5 2003
641.6'92—dc21

                                                                  2003043162

First Edition: July 2003

10 9 8 7 6 5 4 3 2 1

CONTENTS

ACKNOWLEDGMENTS

To begin, it is to the many reporters and contributors to the food pages of *The New York Times,* first as the Living Section, then as Dining In-Dining Out, that I owe my deepest gratitude. Thanks to the resources of *The New York Times,* their fine work as food-savvy reporters taking the culinary pulse of New York City, the rest of the country and indeed the world, has made this book possible, and given it an uncommon richness and unique authority. I am also grateful to have been among them.

The contribution of the many editors who inspired and sculpted the articles and recipes, the copy editors who fine-tune them, and the art directors, artists and photographers who so brilliantly set them forth, must also be recognized.

I also wish to acknowledge the chefs who have been responsible for changing the way we appreciate and prepare seafood today, who opened their kitchens, and who generously shared their recipes and techniques. It is no exaggeration to say that the world is also indebted to the scientists and environmentalists who have made us aware of what seafood represents in the food chain, and how best to protect this precious and delicious resource. They, too, influenced this book.

I was honored that Mike Levitas suggested that I tackle the job of assembling and editing his excellent idea for a cookbook and who actively participated in making it a reality. At St. Martin's Press, Marian Lizzi and her staff, especially Julie Mente, helped bring it about in superb shape. Steve Snider, the art director, Phillip Pascuzzo, the cover designer, and Kathryn Parise, the book designer, at St. Martin's Press were responsible for the book's elegant eye-appeal.

Also deserving my thanks for their hard work in helping to organize the voluminous wealth of available material were Tomi Murata, Deborah Leiderman, Brian Fidelman, Kris Ensminger and Diane Weintraub Pohl.

I owe special thanks to Bruce Stark, who was there for me whenever incompatible formats needed to be put on speaking terms. And, of course, to Richard Fabricant, who cheered me on as I wrestled yet another book project to the ground.

INTRODUCTION

It's not exactly culinary archaeology. But exploring back issues of *The New York Times* to find what has been written in its food pages about seafood and seafood cookery is to discover social, cultural, environmental and economic change, even over just the past decade or two. Globalization, ecology, health issues, cooking techniques and equipment, travel and tastes have all affected what kinds of fish and shellfish are on the plate, and how they are prepared.

Around the middle of the last century, Americans ate much less fish than they do today, less than 10 pounds per person annually, compared with close to 20 pounds now. The numbers are paltry in comparison with those for countries like Japan and Norway, but they represent a decided shift in tastes.

What was once merely the Friday blue plate special is now eaten every day, prepared with much more care and more stylishly appointed. The summer clambake or steamed lobsters in New England, smoked salmon for a New York Sunday brunch, oysters in a fancy San Francisco restaurant, or regional specialties like crayfish in New Orleans and walleye in Wisconsin have become commonplace nationwide. Reservations in elegant seafood restaurants are as sought-after as tables in French haute cuisine establishments. Tuna and sardines are no longer eaten just from cans.

And all the while, the variety and the quality of the seafood available to chefs and in retail markets have improved dramatically. Seafood cookery is as far removed from a fillet of sole dusted with paprika, run under the broiler and served with boiled rice as salad is from a bowl of iceberg lettuce.

It's more of a challenge to do justice to a lovely halibut steak than to toss mesclun with a good shallot vinaigrette, but with the quality of fish that's often available, good fish cooking is actually less daunting than in the past, especially with the heavy-duty nonstick cookware that is sold for preparing it, and other ingredients such as fine olive oil and fresh herbs to enhance it.

A Changing Market and Changing Tastes

Where locally caught fish, such as flounder in the East, redfish in the South and salmon in the West, once dominated the market, it's not unusual now to find dozens of kinds of fish and shellfish, domestic and imported, wild and farmed, on the ice and on menus across the country.

Squid, or calamari, once available for around 30 cents a pound but only in Italian and Greek neighborhoods, is now fried and served from coast to coast, in fast food outlets and fine restaurants. Once discarded as a "trash" fish by fishermen, the hideous monkfish began to be appreciated in the late 1970's by the French chefs who were arriving in America in droves. Consumers became familiar with it, and now it is widely sold, even in supermarkets. The price, of course, has quadrupled. Skate is another former discard that is now prized and even threatened with overfishing.

Thanks to the proliferation of Japanese restaurants in this country, tuna has gone from being exclusively a canned product accounting for the bulk of American fish consumption, to a popular fish sold fresh. And Americans happily feast on sushi, food that most once identified as bait, and they line up for shimmering slices of raw mackerel and meaty dominoes of bluefin. They have ventured into the strange domain of uni, the blobby dollops of sea-urchin roe that can make strong men blanch.

The global nature of the seafood market has distributors promoting fish from North and South America, Europe, Africa and Asia. Fish is shipped frozen or freshly caught and sent by air in a day, so the markets are no longer wedded to the local or seasonal catch.

Even as the country's beloved cod and flounder, bluefin tuna and native swordfish have become scarce, tons of fresh, mild-tasting, white-fleshed fish from far-flung seas are softening the pain of the dwindling supplies. The domestic market routinely imports twice as much seafood, in dollar value, as it harvests from American waters. Think shrimp.

Yellowtail and greentail snapper from South America, onaga and moonfish from Hawaii, turbot from the North Sea, and red mullet or "rouget" and sardines from North Africa have turned airports into fish ports. And they may make the hard times of American fisheries a boon for food lovers in this country, while giving local fish stocks at least a chance to recover.

Today the best-priced and highest-quality fish around are as likely to hail from Icelandic waters or the Indian Ocean as from Cape May or Cape Cod. And some of the immigrant species are richer, more interesting fish.

How these and more commonplace varieties are prepared has affected their popularity.

Americans traveling abroad have tasted bouillabaisse in Marseille, moules-frites in Ostend, grilled sardines in Morocco, butter-basted langoustines in Paris, clams in black bean sauce in China, hamachi in Kyoto, ceviche in Peru and squid in its ink in Venice and Spain. Many willingly order these dishes in restaurants at home and will go into their kitchens to prepare them, often using recipes from chefs and other food authorities who have written for *The New York Times.*

Is there some new fish floating into view? Suddenly popular sablefish, rare white king salmon, curious monkfish livers and yabbies imported from Australia are a few of the news-making varieties that have been described and explained in the Dining pages of *The New York Times,* with recipes. Are warnings needed for potential hazards in eating a fish like escolar, or about alarmingly diminishing supplies of swordfish? The weekly Dining section of *The Times* and the paper's Sunday food page have covered issues like these, too.

Even the ingredients that accompany the seafood and were once considered exotic have become readily available, as recipes that have appeared in *The Times* since the late 1980's clearly show. The ubiquitous wedge of lemon, drawn butter and parsley potato have been moved aside in favor of extra virgin olive oil, toasted sesame oil, fine vinegars, unusual spices like smoked Spanish paprika, wasabi, fresh ginger and jasmine rice, all of which are widely sold in supermarkets, specialty food stores and online. More than merely listing ingredients, *The Times* explains how to select that olive oil from the dozens on store shelves, and what balsamic vinegar is and how to use it.

Environmental Concerns

The access to the global resources also comes at a price—one similar to that inflicted on cod fishermen from Cape Ann to Nova Scotia: dwindling supplies.

Slimehead, a New Zealand fish given the new, improved name of orange roughy, quickly became so popular that 80 percent of the fishery was wiped out in less than a decade. New Zealand took action by putting stringent restrictions on the catch, and the fish all but disappeared from the market. Estimates are that the fishery will be restored in a few years. Orange roughy may become available again, but in more limited quantities.

Patagonian toothfish, marketed as Chilean sea bass, was once unknown to diners outside South America. But a taste for the succulent, snowy fillets was so easily acquired that scientists now say the Antarctic fishery is threatened with depletion and are seeking to strengthen international controls.

More information on the ecological and environmental status of various kinds of fish is available from the Monterey Bay Aquarium at www.monterey bayaquarium.org, and the Living Oceans program of the National Audubon Society at www.audubon.org. These organizations even provide wallet cards with lists of seafood and approval ratings to take along when shopping for fish or when dining out.

Aquaculture

Fish caught in nets or on lines are not yet a thing of the past. But the number of fish raised on farms has doubled in the last decade. This increase in aquaculture is one solution to the problem of depleted supply, but it can also be detrimental to the environment.

Catfish has replaced cotton as the most widely harvested product in Mississippi. Like salmon and shrimp, it is on the National Marine Fisheries Service's Top 10 list of the most consumed fish in the country, although just 20 years ago it was rarely eaten more than 50 miles from the banks of the Mississippi River. Half of the shrimp eaten in this country–and shrimp is hands down the most popular seafood in America–comes from farms.

Salmon is farm-raised in nearly every country with access to cold, deep water. If you order salmon in a restaurant or buy it in a market, you will almost certainly get a farmed fish. Never mind that serving farmed Atlantic salmon from April through September, when wild fish from the Pacific Northwest and Alaska are in season, is the rough equivalent of offering cellophane-wrapped tomatoes in August. What makes farm-raised Atlantic salmon, which is a different species from the Pacific varieties, so popular is its mild but rich flavor from a high fat content (about 10 percent of body weight) and the reliable supply of fresh, consistent fish. Its price is about half that of wild, more muscular and deeply flavorful Pacific salmons, the king or chinook, the silver or coho, and the sockeye.

Aquaculture has also been responsible for introducing varieties like delicate tilapia from Africa, rich, fresh sturgeon from California, rosy arctic char from Iceland and Canada, bay scallops in their shells from Washington, assorted shrimp and prawns from Asia and more than a dozen special kinds of oysters, in a commerce that has gone on since ancient Roman times, including Little Skookums, Fanny Bays and Fisher Islands from the Pacific Northwest and the East Coast. Farm-raised mussels, clustered on cords in seawater off Prince Edward Island, are cleaner and more consistent than mussels gathered by baymen at the shore.

Shellfish and those species of finfish that spend at least some of their lives in freshwater, such as trout, arctic char, salmon, catfish and striped bass, are most easily farmed. And even the variety of striped bass that's farmed is a hybrid, and not the same as the robust wild fish that has made a comeback on the East Coast. But there have been recent experimental successes with a variety of saltwater species, such as halibut, mahimahi and flounder. In Europe, some Mediterranean fish such as branzino and orata are now being farmed, and, have become more widely available in America.

Environmental concerns about aquaculture may seem picayune when compared to those about raising cattle, which have been blamed for everything from the destruction of rain forests to famine. But aquaculture is following the path blazed by the farming of land animals. Part of that path, a part that concerns many experts, is the use of antibiotics and other drugs to treat illnesses, and the impact that the fish, their feed and the pollution from their waste products will eventually have on seas still teeming with wild fish. In Norway, which pioneered salmon farming in the 1970's, fjords have been closed to swimming due to the concentration of fish waste from farms.

Health

Since many people eat fish because they believe it is more healthful than eating other animals—or at least less harmful—another question remains: Is farm-raised fish as healthful as wild fish?

Farmed fish tend to have more fat than the wild. This may not necessarily be a bad thing, however. For example, as total fat increases in salmon, so does the amount of omega-3 fatty acids, widely believed to protect against heart disease and other illnesses, including breast cancer and even clinical depression. Very dark-fleshed fish like sardines, tuna, mackerel and herring have the most Omega-3 fatty acids, and trout and salmon are also well endowed with them.

Although fish farming is regulated, enforcement is limited. And questions have been raised by consumers, chefs and environmental groups about the purity of the fish, its bland flavor and the impact of aquaculture on local and global environments.

A growing demand and profits have led to infusions of capital from multinational corporations–including fish processors, feed producers and drug companies. Farmers can increase the fat content of the farmed salmon's diet to make it extrafatty, which is how sushi chefs prefer it, or they can reduce or withhold fat to make it extralean, which is how the makers of smoked fish like it.

They can feed it more omega-3 fatty acids to improve its nutritional profile. They can augment the feed with pigments–without which its flesh would be pale–to give it the brilliant orange color consumers expect. And they can adjust the feed content to give it a distinctive but rather mild flavor.

At the same time that these concerns are surfacing, the federal government and the industry are addressing concerns about seafood safety. In 1994 a set of standards and regulations called H.A.C.C.P., or Hazard Analysis and Critical Control Point, was set up by the Food and Drug Administration to improve safety in meat and poultry processing facilities. Seafood was added the following year.

But even before H.A.C.C.P., some seafood safety measures were in place. All shellfish, for example, must come from water that is monitored and tested by state and local authorities and must be shipped in bags that are tagged to show the source, so if there is contamination, it can be traced. Problems that may arise from toxins, such as ciguatera from some tropical fish and vibrio bacteria from oysters, are now widely publicized.

And though you will now see sushi chefs wearing gloves, when they are trained in Japan, their first lesson is about hygiene. Eating sushi and sashimi poses minimal health risk; the Food and Drug Administration has reported a relatively small number of parasite infections from fish. Freshwater fish are never served raw, and any parasites in ocean fish are killed by freezing.

A new understanding of the importance of fast-chilling fresh-caught seafood has greatly improved the quality and safety of what is shipped and sold. *The New York Times* has even advised sport fishermen to keep a cooler of ice on board and to put bluefish in it as soon as it is caught.

Fish-market employees are trained to avoid cross-contamination, so that raw seafood does not come in contact with cooked fish, like shrimp, at the retail level. This is something that the home cook should also practice.

For the time being, more of the seafood that is consumed in America still comes from the wild, and not from immense saltwater tanks lined up in the California desert, man-made ponds in the South or pens strung on the ocean floor. Though the amount of farmed fish sold in the United States has doubled in the last decade, in the same period, the amount of fish sold that was caught by conventional means more than doubled, a clear indication of the increased popularity of fish.

But the day when diners speak lovingly of fish that swim freely in the sea, just as they do now of free-range chickens, may not be far off. For now, however, seafood remains the only important category of food that is still hunted.

And on average, it also remains the most expensive protein on the plate, which is why care in its purchase, storage and preparation is so essential. The cost also accounts in part for the trepidation that many cooks feel when they consider cooking fish.

Selecting Seafood

Judging Fish

There are two kinds of cooks: those who go into the market to see what seems to be fresh and appealing before deciding what will be on the dinner menu, and those who shop armed with a list, their recipes and menu decided in advance. Learning to be the first kind of cook is a challenge that takes experience and confidence.

The problem in shopping from a fixed list is that while a fish market is certain to have shrimp and salmon, it may lack fresh tuna in good condition, impeccably fresh cod or a lovely whole red snapper. And rather than settle, it's better to know how to substitute, and to be flexible.

Seafood is fragile and highly perishable. Unless you know that the fish you are buying came off the boat that very morning, it's best to to use fish the same day it's bought. Shellfish, including unopened clams and mussels, cleaned shrimp or crabmeat that's been cooked, is more resilient, providing it is kept cold. After all, 100 years ago they shipped oysters from the East Coast clear to Chicago in winter by barge and rail.

Cooks living in coastal areas, or near lakes and rivers that have important commercial fisheries, should pay attention to seasonality. Fish out of season in one region may have been either frozen or shipped from afar.

But as much as today's good cook and connoisseur might prize freshness, it's nonetheless important not to disparage frozen fish. Once the last choice in the supermarket, frozen fish has new respectability now that varieties like whole salmon are put into blast freezers on board fishing vessels as soon as they are caught and cleaned, resulting in fish that, if carefully thawed, cannot be distinguished from fresh–even by as esteemed an authority as Julia Child–and might even be better.

What is essential–and is rarely seen–is truth in marketing, so that seafood that was once frozen but is sold thawed is labeled as such. At the very least it will prevent consumers from refreezing the fish and greatly damaging its cell structure. Similarly, the consumer should be wary of the tricks, such as bleaches and preservatives, used to enhance some varieties like sea scallops. The days of using cookie cutters to slice disks of monkfish to sell as scallops are over, largely because monkfish has become too expensive. But are the scallops sitting in some telltale whitish fluid? Do not buy.

Fish sold in retail markets is often not as impeccable as what chefs buy. Few consumers demand to know whether the fish came off a day boat that did not stay at sea for a week or more, or whether it was netted or line-caught. How the fish was caught can make a difference, which is why chefs will pay a higher price for sea bass that was not hauled up in a big net and banged around with hundreds of other fish, or for the halibut that was the last one caught on a line with hundreds of hooks, so it will be taken onto the boat first.

Consumers rarely have the luxury of such choices, which is why knowing how to judge fish in the market is important. Freshness usually determines flavor and the overall quality of the dish.

The basic rules that apply to whole fish, that the eyes should be bright and the gills red, are often irrelevant. Though any fish market will clean and fillet a fresh whole fish while you wait–and it remains the best way to buy fish–most consumers do not bother. They see the fillets and pick and choose the size they want. Also, many kinds of fish, such as tuna and monkfish, are never on display whole, in the round.

So how do you judge a halibut steak, a cod fillet or a piece of tuna?

First of all, fresh fish has no fishy smell. If there is any odor at all, it should be mildly oceanic. White-fleshed fish has an almost pearly transluscence when very fresh, and it should look as though it will spring back if you touched it. It should never be dull, spongy-looking (which might indicate fish that's been frozen and improperly thawed), dried or dull white around the edges, cracking or sitting in liquid. Luster and shine indicate freshness, while drooping and browning are signs of fatigue. Some fish, especially the darker-fleshed varieties, have a deep red bloodline. The smaller the bloodline the more likely the fish was properly handled after it was caught.

Evaluating shellfish in the market is easier. Lobsters should be active, uncooked crabs (including soft-shells) alive, mollusks closed or, if slightly agape, they should close when touched. And shrimp in the shell should have no browning or black spots.

Knowing How to Substitute

Suppose you do not find the fillet of cod you had planned on serving for dinner?

Throughout this book, for each type of seafood, appropriate substitutes are suggested. Sometimes they are not the same for a fish in steak form as for the fillet or the whole fish. What is paramount is not necessarily the similarity but, rather, how the fish behaves in the pan and in the particular recipes in the book. In general, the main considerations are flavor, texture, fat content, size and, to a lesser extent, bone structure.

There are no hard-and-fast rules. Indeed, some fish that might seem easy to interchange, such as fillets of farmed striped bass for wild, are very different. The rich, muscular flesh of big wild striped bass, which run six pounds or more, bears almost no resemblance to farmed striped bass, a hybrid fish with soft texture and little flavor.

Many of the oilier, dark-fleshed fish make good substitutes for each other—mackerel for bluefish and sardines for red mullet, for example. But white-fleshed fish are not so easily interchanged.

A recipe that can be prepared with monkfish, which has relatively little grain and a dense, almost lobsterlike quality, would not be as successful with red snapper. Swordfish can be used in place of tuna in some recipes, but not if the fish is to be cooked rare. Though swordfish dries out when overcooked, it is rubbery if it's not at least medium-well.

When shopping for seafood, if you start by knowing the characteristics of the fish you plan to buy or want to cook, you can then talk to a clerk at the store to find out which other fish are likely to deliver the same qualities.

The flake, the overlapping layers of flesh in the fillet, is a critical factor. For a fillet that has a broad flake, evident from the grain or subtle whitish striations you can see, it's best to choose another type of fish with similar grain. And fish with a larger flake tends to be relatively forgiving, harder to overcook and therefore capable of reaching gastronomic heights unmatched by the more delicate varieties.

For fillets that are flat and thin, like flounder, try to find another flat, thin fillet, like gray sole, fluke or catfish. Sometimes staying in the same fish family is helpful, which is why fluke, flounder and sole can replace each other. But halibut, which is a much larger flatfish, would not be a good substitute.

If you have a Mexican recipe with a spicy salsa but the market has no red snapper, look for another fish from around the Caribbean, such as mahimahi, because it should complement the seasonings nicely.

Cuts and Portion Size for Finfish

There are essentially three ways to buy fish: whole, steaks and fillets. Within these categories there are certain distinctions.

Whole fish: These can be as small as whitebait, to be fried whole, with dozens to a serving, or as large as a 10-pound wild striped bass or king salmon to roast for 10 people. On the bone calculate about a pound of fish per serving. A fish that weighs about a pound, like trout, will provide a single serving. A two- to two-and-one-half-pound black bass serves two, and so on. Whole fish can simply be cleaned and gutted for roasting or grilling or, with smaller fish like whiting, smelts and flatfish like sole, sautéed. Another option is to have the fish filleted but left whole, so it can be stuffed. Mackerel is prepared in this fashion in Istanbul, with a savory rice and pine-nut stuffing scented with cinnamon. Or a whole fish can be boned and butterflied, for grilling or sautéing. Arctic char is an excellent choice for this treatment.

Few fish dishes are as impressive as a whole roasted or grilled fish brought to the table or set out on a buffet. And serving whole fish is usually not a complicated affair. The general rule is to take a sharp knife and make a cut just along the top or dorsal edge of the fish. This cut will release the top fillet from the bony edge of the fish. Then cut along the belly edge and, using a spatula, a knife and fork or even a large spoon, lift off the top fillet. If the fish is properly cooked, the bone will come away easily and can be removed along with the head. Then serve the bottom fillet.

Steaks: What distinguishes a steak from a fillet is that it is a crosscut slice of the fish, usually about an inch thick. Depending on the size of the fish and its bone structure, a steak can be a thick boneless slab–think swordfish or tuna–or it can have a bone running through the center, like salmon or halibut. Steaks are best broiled or grilled, though sautéing and roasting are other options. A portion of boneless steak fish is usually around six ounces, or eight ounces with bone.

Fillets: In contrast to the steak, a fillet is cut through the length of the fish, off the bone, to make a long slab with the grain running its length, or on the bias. Depending on the preparation, about six ounces is an ample serving for one person. Though most shoppers purchase fillets out of convenience, it's better to select a good-looking whole fish and have it filleted at the market. Take the head and bones home to make stock.

Fillets of whole fish are not uniform in shape, and this must be considered when more than one serving is cut from a large fillet. The fillet is thicker near the head and narrows toward the tail. Furthermore, near the thickest part of the fillet there is usually a thin, flat area, called the belly flap, which is fine to serve when a single six-ounce fillet of sea bass or red snapper, for example, is used for each portion. But the belly flap should be removed and either discarded or saved for making stock when a large fillet, like a three-pound slab of salmon, is used for several servings.

Depending on the recipe, you may or may not want the skin left on the fillet. With some fish, like salmon, striped bass and sea bass, the skin of the fillet can be seared for an attractive, crisp contrast to the tender, voluptuous flesh.

With fillets of some fish, notably salmon, it's important to remove the pin bones, the small vertical bones that are not taken out during filleting. While some fish markets do this, it's easily done at home with a small pair of needlenose pliers, or heavy tweezers. Lightly run your hand over the surface of the fish, and if you feel these little bones sticking out, yank them straight out.

Some fillets also have a right side and a wrong side. With flounder, for example, the skin side of the fillet will be darker, something you may want to take into account before serving, especially with fish that is baked, steamed or poached.

Portion Size for Shellfish

It's easier to buy shellfish than finfish. With many varieties, you know just how much everyone is likely to eat. A whole one-and-one-half-pound lobster, six oysters, three big sea scallops, six jumbo shrimp and so on. When the seafood is all meat, no shell, the rule of thumb is four to six ounces per person. With shell, about a pound. Of course, how the seafood is prepared will also affect the quantity. You need less lobster in a risotto or pasta sauce than if you're serving lobsters simply boiled or broiled.

All seafood should be kept refrigerated, wrapped in plastic film, until it is ready to be cooked. If you will not be returning home as soon as you have made a purchase, ask the fish market to put a frozen gel pack in with your order.

Preparing Seafood

There are more than a dozen ways to prepare seafood, and not all are appropriate for every variety.

1. Raw

Only the freshest fish is suitable for serving raw, and even then there are limitations. Freshwater fish, like trout or whitefish, should never be served raw. Fish that may harbor parasites, like cod, are also to be avoided. A sushi bar menu will provide an excellent guide to what fish can be served raw.

Clams and oysters (and occasionally mussels) are routinely served raw, on the half shell. They should be opened just before serving and not rinsed. Fresh scallops, either sea scallops in thin slices or bay scallops, are also delicious raw, but be sure they are fresh, never frozen.

Among the ways to serve raw fish are tartare, made with fine dicings of fish; sashimi, made with small slabs of fish about one-quarter inch thick; tiradito, which is South American sashimi, with the fish cut in thin slices and seasoned with a piquant sauce; and usuzukuri, like carpaccio, with fish shaved in the sheerest slices of all.

2. Marinating

The most popular style of marinated fish is ceviche, which can be made with fish or shellfish, including squid and scallops cut in uniform dice. Years ago, ceviches were made by marinating the fish overnight in an acid-based mixture, usually with citrus juice. The result was a seafood cocktail in which the fish's flavor and texture were completely changed. The long marinating was a kind of pickling. Today, the style is for much briefer marinating, an hour or so, with fresher-tasting results.

Escabeche is another marinated dish, but the fish is fully cooked first.

Fresh herring is often marinated in season, to make matjes herring. And fresh anchovies are often marinated in vinegar, then used in salads. Another technique, using sugar, salt and herbs, cures salmon for gravlax.

Marinating can also enhance the flavor of seafood that is to be cooked by other means, notably grilling, broiling and roasting. The marinating is for flavor, not tenderness. But most fish should not sit in an acid marinade for more than an hour, otherwise there will be changes in the cellular structure. And before any marinade is used as a sauce, it must be heated thoroughly, for safety.

3. Poaching

Poaching is the low-fat technique for preparing fish and is especially suited to fish that will be served cold. Whole fish, thick fillets or steaks are submerged in a well-seasoned fish broth (court bouillon) and barely simmered until done. Another poaching method is to place the fish in the liquid, bring it to a simmer, shut off the heat and allow the fish to remain in the broth until it cools to room temperature. This technique is a safeguard against overcooking. Smaller portions of fish—an individual fillet or fish steak, for example—can be "poached" for two minutes in a microwave oven, without any liquid.

For great succulence, fish can also be poached in an olive oil bath. This method, similar to making confit, is excellent for fresh tuna, producing thick chunks that resemble canned tuna in oil, but which are far more delicious.

4. Boiling

Some kinds of seafood call for cooking in water or broth that's not quite at a rollicking boil, but is stronger than the bare shiver of the poaching bath. Live crabs, crayfish and lobsters must be boiled to kill them fast. Peppery seasonings are often used to flavor crabs and crayfish. Shrimp should also be added to boiling water or court bouillon, but often they're cooked through before the liquid has even had a chance to return to the boil. Squid sliced into rings require no more than a minute in boiling water; longer than that will toughen them.

With some quick-cooking seafood, like shrimp, it's a good idea to have a bowl of ice water nearby in which the seafood can be chilled to stop the cooking as soon as it is drained.

5. Steaming

Small whole fish, fillets and steaks can all be steamed. Steaming is a gentle cooking method, one that virtually guarantees against overcooking. The fish can either be seasoned first or simply steamed on a layer of flavorful ingredients, such as pieces of fresh ginger, sprigs of herbs, scallions, slices of lemon or roasted chili. If the seafood is steamed on a plate, the liquid it gives off can be captured to use as a sauce. Fish can also be steamed in a microwave oven.

Mollusks like mussels and clams are frequently steamed until they open, then served in the steaming broth.

Another steaming technique is to cook seafood wrapped in foil, in an envelope of parchment or covered with banana leaves, grape leaves, cabbage leaves or corn husks. The packages can be steamed or baked. Baking fish covered with a thick crust of salt or a salt and flour dough is also tantamount to steaming it.

6. Sautéing

A popular method for preparing many kinds of seafood is sautéing. A small amount of fat is heated in a skillet or a sauté pan, and then anything from whole fillets to small pieces of fish or shellfish like shrimp is browned. For effective sautéing, for achieving a golden finish, the seafood must be dry before it goes into the pan. Sometimes a light coating of flour, bread crumbs or cracker crumbs will add a crusty seal.

Fish can also be sautéed on the skin side, to brown and crisp it, then finished by baking in the oven. And dishes like fish stews often begin with sautéing seafood, including raw, cut-up lobster in the shell.

Stir-frying is essentially a sautéing method, using small pieces of seafood to which ingredients for a sauce are added.

7. Frying

In deep-frying, pieces of seafood are cooked in hot oil. The oil must be at least two inches deep and heated to about 375 degrees. The seafood usually has a crumb, flour or batter coating. When serving deep-fried food, bring it to the table as soon as it has been cooked and briefly drained.

8. Grilling

Grilling means putting the seafood in contact with direct heat from below. Because fish cooks quickly, it's important that the grill fire be hot, otherwise the fish will be done before it has acquired an attractive burnish and perhaps the merest char on the surface, which is, after all, one of the main reasons to light a grill.

Whole fish, steaks and thick fillets are best to grill and will be easiest to turn. Well-oiled grates are necessary. The hotter the fire, the less likely the fish will stick. The surface of the fish should be dried on paper towels, even if it has been marinated. A gloss of oil should then be applied. The fish can be basted with its marinade as it cooks. A wide spatula is extremely useful for turning the fish. If the fish is sufficiently brown before it has cooked through, move it to a place on the grill where the fire is not as intense.

Whole fish for the grill will benefit from having a bunch of herbs stuffed into the cavity. Some recipes call for scoring each side in three or four places and adding seasonings, such as a pesto. It's a trade-off, because the juices will run out of the slits and the fish might dry somewhat. Placing fish to be grilled on a bed of herbs such as fennel fronds, branches of rosemary or bunches of mint will certainly add a whiff of flavor and also make the fish easier to turn.

Grilling is not suited for recipes that require the cooking juices. Lobsters, for example, can be split and put on a grill, but if the cut side is facedown to sear the flesh, they will dry out. Grilling is not recommended. Clams and oysters will open on a hot grill, but putting them on a double thickness of heavy-duty foil first will allow the cook to keep the juice. They can even be grilled wrapped loosely in a foil package. Squid and octopus are first-rate when grilled, but the octopus should be parboiled.

Pieces of dense fish like swordfish, and shellfish like shrimp, are excellent to string on long skewers, then grill. Small bamboo skewers, soaked in water first, or even branches of rosemary, can be used to make hors d'oeuvre skewers of smaller shrimp, bay scallops, shucked oysters or crayfish tails.

9. Broiling

Like grilling, broiling is a direct-heat cooking method, but the source of heat is above, not below, the food. Because seafood being broiled is usually placed on a pan, the juices are not lost as the flames lick the surface or the electric heat element gets it sizzling. If the slice of fish, fillet or steak, is less than one inch thick, do not plan to turn it. Just broil it on one side. Even with thicker steaks, if the broiling pan is preheated, turning will not be necessary. Split lobsters brushed with butter are excellent to broil. Clams or oysters on the half shell with a savory topping can also be broiled.

In the past, a dusting of paprika stood in for actual browning on a fillet of sole, which was done in minutes. But there are better, more flavorful color-enhancers. A buttery crumb coating patted on over a slick of mustard is one easy technique.

And here is a great tip to remember: a slather of mayonnaise, even commercial mayonnaise straight out of the jar, or seasoned with herbs, capers, or curry, will not only enhance browning, it will prevent the fish from drying out.

10. Roasting

Roasting is useful for cooking whole fish that has been seasoned with an herbal rub, some lemon juice or even just salt and pepper. The best way to roast fish is in the hottest possible oven, 500 or 550 degrees. Fear not. A small whole fish, like trout, will be done in less than 15 minutes and the skin will have a chance to acquire more than a tan. A three-pound arctic char or sea bass will need 20 minutes or so, and even a huge wild striped bass or king salmon, tipping the scale at seven pounds, will be done in a mere five minutes per pound. If you plan to roast a large whole fish, be sure it will fit into the oven. Remove the head if necessary.

But, as with the Thanksgiving turkey or the Sunday standing rib roast, it's important to allow roasted fish to rest after coming out of the oven, for about half the time it took to roast. Any concern that the fish will not stay hot can be alleviated by lightly tenting the fish with foil.

Mussels or small clams that have been glossed with olive oil, then put in a cast-iron skillet in a hot oven, will emerge opened, sizzling and delectable. Toss in diced bacon or sausage if you like.

Not all roasting requires high heat, however. For example, a thick fillet seared on the skin in a heavy, ovenproof sauté pan can then be turned so the skin side is up and put into a moderate, 350-degree oven, to finish cooking in five to eight minutes.

There are even effective slow-roasting methods for fish. A steak cut or thick fillet laid on a rack or a bed of greens so the fish does not touch the roasting pan, then put in a 225-degree oven for 20 to 25 minutes, will not overcook and will emerge with an almost custardy texture, not unlike steamed fish. But do not expect it to brown. This method works best with fish that has some fattiness, like salmon and sablefish, or a fairly dense texture, like halibut or swordfish.

11. Baking

When it comes to oven cooking, baking is not the same as roasting. It usually means cooking the seafood in a sauce, either covered or uncovered, and at a moderate temperature. To prevent having to handle fragile fish, use a baking dish or casserole that can go directly from oven to table.

Baking fillets of fish with a crumb coating on an oiled baking sheet can yield results that are similar to those from frying, with less fat.

12. Braising

Like braising meat, braising fish involves first briefly browning it in fat on top of the stove, then adding seasonings and a little liquid like wine, covering the pan and allowing the cooking to continue on top of the stove or in the oven at low to moderate heat. The juices that exude from the food mingle with the wine and seasonings and create a flavorful sauce. Though the technique may be the same, the purpose is quite different. With meat, it's the tough muscle, like shoulder cuts, that needs a long, slow braise to become tender. The purpose of braising for seafood is not to tenderize but to infuse flavor. Thick fillets, not steak cuts, are best to braise.

13. Smoking

Two kinds of smoking are commonly used for fish: cold and hot. Cold-smoking adds flavor and results in the typical thin slices of smoked salmon to put on a bagel. In fact, few other types of fish are as suited to cold-smoking as rich, fatty salmon. When cold-smoked, the fish is seasoned with a wet or dry rub, then placed in the smoker for many hours, but never heated enough to cook it. It is not recommended for the home kitchen.

Hot-smoking is another matter and can both flavor and cook seafood. Big backyard smokers, smoke boxes attached to an outdoor grill and stovetop smokers are widely available. They take flavorful woods or wood chips, which may require soaking, and produce enough heat and smoke to cook and season. A wok can be used as a smoker. Line the wok and its cover with foil and place a mixture of raw rice, black tea leaves and sugar in the bottom and place the wok over medium heat. As soon as smoke begins to rise, put a rack or a heat-proof plate in the wok, place the seafood on the rack or plate and cover the wok. It will take about 20 minutes to cook and flavor the seafood.

Marinating the seafood first, or applying a dry seasoning rub some 30 minutes or so before smoking, will boost the flavor. Some of the seafood suitable for hot-smoking are trout, sturgeon, tuna, eel, salmon, monkfish, whitefish, sablefish, cobia, bluefish, sardines, scallops, mussels, oysters, shrimp and lobster.

14. Planking

This traditional method used by Indians in the Pacific Northwest for salmon and along the East Coast with shad has become popular. The fish is usually butterflied and attached, skin-side down, to a wooden plank with pegs. The plank is placed at an angle at the edge of a fire and the fish cooks until done. Now, special planks are sold for use in home ovens. Untreated cedar, fruitwoods and hardwoods like hickory and alder are best. A simple cedar shingle purchased from a lumber yard will do the trick. The wood adds a bit of flavor and makes for handsome presentation at the table. Some Japanese restaurants even cook small fillets on a slab of slate that has been heated on a grill.

Doneness

Many cooks are nervous about preparing fish for fear of overcooking. Indeed, on this score, tastes have changed somewhat. A familiarity with raw fish has affected how some varieties, notably tuna and salmon, are routinely cooked–or rather, undercooked–so the interior is anything from raw to barely medium.

It is impossible to generalize as to when fish and seafood are done, which is why rules of thumb, such as the popular Canadian method of 10 minutes per inch of thickness, are fairly useless.

A hunk of tuna can be delicious merely seared on the outside and raw in the center, but with swordfish, a similar steak fish, the results will be like rubber. A delicate balance has to be achieved. With just a few exceptions, seafood should come off the fire as soon as the juices coagulate and it turns opaque. After that, the internal juices will begin to escape and the fish will become dried out. With some fish, a moment or two before this point is reached is best, since cooking will continue from the retained heat in the fish, especially if it has been cooked on the bone. Waiting until the fish "flakes" usually means waiting until it is overcooked.

There are several ways to test fish for doneness, and familiarity with these will eventually enable the cook to rely less on mechanical tools and more on eye and feel.

The point of a sharp paring knife inserted into the fish will provide two clues. First, insert the point of the knife into the middle of the fish, not touching any bone, then touch the point to your skin just below your lower lip. If the knife is cold, the center is raw. Barely warm will indicate fish is cooked about medium, and warm to hot tells that the center is thoroughly cooked. Second, try to insert the knife all the way through. If it meets no resistance, the chances are that the fish is cooked through. With whole fish, peek into the belly cavity and poke gently with a knife to see whether the bone separates easily from the flesh, indicating the fish is done.

An instant-read thermometer is also useful. Fish does not have to cook beyond 140 degrees. And if you like your salmon medium to medium-rare, aim for 125 degrees in the center.

With shellfish, it's much easier. Crustaceans are done the moment they turn opaque and mollusks as soon as they open.

Because different varieties cook at different rates, it's important to take this into account when preparing dishes made with clams and cod, say, or a paella or a bouillabaisse. Do not put all the seafood in the pot at one time. Instead, to prevent overcooking, add the fish that take longest to cook to the casserole or pan first, then a shorter-cooking batch, and so on.

To the Rescue

How can you save that fish or shellfish that waited an extra day to be cooked or stayed in the pan too long or fell apart as you tried to take it off the grill? Here are a few tricks.

If something comes up and the fish you purchased for dinner will not be used that evening, try sprinkling it with a few drops of vodka, then rewrapping it, to keep it fresh. Apply a stronger seasoning than you originally planned, or marinate the fish for 30 minutes or so before cooking it. Bake it in a sauce instead of simply sautéing it in butter.

The texture of some seafood, notably shrimp and dense fish like monkfish, can be improved by brining, allowing the seafood to soak in water that tastes about as salty as seawater for about 30 minutes, then rinsing and drying it before cooking. Shrimp will acquire a toothsome crispness and fish will have a firmer succulence.

The result of overcooking is drying. The best solution is to add moisture. Liberally brush the fish with good extra virgin olive oil or melted butter that has been warmed with a little lemon juice. Serving plenty of sauce is another quick fix.

If what were supposed to be nice, whole fillets became broken pieces, one cosmetic repair is to cut all the fish in smaller portions and arrange them, with a fresh herb garnish, on a platter or individual plates.

Because timing is so critical, it's also important to know what to do if dinner is suddenly delayed. Fish that has been partially cooked, on one side in the sauté pan, under the broiler or on the grill, or which has not finished roasting, can be put into a slow oven, 150 degrees, where it can remain, without over-cooking, for 30 minutes or more.

Putting fish that has been roasted, broiled, grilled, steamed, poached or baked into a slow oven, about 150 degrees, is also the best way to reheat it, though a microwave oven can also be used.

Sauce for Fish

While a splash of lemon might be fine for some fish preprations, something a bit more elaborate is often appropriate. One of the best and quickest sauces is made by simply deglazing the cooking pan used for sautéing, roasting or broiling with wine, water, beer or broth, then whisking in a nugget of butter to add flavor, body and shine.

Brown butter makes an excellent sauce for fish. Heat fresh butter gently until it turns a hazelnut color and pour it over the fish, or first add a bit of acid, like some capers, lemon juice or a splash of vinegar.

Olive oil can also be the finishing touch that transforms something simple into something irresistible, providing the olive oil is herbaceous and flavorful, fresh and has been warmed a bit before it is spooned on the fish. Toasted sesame and nut oils, and herb-infused oils, are also good to use.

It takes only a little traditional balsamic vinegar—a dark, syrupy and costly condiment that has an intensity of flavor not found in cheaper salad-dressing vinegars—drizzled on the fish to add a beautiful finishing touch.

A compound butter, made by seasoning soft butter with herbs or spices and then chilling it again, can add luster to seafood. Allow a cold slice to melt onto hot broiled fish.

Pesto and green sauces, spicy salsas, and even mayonnaise (seasoned, perhaps with pickles to make tartar sauce) are all appropriate dressings for seafood.

Beurre blanc is a sauce that looks light on the plate but is actually almost pure butter. Vinegar or wine is boiled with shallots until the liquid is just a glaze, then slices of cold butter are whisked in until a thick, emulsified sauce forms.

Equipment

Relatively little specialized equipment is essential for preparing seafood.

In general, heavy-duty skillets, saucepans and roasting pans are best. At least one skillet with a sturdy nonstick finish is important in any kitchen. Bear in mind that unlike a cut-up three-pound chicken, which will easily fit into a 12-inch sauté pan, fish fillets for four people may take up much more space. Consider a larger pan, but only if your burners can accommodate it. Or buy two pans.

An oval fish-poacher with a rack that will fit over two burners may be useful.

A steamer, either large for a mess of crabs or lobsters, or a smaller one, or both, is good to have.

Some kind of basket or grate with small holes can be placed on a grill for cooking shrimp, squid and other small seafood.

A skimmer, wide spatulas, a colander, a wooden mallet and utensils like clam and oyster knives (they are not the same), lobster crackers and picks, skewers and, for the table, cocktail forks, fish knives and forks are all useful. Needlenose pliers work best for extracting pin bones from fish fillets.

Notes on Ingredients

Need one be reminded that seafood, for the most part, is expensive? For that reason, it is important to use the highest-quality ingredients when preparing it. Fortunately, they have become widely available.

Oils and Fats

Throughout this book, the only kind of olive oil that is recommended is extra virgin. There are many types and qualities from many countries, and the rarest, most costly estate-bottled oil is hardly necessary. But the oil should be cold-pressed and have a pleasant flavor. Look for oil that bears a use-by date so it is fresh. And an oil in a can or a dark bottle will be less likely to turn rancid. Oils from Spain and Greece are often best on a price-quality ratio.

For deep-frying, an oil with a high smoke point such as canola or peanut is recommended. If you prefer not to use an industrial oil, cold-pressed grape-seed oil is the best neutral choice.

The butter listed in most of the recipes is unsalted. Though the federal standard for butter is 80 percent butterfat, some higher-fat butters are on the market, even in supermarkets. A butter with 84 percent fat will give your sauce a better gloss and richness, and you may even wind up using a bit less.

Herbs and Spices

Unless dried herbs are specified, the recipes in this book call for fresh herbs. With fresh herbs, they should be bright and lively looking, not browning or wilting. In some instances, with stronger perennial herbs such as thyme, oregano and rosemary, dried can be substituted for fresh, providing the dried herbs you have on hand are not pale, faded and stale. When using tender leafy herbs like cilantro, parsley, mint and basil, it's often advisable to take the time to pluck the leaves from the stems. The stems may be woody and often do not have quite the same flavor as the leaves. Some exotic herbs, like lemongrass, Kaffir lime leaves and epazote are increasingly available in stores and from online services.

Like dried herbs, the spices on your rack should be fresh and fragrant. Some recipes call for freshly ground whole spices like fennel seeds. An electric spice grinder or an old-fashioned mortar can be used. Depending on the recipe, dried chili flakes or whole dried chilies are appropriate, though for some dishes, fresh jalapeños, serranos or other fresh chilies are necessary. It's a good idea to wear gloves or cover your hands with baggies to protect them when handling chilis.

Pepper should be freshly ground. Two pepper mills, one for black pepper, the other for white, are a good idea. White pepper is less likely to be evident on the surface of a fillet or in a sauce, though it tends to have a stronger flavor.

Salt can mean anything from regular table salt to exotic and costly sea salts. In general, kosher or sea salt is best to use because it is easier to control its quantity. Coarse sea salt or fleur de sel sprinkled on just before serving adds a bit of crunchy texture in addition to flavor. When considering salting, bear in mind that most seafood came from the sea. Some varieties, such as clams and oysters, are naturally salty, but most finfish benefit from proper seasoning.

Vinegars

A wardrobe of vinegars lines store shelves. For preparing fish, it's useful to have good-quality red and white wine vinegars on hand. Spanish sherry vinegar, French Champagne vinegar and cider vinegar are useful additions. As for balsamic vinegar, the cheaper supermarket varieties are too harsh and too sweet at the same time, without the complexity of a true well-aged balsamico from Modena, Italy. The most expensive artisanal varieties are syrupy and concentrated, but as a compromise, a balsamic that has been aged 20 years or so can be acceptable.

Citrus Juices

Though refrigerated orange juice or orange juice from concentrate can be used in a pinch, fresh-squeezed is better. Lemon and lime juices must be fresh. Grapefruit juice must also be fresh.

Clam Juice and Sauce Bases

Bottled clam juice is good to keep on hand for emergency stock-making. But a better alternative is to steam a few dozen clams in a little white wine, strain the broth that results and freeze it. Mussel broth is sweeter and less salty than clam broth. Some fish markets sell frozen homemade stocks, which are also good to keep on hand. They are preferable to often acrid-tasting stock made from fish bouillon cubes.

Seasonality

It pays to keep the calendar in mind when planning to prepare seafood. Not only are some varieties better at different times of the year—oysters are sold year-round but they are plumper and more flavorful in cold weather; some kinds of wild salmon and bay and sea scallops have definite seasons—but the other ingredients in the dish may also be seasonal. Do not consider a dish that requires basil or ripe tomatoes in January.

Wine

Has "red wine with fish" become a cliché? Since the days of serving only white wine with seafood, the pendulum is threatening to swing the other way. There are few hard-and-fast rules.

White Wine

Obviously, fish served in a white wine sauce, in a cream sauce or some kinds of seafood like oysters on the half shell, moules marinières or New England clam chowder demand white wine.

Lively whites, with some acidity, suit all but the richest and creamiest fish dishes. These include French muscadet; sauvignon blanc from France, New Zealand or California; pinot grigio from Italy and other wines from the same grape like pinot gris from Oregon or tokay pinot gris from Alsace; albariño from northern Spain or alvarinho from Portugal; grüner veltliner from Austria; and Champagne.

Richer whites, especially fine chardonnays, but also varietals like viognier, riesling and gewürztraminer, deserve that lobster thermidor, poached white king salmon, oyster stew and skate in butter sauce.

Red Wine

Red wine has become more accepted alongside fish these days. Dark-fleshed fish, fish that has been prepared with assertive spices or sauces, and fish in red wine sauce all marry well with red wine. Meaty or rich fish, such as swordfish and salmon, can also take red wine, as can many dishes made with tomatoes. The guidelines as to which red are the same as for other foods: the heavier the dish, the heavier the wine. But for the most part, a red with good acidity and perhaps, because fish does not have the meatiness needed to stand up to strong tannins, a lighter, silkier red is most appropriate. Think pinot noir instead of zinfandel or blockbuster cabernet, and aged Rioja rather than Barolo.

Rosé Wine

Some fish dishes, such as bouillabaisse, beg for a rosé. And since rosés that offer more than mellow pinkness are now being made, it pays not to ignore them. Those fish stews, summer salads, spicy crab boils and fish from the grill that may not demand a red but need something more rounded than many whites are all candidates for a high-quality rosé.

About the Recipes and Text

The recipes in this book have all been attributed to writers and contributors to *The New York Times*, to cookbook authors and to chefs. For chef's recipes, the chefs have been identified with the restaurants at which they were cooking when the recipes were first published—and not necessarily the restaurants where they are working now. Indeed, some of the restaurants cited are no longer in business.

The essays that appear alongside the recipes have been adapted from articles that were published in *The New York Times*, and usually include the byline of the writer.

CHAPTER ONE

Fish A to Z

Anchovies

That anchovies could be anything but dark, salty, oily canned little strips of fish, either flat or rolled around a caper, might come as a pleasant surprise to those who detest them. And people who adore them on a pizza or in a salad may be delighted to find a new way to enjoy them.

When freshly scooped from the sea, anchovies are bright-eyed silver darts that resemble small sardines. Once they have been deboned and gutted, they can be cooked fresh, but more often the fillets are marinated in a mixture of lemon juice and vinegar for six hours to several days. The normally gray flesh turns an opaque whitish color, which is why they are called white anchovies, and they wind up with a taste that suggests pickled herring.

Anchovies are caught in the Atlantic, off the coasts of Portugal, Spain and Morocco, and throughout the Mediterranean. Unmarinated fresh anchovies are sometimes breaded and fried to serve at once. They may also be baked in casseroles or with potatoes. In Turkey, where they extremely popular, they may be fried, then baked in a pilaf.

The fresh ones, which are seasonal in spring, are often imported from Agadir, in Morocco. When buying fresh anchovies to marinate, it's best to select large ones, if possible, no more than 24 to 30 per pound. They will be meatier and easier to clean.

Substitutes: none

ANCHOVY VINAIGRETTE
Time: 5 minutes

Anchovy paste can be used in place of fillets.

½ cup extra virgin olive oil
3 tablespoons or more good red or white wine vinegar
Salt and freshly ground black pepper to taste
1 heaping teaspoon Dijon mustard, optional
3 canned anchovy fillets, or more to taste, with some of their oil
1 large shallot, peeled and cut into chunks

1. Place all ingredients except shallot in a blender and combine. A creamy emulsion will form within 30 seconds. Taste, and add more vinegar if necessary, about a teaspoon at a time, until the balance is right.

2. Add shallot, and turn machine on and off a few times, until shallot is minced within the dressing. Taste, adjust seasoning and serve. (This vinaigrette is best made fresh but will keep refrigerated for a few days. Before using, bring it back to room temperature, and whisk briefly.)

Yield: 4 servings
(Mark Bittman)

WHITE ANCHOVY AND ORANGE SALAD
Time: 15 minutes

6 oranges, preferably blood oranges
48 marinated fresh anchovy fillets (white anchovies)
Juice of 1 lemon
⅓ cup extra virgin olive oil
Salt and freshly ground black pepper
6 ounces mesclun
2 tablespoons minced flat-leaf parsley

1. Use a sharp knife to cut peel from oranges, removing all the white pith. Cut sections out, slicing close to membrane. On 6 salad plates, arrange orange sections like spokes of a wheel, alternating with anchovy fillets, leaving a space in the center.

2. Beat lemon juice and olive oil together and season. Toss with mesclun and put in center of each plate. Scatter parsley over anchovies and oranges. Season with pepper and serve.

Yield: 6 servings
(Mario Batali, Babbo,
New York City)

PUNTARELLE WITH ANCHOVIES
Time: 25 minutes, plus soaking time

> 1 head puntarelle, about 1 pound, or frisée
> 3 anchovies, canned in oil or salted and rinsed
> 1 clove garlic
> 1½ tablespoons red wine vinegar
> Salt and fresh black pepper
> ¼ cup extra virgin olive oil

1. Clean puntarelle, removing tough outer leaves. Cut off tough base and separate stalks. Wash and dry well, then cut into thin strips. Soak in water 2 to 3 hours. Drain, dry and place in a large salad bowl.

2. Place anchovies and garlic in a mortar. Use pestle to mash until creamy and smooth. Transfer to a bowl and add the vinegar and salt and pepper to taste. Whisk in oil until emulsified.

3. Pour the dressing over the greens, toss well and serve.

Yield: 4 servings
(Sandro Fioriti, Sandro's,
New York City)

Salted anchovies are often meatier than canned fillets in oil, but they should be rinsed and patted dry before using.

LINGUINE WITH ANCHOVIES AND ARUGULA

Time: 30 minutes

Salt
4 tablespoons extra virgin olive oil
4 large cloves garlic, peeled and slivered
8 canned anchovy fillets, or more to taste, with some oil
1 pound linguine or other long pasta
2 cups arugula leaves, rinsed, dried and chopped
Freshly ground black pepper
½ teaspoon or more red chili flakes

1. Set a large pot of salted water to a boil.
2. Put 2 tablespoons of the olive oil in a deep skillet over medium heat. Add garlic and anchovies. When the garlic sizzles and the anchovies break up, turn the heat to low.
3. Cook the pasta until it is al dente, about 6 minutes. Drain, reserving 1 cup of the cooking water. Add pasta and arugula to skillet, along with enough of the reserved cooking water to make a sauce. Turn heat to medium, and stir for a minute. Add salt and pepper to taste, plus red chili flakes to taste.
4. Transfer pasta and sauce to a bowl, toss with remaining olive oil and serve.

Yield: 4 servings
(Florence Fabricant)

Arctic Char

Arctic char, a member of the trout family, is mostly farmed in Canada and Maine. It's a handsome fish, silver-black with random spots and a small head, and succulent pink flesh. Most chars in the market are two and one-half to three pounds. Wild arctic char with deep red flesh are also fished in Hudson Bay and sometimes reach restaurants in Quebec and Montreal.

Substitutes: coho salmon, trout, salmon fillets

ARCTIC CHAR WITH CARROTS AND HONEY

Time: 40 minutes

12 tablespoons unsalted butter, at room temperature
1 3-pound arctic char, cleaned, head and tail removed, rinsed
    and dried
16 baby carrots, peeled, stems trimmed
1½ tablespoons evergreen, acacia or other strong honey
Sea salt and freshly ground black pepper
¼ cup vegetable broth
1 teaspoon lemon juice
20 white peppercorns, crushed

1. Preheat oven to 300 degrees. Place a skillet or flameproof baking pan large enough to hold fish over medium heat. Add 5 tablespoons butter. When it is foamy, add fish. Cook for 4 minutes on each side, adjusting heat so butter does not brown.

2. Place a large sheet of heavy-duty foil on a work surface. Transfer fish to foil and wrap it, sealing tightly. Set foil-wrapped fish on a baking sheet, and place in oven for 5 minutes. Remove from oven, and set aside; fish will continue to cook in foil.

3. Fill a small saucepan with 3 cups water, and bring to a boil. Add carrots, 1 tablespoon honey and ½ teaspoon salt. Reduce heat and simmer until carrots are tender, about 6 minutes. Drain, set aside and keep warm.

4. In a small saucepan, combine vegetable broth and lemon juice. Bring to a boil, cook 2 minutes, then turn heat to low. Whisk in remaining butter a tablespoon at a time. Season to taste with salt and pepper and keep warm over low heat.

5. Check fish by opening foil and making a small cut into the thickest part. It should be slightly rare in the center. If additional cooking is needed, return to oven for a few more minutes.

6. To serve, remove fish from foil, and place on serving platter. Spoon butter sauce over and around fish, and sprinkle with crushed white peppercorns. Arrange carrots on platter, drizzle with remaining ½ tablespoon honey and serve.

Yield: 4 servings
(Marc Veyrat, L'Auberge d'Éridan,
Veyrier-du-Lac, France)

Marc Veyrat, whose restaurants are near Lake Annecy in the French Alps, gets a fish called omble chevalier from Lake Geneva. It's a close cousin to arctic char.

ARCTIC CHAR WITH THYME VINAIGRETTE

Time: 30 minutes

A 3-pound arctic char, cleaned and left whole
6 tablespoons extra virgin olive oil
Salt and freshly ground black pepper
1 bunch thyme
½ red onion, finely minced
1 jalapeño chili, seeded and minced
½ cup dry white wine
2 tablespoons white wine vinegar

1. Preheat oven to 500 degrees. Line a baking pan large enough to hold the fish with heavy-duty foil.

2. Rub fish with a tablespoon of the oil and season with salt and pepper, inside and out. Remove a tablespoon of leaves from the bunch of thyme and tuck the rest of the bunch inside the fish. Put the fish in the oven and roast for 15 minutes. The fish will be slightly undercooked in the center. If you prefer it well done, roast it for 20 to 25 minutes.

3. While the fish is cooking, heat a tablespoon of the olive oil in a small skillet. Add the onion and jalapeño and sauté over medium heat until soft. Add the wine and simmer until it is reduced to about three tablespoons, enough to film the bottom of the pan. Stir in vinegar and the tablespoon of thyme leaves, cook briefly, then remove from heat. Transfer to a bowl, stir in the remaining olive oil, season to taste with salt and pepper and cover to keep warm.

4. Remove the fish from the oven and allow to rest for about five minutes. Using a broad spatula, carefully lift it from the pan and transfer it to a serving platter. Remove the thyme from the cavity.

5. Serve, lifting off the top fillet and removing the bones. Spoon some of the sauce over each portion and pass the rest alongside.

Yield: 4 servings
(Moira Hodgson)

CHARRED ARCTIC CHAR

Time: 20 minutes

2½ tablespoons extra virgin olive oil

A 3-pound arctic char, filleted but not skinned

1 lemon

Salt and freshly ground black pepper

4 tablespoons dry bread crumbs

2 teaspoons minced parsley

This recipe is a play on words, but lightly charring the char adds an edge of flavor.

1. Preheat a broiler. Line a broiling pan with foil and use one-half table-spoon of the oil to grease the foil. Mix bread crumbs with remaining oil and the parsley and spread on the foil. Broil until crumbs are browned. Scrape crumbs off foil.

2. Put the fillets on the foil skin side down. Cut the lemon in half verti-cally, cut one-half into 4 wedges and reserve. Juice the rest and moisten the fish with the juice. Season fillets with salt and pepper.

3. Put under the broiler, as close to the source of heat as possible, and cook until the fish is cooked and lightly charred at the edges, about 8 minutes. Spread crumbs on top and serve with lemon wedges.

Yield: 4 serving
(Florence Fabricant)

Blackfish

Blackfish is a New England catch, also called tautog. The fillets are meaty and excellent in stews, even bouillabaisse.

Substitutes: monkfish, tilefish, mahimahi, grouper

BLACKFISH STEW
Time: 1 hour

Though half-and-half can be used intead of milk for a richer version, the lightness of this stew is appealing.

2 tablespoons extra virgin olive oil
½ cup chopped onion
1 cup finely julienned leeks, white and light green part only
2 cloves garlic, crushed
½ pound red-skinned potatoes, peeled and sliced thin
2 cups whole milk
Salt and freshly ground black pepper to taste
Pinch nutmeg
1½ pounds blackfish fillets, in 2-inch chunks
1 tablespoon minced chives

1. Heat oil in a 3-to-4-quart casserole. Add onion and sauté over medium low heat until soft but not brown. Stir in leeks and garlic, sauté a minute or two longer, then stir in potatoes.

2. Add milk, bring to a low simmer, cover and cook until the potatoes are just tender, about 10 minutes. Season with salt and pepper to taste, then stir in nutmeg. The recipe can be prepared up to an hour in advance up to this point.

3. Reheat milk and vegetable mixture to a low simmer. Add fish. Cover and simmer about 10 minutes, just until the fish is cooked through. Recheck seasoning and sprinkle with chives. Serve in soup plates.

Yield: 4 servings
(Gail Arnold, Nick and Toni's,
East Hampton, N.Y.)

BLACKFISH WITH PINEAU DES CHARENTES AND SPRING VEGETABLES

Time: 30 minutes

2 cups fish broth (recipe page 321)

1 cup Pineau des Charentes wine or dry vermouth

3 tablespoons unsalted butter (optional, or to taste)

2 teaspons minced garlic

1 tablespoon minced fresh ginger

6 carrots, peeled and diagonally sliced ¼ inch thick

Salt and freshly ground black pepper

1 cucumber, peeled, halved lengthwise, seeded and sliced
   ½ inch thick

3 medium-size zucchini or yellow squash, halved lengthwise
   and sliced ½ inch thick

3 medium-size ripe tomatoes, halved, seeded and cut in 1-inch
   dice

3 pounds blackfish fillets, cut in 12 equal pieces

1 tablespoon minced chervil

Fresh chervil sprigs for garnish

1. Combine fish broth, wine, butter, garlic, ginger and carrots in a large sauté pan. Bring to a simmer. Taste for seasoning and add salt and pepper if desired.

2. Add the cucumber, zucchini and tomatoes to the pan, then add fish. Reduce heat to a slow simmer, cover and cook about 8 minutes, until the fish is just cooked through. Reseason if necessary. Sprinkle with chervil.

3. Spoon the stew into 6 soup plates and garnish each with sprigs of chervil. Serve at once, with crusty bread on the side.

Yield: 6 servings
(Gail Arnold, Nick and Toni's,
East Hampton, N.Y.)

An herbaceous sauvignon blanc goes with this springtime stew, a variation on the preceeding recipe.

Bluefish

On the East End of Long Island in summer, bluefish, some of the fiercest fish in the sea, roil the waters. They're called choppers by the local fishermen because they can slash their hungry way through schools of less predatory species. Baby blues, which are delicious, are called snappers.

When a fisherman brings in a bluefish, the fish should be put in seawater and ice immediately to shock it, as is done with tuna. Otherwise it will deteriorate. You'll see recreational fishermen just throw it on the deck or put it in a burlap sack in the sun. That ruins it. Bluefish have to be very fresh and handled with care. Otherwise they'll deserve their often negative reputation for being strong in taste.

When you buy a whole fish, one that's bright and firm and no bigger than about three and one-half pounds, have it filleted in front of you. A bluefish that's been properly handled will have a thin bloodline, that dark line up the middle of the fillet. A thin bloodline is a good sign in any fish.

Substitutes: mackerel, rouget

BLUEFISH WITH ASIAN SLAW
Time: 40 minutes

Because the skin of bluefish is extremely thin, it is rarely removed from the fillets.

½ pound jicama, peeled and in julienne slivers

1 medium carrot, peeled and grated

1 cup shredded napa cabbage

Juice of 2 limes

2 tablespoons rice vinegar

1 teaspoon grated fresh ginger

3 tablespoons Asian, or toasted sesame oil

3 scallions, trimmed and chopped

Salt and freshly ground black pepper to taste

¼ cup rice flour

1 teaspoon five-spice powder

4 bluefish fillets, each about 6 ounces

2 tablespoons peanut oil

1 tablespoon Chinese oyster sauce

1 tablespoon finely chopped cilantro

1. Combine jicama, carrot and cabbage in a bowl. Mix lime juice, rice vinegar, ginger and sesame oil together, pour over vegetables and toss. Mix in scallions. Season with salt and pepper. Set aside.

2. Mix rice flour and five-spice powder. Season to taste with salt and pepper. Spread on a plate and dip fish fillets in to coat both sides. Heat peanut oil in a large, heavy skillet, nonstick or cast iron. Sauté the fish, skin side up, about 2 minutes. Turn fillets over, brush fish with oyster sauce and sauté on skin side another 2 to 3 minutes, until lightly browned. Remove from heat.

3. Spread vegetable slaw on a platter large enough to hold fish. Put fish, skin side up, on top of slaw, sprinkle with cilantro and serve.

Yield: 4 servings

(Florence Fabricant)

CURRIED BLUEFISH WITH CUCUMBER-MINT SAUCE

Time: 20 minutes

¼ cup yellow cornmeal

1 tablespoon curry powder

Salt and freshly ground black pepper to taste

4 bluefish fillets, each about 6 ounces

2 tablespoons grape-seed oil

Juice of 1 lime

2 medium-size cucumbers, peeled, seeded and chopped

3 tablespoons finely minced mint leaves

1 teaspoon minced, seeded jalapeño chili

1⅓ cups plain yogurt

1. Mix cornmeal, curry powder and salt and pepper to taste on a plate. Dip fish in this mixture to coat both sides.

2. Heat oil in heavy skillet, nonstick or cast iron. Sauté fish, skin side |down, until lightly browned, about 3 minutes. Turn and sauté other side about 2 minutes. Transfer to platter. Sprinkle with lime juice.

The sauce is best made at the last minute, otherwise the cucumbers will release too much liquid. To prepare it in advance, salt the cucumbers and allow them to sit for 30 minutes, then rinse, drain and dry them.

3. Combine cucumbers, mint and jalapeño in a bowl. Fold in yogurt. Season with salt and pepper. Spoon over fish and serve.

Yield: 4 servings
(Florence Fabricant

Carp

Rich, meaty carp are extremely popular in China, where they have been cultivated since 500 B.C. The dark meat of the fish can be tougher than the lighter flesh, which is why braising, a cooking method that tenderizes, is especially appropriate.

Substitutes: whitefish, shad, salmon

BRAISED CARP

Time: 1 hour

Chinese five-spice powder, which has an earthy, anise flavor, is suited to the fish.

1 4-pound carp cleaned, gutted and scaled, preferably
   with head on
Salt to taste
Flour for dredging fish
½ cup peanut oil
20 pearl onions, peeled
1 pound small white mushrooms, halved
¼ pound oyster mushrooms
5 pieces star anise
1 tablespoon minced garlic
1 tablespoon dark soy sauce
4 cups rich chicken stock

¼ cup sherry vinegar

Freshly ground black pepper to taste

½ **cup minced chives or garlic chives for garnish**

1. Preheat oven to 400 degrees. Rinse and dry fish; cut 3 or 4 vertical gashes on each side of fish, an inch or two apart. Heat a heavy roasting pan long enough to fit fish (cut off the head, if necessary) over medium-high heat for a few minutes.

2. Salt fish inside and out, and dredge lightly in flour. Add peanut oil to the pan and raise heat to high. When oil is hot, add fish and sear on both sides. Remove to a plate.

3. Add onions and mushrooms to the pan and sauté over medium-high heat until lightly browned. Add star anise, garlic, soy sauce, stock, vinegar, salt and pepper, and stir. Return fish to pan, cover with aluminum foil, and place in the oven. Bake about 30 minutes, or until flesh comes off the bone with ease.

4. Remove fish to a platter and keep warm. Over high heat, reduce liquid in the pan by half. Remove star anise, check sauce for seasoning, pour over fish, and garnish with chives. Serve by spooning portions of fish off the bone and topping with sauce.

Yield: 4 to 6 servings
(Lynne Aronson)

Catfish

Catfish, a bottom-feeder, is the biggest farmed-fish industry in America. The farmed fish are grain-fed and do not have the somewhat muddy flavor found in the wild variety.

Substitutes: tilapia, flounder

CATFISH AMOK

Time: 90 minutes, plus 24 hours marinating

1 teaspoon thin slices peeled galingale root or ginger
1 clove garlic, peeled
1½ tablespoons finely julienned fresh Kaffir lime leaves
¼ teaspoon turmeric
4 tablespoons fresh minced lemongrass
5 dried red Asian chilies, deveined and deseeded, soaked
    10 minutes in lukewarm water and chopped fine
2 tablespoons Thai fish sauce
1 egg, well beaten
2 tablespoons sugar
1 16-ounce can unsweetened coconut milk
1½ pounds catfish fillets, sliced width-wise in strips ¼ inch thick
8 pieces banana leaf, cut 14 inches by 10 inches
½ pound spinach leaves

Amok is a steamed fish pâté that is served in Laos and Cambodia. If banana leaves are not available, foil can be used as a wrapper. Even fresh corn husks would work, though they would never be used in Southeast Asia.

1. In a blender or food processor, combine the galingale root or ginger, garlic, 1 teaspoon of the Kaffir lime leaves, turmeric, lemongrass, chilies, fish sauce, egg, sugar and coconut milk. Pulse, scraping the sides of the container occasionally, until ingredients are pureed.

2. Combine contents of blender and catfish in a glass bowl, coating fish thoroughly. Cover and refrigerate overnight, or at least 5 hours.

3. Put 1 piece of washed banana leaf atop another, to make a double thickness. Place one-quarter of the washed spinach leaves in the center, and top with one-quarter of the fish mixture, about 1 cup. Garnish with a pinch of julienned Kaffir lime leaves. Fold the 2 layers of banana leaves lengthwise in

thirds. Then fold the ends up to the top, and secure with toothpicks. Keep this side up to prevent leaking. Repeat procedure, making 4 packages. If banana leaves are not available, parchment paper or foil can be substituted.

4. Place the bottom rack of a 9- or 10-inch bamboo steamer in a wok and pour in enough water to come to about an inch below the steamer. Put 2 fish packages on the bottom rack. Fit a second rack above it, and put in the remaining 2 packages. Cover, and place over high heat for about 5 minutes, to bring to a boil. Reduce heat to medium low, and cook for 45 minutes. To serve, remove the toothpicks and open packages. Serve with rice.

Yield: 4 servings
(Sovan Boun Thuy)

SOUTHERN-FRIED CATFISH AND HUSH PUPPIES

Time: 45 minutes

> **Peanut oil for frying**
> **1½ cups corn flour, preferably stone-ground**
> **Salt**
> **½ teaspoon freshly ground black pepper**
> **¼ teaspoon cayenne pepper, or to taste**
> **3 pounds small, cleaned catfish fillets**
> **1 large egg**
> **2 cups buttermilk**
> **1¾ cups stone-ground yellow cornmeal**
> **½ cup minced onion**
> **1 scant teaspoon baking powder**
> **1 scant teaspoon baking soda**

Corn flour, the finest grind of cornmeal, can be made by grinding cornmeal in a blender or food processor. Masa harina, sold in Mexican stores, can be substituted.

1. Preheat oven to 200 degrees. In a stockpot or Dutch oven, pour oil to a depth of at least 1½ inches, and heat the oil at medium high until the temperature reaches 375 degrees. Place wire racks on 2 baking sheets and set aside.

2. In a wide bowl, mix the corn flour, 1 teaspoon salt, pepper and cayenne.

3. In a medium-size bowl, mix the egg and buttermilk well, then stir in the cornmeal until well blended. Add the onion and stir in. Set aside. Place the baking powder, baking soda and a scant teaspoon salt in a separate bowl and set aside while you fry the fish.

4. Dip each fish or fillet into the seasoned corn flour, coating it well and shaking off any excess. Carefully lower each piece into the oil. Fill the pot, but do not crowd. The oil should bubble up around each piece. Make sure the temperature stays between 365 and 375 degrees. Fry the fish until it is golden all over, about 2 or 3 minutes on each side. Set remaining corn flour mixture aside.

5. Remove fish pieces from the oil in the same order in which they were immersed, using a wire-mesh strainer or tongs to let excess grease drain. When the fish stops dripping, place it on one of the prepared baking sheets. Place in the oven.

6. Continue until all fish is fried.

7. For the hush puppies, add baking powder, baking soda and salt mixture to the buttermilk batter and mix well. Add the leftover seasoned corn flour to the batter a little at a time, until the batter is thick enough to be spooned. You will have added about ¼ to ½ cup of the corn flour.

8. Make sure the oil has returned to 375 degrees; then, drop the batter by spoonfuls into the oil, using 2 teaspoons dipped in cold water. Fry the hush puppies until golden brown all over, about 3 minutes. Drain each well over the pot, and place on the second prepared sheet pan. Repeat the process until all the batter is fried. Serve the fish and hush puppies immediately.

Yield: 8 servings
(John Martin Taylor)

Chilean Sea Bass (Patagonian Toothfish)

Chilean Sea Bass: More Than an Identity Problem
By FLORENCE FABRICANT

In the late 1990's, responding to preliminary reports that the meteoric popularity of Chilean sea bass might eventually deplete the fishery, chefs started taking the fish off their menus. It developed into a full-fledged boycott. A host of other environmental and seafood organizations and lobbying groups, including the Seafood Choices Alliance, the Marine Fish Conservation Network and the Monterey Bay Aquarium support the growing boycott.

Some scientists believe that if the fishery is not largely curtailed, it may collapse within five years. Signs of danger include lower catches in once-thriving parts of the icy southern and Antarctic seas and smaller fish, often those that have not reached sexual maturity. Chilean sea bass is actually Patagonian toothfish (Dissostichus eleginoides), a slow grower, but it can reach 100 pounds and live for 80 years.

Until about 10 years ago, it took a trip to Chile or Argentina to sample thick, succulent, snow-white fillets of toothfish. But when marketing experts came up with the attractive but meaningless name—it's not a sea bass at all—the fish was on its way to commercial stardom.

Whether the fish coming into this country is part of the legal catch is at the heart of a controversy about the boycott. An international licensing and conservation agreement, the Convention on the Conservation of Antarctic Marine Living Resources, or C.C.A.M.L.R., among 24 nations is in place. But, say those who support the boycott, it is difficult to enforce.

Illegal fishing accounts for up to two-thirds of the total harvest and, according to a fact sheet issued by the federal Department of Commerce and the State Department, "some illegally harvested Chilean sea bass does enter the United States."

Substitutes: sablefish, mahimahi, wild striped bass, shad

STEAMED CHILEAN SEA BASS WITH CHINESE BLACK BEAN BROTH

Time: 30 minutes

> 5 tablespoons unsalted butter
>
> 2 tablespoons minced garlic
>
> 2 tablespoons fresh ginger, minced, plus 1 tablespoon slivered
>
> 2 tablespoons minced lemongrass bulb
>
> 1 tablespoon fermented Chinese black beans, rinsed and coarsely chopped
>
> 1 cup sake
>
> 1 cup chicken stock
>
> 1 tablespoon soy sauce
>
> 1 tablespoon rice vinegar
>
> 1 tablespoon kejup manis (Indonesian soy sauce), optional
>
> 4 fillets Chilean sea bass, 6 ounces each

Salt
¼ cup thinly sliced scallions
1 cup fresh bean sprouts

1. In a small nonreactive saucepan over medium-low heat, melt 1 tablespoon butter. Add minced garlic, ginger, lemongrass and black beans. Sauté until softened and garlic is translucent, about 3 minutes.

2. Add sake and stock, and mix well. Increase heat to medium-high, and boil until reduced by two-thirds, about 10 minutes. Remove from heat, and whisk in soy sauce, vinegar and kejup manis. Set aside, and keep warm.

3. Season fillets with salt. Place a bamboo steamer over simmering water, or set a rack or heat-proof plate over simmering water in a covered wok. Add fillets and scatter silvered ginger on each. Place 1 tablespoon butter on each. Cover, and steam until fish is opaque and ginger is softened, about 4 minutes.

4. Place a fillet in each of four shallow soup plates and spoon broth liberally over. Garnish with scallions and bean sprouts.

Yield: 4 servings
(Julian Alonzo, Brasserie 8½,
New York City)

Cobia

A popular Caribbean fish, cobia is most readily available in spring. It's a meaty fish, best used in steak form or as thick fillets.

Substitutes: swordfish, albacore tuna

COBIA WITH TOMATILLO SALSA
Time: 20 minutes

24-to-28-ounce cobia steak
⅓ cup extra virgin olive oil
12 small tomatillos, husked and diced
20 basil leaves, rinsed and patted dry and coarsely shredded

Juice of 1 lime

2 tablespoons light soy sauce

Salt and freshly ground black pepper

1. Cut fish sharply on the bias into 8 slices like veal scallopini. Brush on both sides with 3 tablespoons of the olive oil and set aside.

2. Combine tomatillos and basil leaves in a bowl. Beat the lime juice and soy sauce together and slowly beat in the remaining olive oil. Mix with tomatillos and basil. Season to taste with salt and pepper and set aside.

3. Heat a heavy, seasoned griddle, cast-iron skillet or a heavy nonstick skillet over very high heat. Add the fish slices and sear quickly, 2 to 3 minutes on each side until lightly browned on the outside and just barely cooked in the middle. Transfer fish to each of 4 warm plates and season to taste with salt and pepper.

4. Spoon salsa over the fish and serve.

Yield: 4 servings

(Ed Brown, Sea Grill, New York City)

Cod

A Cod's Swift Journey From Sea to Plate
By AMANDA HESSER

Casco Bay cod can go from 20 miles off the coast of Maine to a Manhattan dining room in 36 hours. In the trade it might be called day-boat cod. Chefs will pay more for it because it's fresher. Day boats carry a smaller load and do not go out as far into the ocean. (Fish that require a longer trip into deep water, such as tuna and swordfish, are generally not caught on day boats.)

Portland, Me., has an open-display auction, so the fish from a dozen boats are labeled and grouped together in large plastic bins. Buyers can inspect the fish before bidding. The buyers often pack their fish on salt flake ice, which is colder than regular crushed ice and helps keep the bacteria down on the fish skin. It is also shaved, to cushion the fish without bruising. Boxes are lined with cardboard cushioning and bubble wrap. Anyone would think they were packing fine china.

By evening, trucks are heading out to cities in the Northeast with their cargo of fresh fish. And by the next day, the fish is on the plate, fresh-tasting, almost as if you could still taste the sea. Maybe you can. It came ashore just the day before. 🐚

Substitutes: sablefish, scrod, hake, grouper; for steaks: halibut

POACHED COD WITH LEMON-PARSLEY SAUCE

Time: 10 minutes

Fish broth (recipe p. 321) can be used instead of water for poaching.

2½ tablespoons lemon juice
2½ tablespoons extra virgin olive oil
½ teaspoon salt
¼ teaspoon freshly ground black pepper
¼ cup chopped flat-leaf parsley
6 pieces of thick cod fillets, 4 to 5 ounces each

1. Combine lemon juice, olive oil, salt, pepper and parsley in a small bowl. Set aside.

2. Bring 6 cups of water to a boil in a large saucepan. Holding the fish fillets with a slotted spoon or skimmer, lower them individually into the pan, and bring the water back to a boil. Reduce the heat to low, and poach the fish in barely simmering water for 3 to 4 minutes, until they are barely cooked through.

3. Using a slotted spoon or skimmer, lift the fish from the water, drain thoroughly, and arrange 1 fillet on each of 6 warm plates. Press the fish lightly with a spatula or fork to make it separate a little at the grain.

4. Add 2 tablespoons hot poaching liquid to lemon juice mixture, beat briefly, then spoon the sauce over the fish. Serve.

Yield: 6 servings
(Jacques Pépin)

ROASTED COD WITH NIÇOISE VINAIGRETTE

Time: 30 minutes

8 anchovy fillets, drained and minced
1 tablespoon capers, minced
1 tablespoon niçoise olives, pitted and minced
1 tablespoon minced shallot
1 teaspoon finely slivered garlic
½ cup extra virgin olive oil
3 tablespoons sherry wine vinegar
Salt and freshly ground black pepper
4 cod fillets, each about 6 ounces

1. Preheat oven to 500 degrees. Mix anchovies, capers, olives, shallot and garlic with ⅓ cup olive oil and the vinegar. Season with salt and pepper. Set aside.

2. Heat remaining oil in an ovenproof skillet. Season cod with salt and pepper, place in skillet and sear on one side until golden, about 2 minutes. Turn and place in oven until done, about 5 minutes.

3. Place a cod fillet on each of 4 plates. Spoon about 2 tablespoons anchovy sauce on top.

Yield: 4 servings
(Stephen Kalt, Spartina,
New York City)

When buying cod, examine it carefully. Any signs of splitting indicate that the fish could be fresher.

COD STRUDEL WITH SAUERKRAUT IN RIESLING SAUCE

Time: 1½ hours

Except for the final cooking, this dish can be prepared in advance. Serve it with a good Austrian white wine, such as a grüner veltliner from the Wachau Valley.

1 tablespoon duck fat or unsalted butter

1 medium onion, finely chopped

10 ounces sauerkraut, well drained

A 2-inch chunk smoked bacon

2 bay leaves, 12 black peppercorns, 6 juniper berries–
all tied in cheesecloth

½ cup chicken stock or water

20 ounces cod fillet in 4 equal portions

Salt and freshly ground white pepper

Leaves from 4 stems tarragon

8 sprigs chervil or 16 opal basil leaves

10 full-size sheets phyllo

6 tablespoons clarified butter

½ medium-size baking potato, peeled and diced

1 cup dry riesling, preferably Austrian

⅓ cup dry vermouth

Juice of ½ lemon

½ cup heavy cream

1. Melt fat or butter in heavy saucepan. Add onion and cook over medium heat until just golden. Add sauerkraut, bacon, spices in cheesecloth and stock or water. Bring to simmer. Cover and cook over low heat 45 minutes.

2. Meanwhile, season cod with salt and pepper. Each piece should measure about 2 by 5 inches and about 1½ inches thick. If the pieces are larger and flatter, cut them to size and stack 2 pieces for each portion. Divide herbs among each portion, placing them on the top and underside.

3. Cut sheets of phyllo in half across the width. Stack them and cover with a damp cloth. Place one of the half sheets on work surface. Brush with butter. Top with four more sheets, brushing each with butter. Center a portion of cod at the bottom of buttered sheets. Roll cod in phyllo like a jelly roll, to make a package. Press down on the ends to seal. Cut off and discard excess phyllo at ends, taking care that fish is enclosed. Butter the outside of the package and place on a parchment-lined baking sheet. Repeat with the remaining cod and phyllo. Refrigerate until 15 minutes before serving.

4. Stir sauerkraut. Remove bacon and spice bag. Add potato, riesling and vermouth. Simmer uncovered about 10 minutes. Add lemon. Simmer a few minutes longer, then stir in cream. Bring to simmer and set aside until ready to serve.

5. Preheat oven to 450 degrees. Place baking sheet in oven and bake 15 to 20 minutes, until strudel is lightly browned.

6. Remove sauerkraut from pan, draining juices well into pan, and divide sauerkraut among 4 warm soup plates. Cut each strudel in half and place 2 pieces on top of sauerkraut. Bring juices remaining in pan to a simmer and strain into blender. Process briefly at high speed, then pour around sauerkraut in each dish and serve.

Yield: 4 servings

(Kurt Gutenbrunner, Wallsé, New York City)

ROASTED COD WITH SWEET BRANDADE AND OLIVE SAUCE

Time: 1¼ hours

¼ cup black olive paste
½ tablespoon Dijon mustard
2 tablespoons red wine vinegar
½ cup extra virgin olive oil
5 medium Yukon gold potatoes, peeled
Kosher salt, to taste
6 cloves garlic, peeled
1 cup milk
5 7-ounce boneless, skinless cod steaks, 2 inches thick
¼ cup unsalted butter
1 tablespoon chopped flat-leaf parsley
Fine sea salt, to taste
Freshly ground white pepper, to taste
Quick mixing flour (Wondra) or sifted all-purpose flour
2 tablespoons canola oil

1. To make olive sauce, in a small saucepan whisk together olive paste, mustard and vinegar. Slowly whisk in ¼ cup olive oil until smooth and emulsi-

The sweet brandade in this recipe is made with fresh, not salted, cod and mashed potatoes.

COD   47

fied. It should pour like a sauce; if it is thick, thin with a little warm water. Set aside.

2. Place potatoes in a medium-size pan. Cover with water; season with kosher salt. Bring to a boil, reduce heat and simmer until tender, 20 to 25 minutes. Drain.

3. Meanwhile, preheat oven to 400 degrees. In a small skillet, combine garlic cloves and remaining oil, and roast in oven until garlic is tender and lightly browned, about 15 minutes. Remove from oven and set aside. In a small pan, bring milk to a simmer. Add 1 cod steak, and simmer until it is fully cooked, 5 to 7 minutes. Remove cod from milk, reserving both.

4. To assemble the brandade, in a large pan combine potatoes, poached cod, butter and olive oil–garlic mixture. Mash with a fork into a well-blended, slightly lumpy mixture. Add ½ cup reserved milk and the parsley, and stir until smooth. Season to taste with sea salt and white pepper. Cover this mixture and set aside.

5. Preheat oven to 400 degrees. Season the 4 remaining cod steaks with sea salt and pepper, and dust lightly with flour. In a large nonstick sauté pan, heat canola oil over medium-high heat. Add the cod steaks to the pan, and sauté until light golden brown on the bottom, 5 minutes. Transfer pan to the oven, and roast 3 to 4 minutes, until bottom of fish is well browned and fish has begun to cook on the sides and top. Flip the cod steaks, and continue roasting 3 to 4 minutes longer. Test for doneness: a metal skewer should slide into the middle easily and be warm to the touch after it is withdrawn. Remove cod from the oven, and transfer to a plate. Let it rest while you finish the sauce.

6. Place olive sauce over medium-low heat, and warm through. Place the brandade over medium heat, and stir until warm. To serve: on each of 4 plates, place a cod steak on one-half of the plate. Spoon a little sauce around it (not on it). Spoon the brandade on the other half of the plate. Serve.

Yield: 4 servings
(Eric Ripert, Le Bernardin,
New York City)

FOCACCIA WITH BRANDADE

Time: 2½ hours, plus overnight soaking

½ pound boneless salt cod

1 packet dry yeast

Pinch sugar

½ teaspoon salt

4 tablespoons extra virgin olive oil

3 cups flour, approximately

1½ cups milk

2 large baking potatoes, peeled and cut into 1-inch cubes

6 cloves garlic, peeled and minced

1 teaspoon freshly ground black pepper

3 tablespoons heavy cream

2 teaspoons chopped flat-leaf parsley

Not all salted, dried codfish is the same. Look for boneless salt cod, preferably vacuum-packed. A few sprigs of rosemary can be strewn over the focaccia before baking.

1. Place salt cod in a dish, cover with cold water and soak for 24 hours, changing water twice.

2. Mix yeast, sugar and salt in mixing bowl. Add ½ cup warm water and set aside 5 minutes to proof. Stir in 1 tablespoon olive oil and ¾ cup warm water. Gradually add enough of the flour to make a firm but pliable dough. Knead 5 minutes, then place in an oiled bowl and set aside to rise until doubled, about 1 hour.

3. Drain and rinse the salt cod, and cut it into 2-inch pieces. Place in a medium saucepan, and cover with milk. Bring to a simmer over medium heat, and simmer slowly for 10 minutes. Drain and coarsely chop. Place in a large bowl, and set aside.

4. Place the potatoes in a medium saucepan, and cover with water. Bring to a boil, reduce to a simmer and cook until the potatoes are tender, about 10 minutes. Drain and add potatoes to the cod. Use the back of a fork to coarsely mash them together. The mixture should be rough. Gently stir in the garlic and pepper. Fold in 2 tablespoons olive oil and then the cream.

5. Preheat oven to 425 degrees.

6. Roll out dough on floured board to 12-inch circle. Place on baking sheet and prick. Spread salt cod mixture on top, leaving a ½-inch border around the circumference. Bake until crust is golden brown, about 20 minutes. Sprinkle with parsley, drizzle with remaining olive oil, cut into wedges and serve hot.

Yield: 4 to 6 servings

(Molly O'Neill)

SCRAMBLED EGGS WITH SALT COD AND POTATOES

Time: 40 minutes, plus overnight soaking

This is a cousin to the New York Sunday brunch favorite, lox and eggs.

½ pound boneless salt cod

9 tablespoons extra virgin olive oil

6 cloves garlic, smashed

Kosher salt

Canola oil

2 medium Idaho potatoes, peeled and cut into matchsticks

8 eggs

2 tablespoons chopped flat-leaf parsley

1. Soak salt cod in water for 24 hours, changing water twice. Bring a medium pan of water to a boil. Add salt cod, and simmer for 5 minutes. Drain.

2. Heat 4 tablespoons olive oil in a saucepan. Add garlic and salt cod, breaking it into walnut-size pieces with a wooden spoon. Cook over medium-low heat, stirring occasionally, until salt cod has absorbed oil and garlic has softened, about 10 minutes. Remove from heat, season to taste with salt if needed and let cool.

3. Pour 1 inch of canola oil into a medium saucepan. Heat to 375 degrees. Add as many potatoes as will fit comfortably without lowering temperature of oil. Fry until potatoes are tender but not browned, about 5 minutes. Drain on paper towels, and season lightly with salt. Repeat with remaining potatoes.

4. Crack eggs into a bowl, and set near stove. Place a 12-inch, nonstick sauté pan over medium-high heat. Add 2½ tablespoons olive oil. When it shimmers, add half the salt cod and half the potatoes, scattering them around pan. Once they are hot, add half the parsley. Working quickly, pour half the eggs into pan, and stir vigorously with a wooden spoon or spatula. Eggs should just set and should not brown. While they are still a little wet, pour eggs onto a serving dish. Keep warm. Repeat with remaining ingredients, transfer to serving dish and serve.

Yield: 4 to 6 servings
(Casa Robles, Seville, Spain)

Croaker

Croakers are so-called because they make a sound. They belong to a family of fish called drums, which includes the redfish of "blackened redfish" fame and also weakfish (sea trout, page 126). Now that redfish are near depletion and are mainly a sport fish, croaker fillets can be blackened instead. Croaker is also popular among the Chinese and is a deliciously meaty fish to steam whole.

Substitutes: porgy, pompano

STEAMED CROAKER WITH SCALLIONS AND GINGER
Time: 40 minutes

2 whole croakers, about 1½ pounds each, cleaned
3 tablespoons Asian, or toasted sesame oil
1 bunch scallions
Ginger slice, 1 inch thick, peeled and slivered
2 tablespoons light soy sauce
3 tablespoons rice vinegar

1. Set a large Chinese steamer basket over a wok. Oil a heat-proof plate that will hold the fish and can fit into the basket with 1 tablespoon sesame oil.

2. Remove roots from the scallions, then quarter scallions lengthwise. Cut into 3-inch lengths.

3. Scatter half the scallions and half the ginger over the platter. Place fish on the platter, put some of the scallions and ginger inside each fish and scatter the rest over the top.

4. Bring an inch of water to a boil in the wok. Place the platter on the steamer rack over the water, cover steamer and steam the fish about 15 minutes.

5. Carefully remove the platter from the steamer and transfer fish to a serving platter. Drain all but a few spoonfuls of liquid from the platter, reserving all the scallions and ginger as well. Scrape reserved cooking juices, scallions and ginger into a dish, add soy sauce, vinegar and remaining sesame oil, stir and spoon over the fish. Serve.

Yield: 4 servings
(Florence Fabricant)

Another way to steam the fish is to place it in a microwavable container, loosely covered, and microwave it about 6 minutes.

Dorade

Also called dorade royale, this fish, which usually comes from the Atlantic and the Mediterranean, is in the porgy family. In Europe it's also known as sea bream, orata and gilthead bream. Under the name orata, its increasingly available in the United States, shipped in fresh from fish farms in southern Europe.

Substitutes: porgy, red snapper, sea bass, wild striped bass, fluke, mahimahi

PAN-SEARED DORADE FILLETS
Time: 20 minutes

Consider serving mashed potatoes alongside.

> 2 dorade fillets, 6 to 7 ounces each, with skin
> 2 teaspoons melted unsalted butter
> Salt and pepper to taste
> 1 teaspoon extra virgin olive oil
> 2 lemon wedges

1. Preheat the oven to 450 degrees. Set rack in middle postion.

2. On top of the stove, over medium-high heat, preheat cast-iron or other heavy ovenproof skillet large enough to hold fish in a single layer.

3. Brush the skin side of each fillet with melted butter, and sprinkle with salt and pepper. When the pan is smoking hot, add olive oil.

4. Put the fillets in pan, skin side down. Adjust heat to medium, and cook for 2 to 3 minutes, or until the edges of the fillets start to brown. Transfer pan to preheated oven for another 2 to 3 minutes, until fish is just cooked through. Turn skin side up and serve immediately, drizzled with pan juices and lemon wedges on the side.

Yield: 2 servings
(Rick Moonen, Oceana,
New York City)

Eel

Spaghetti From the Sea
By AMANDA HESSER

The real eel delicacy is baby eel, which is as thin as string, its noodlelike body absent of color. In the spring eels pass through tidal areas on the East Coast en route to lake waters. During their infancy, predators are a problem, none more so than chefs. In France and Spain fresh baby eels are sautéed, live, in olive oil infused with chili and garlic. They're eaten with wooden forks and could be mistaken for linguine.

As for mature eel, more smoked than fresh makes it into the market. But fresh eel, which is rich and succulent, deserves attention. Skinning an eel is like peeling off a stocking. But the fish market will do it for you. ❧

Substitutes: none

BROILED EEL WITH MUSTARD BUTTER
Time: 20 minutes

> 7 tablespoons soft unsalted butter
> Juice of ½ lemon
> 2 teaspoons Dijon mustard
> 3 tablespoons minced curly parsley
> ¼ teaspoon Worcestershire sauce
> Tabasco sauce to taste
> Salt and freshly ground black pepper
> 1 skinned eel, 1¼ to 1½ pounds, cleaned

1. Preheat broiler.

2. Combine 4 tablespoons butter with lemon juice, mustard, parsley, Worcestershire sauce and Tabasco. Beat well with a whisk until well blended. Season to taste with salt and pepper. Set aside.

3. Score eel by making parallel incisions, ⅛ inch deep, at half-inch intervals. Cut eel into 6-inch lengths.

This dish, which was devised by Craig Claiborne, can be served either as an appetizer or a main course.

4. In a baking dish melt remaining butter. Add eel pieces, season to taste with salt and pepper and turn to coat eel well with butter. Place under broiler and broil about 2 minutes. Turn and broil 2 to 3 minutes longer. Pour off fat from pan. Top eel with mustard butter and serve.

Yield: 6 servings
(Craig Claiborne)

Escolar

A Fish Puts Chefs in a Quandary
By MARIAN BURROS

Some restaurants have been offering a fish of unparalleled richness. It's called escolar, but for a significant number of people, the flesh of this fish acts like a laxative. This is the same fish that has been banned in Japan since 1977 because the Japanese government believes it is toxic.

In this country, enough people complained about escolar's purgative effect for the Food and Drug Administration to issue an import bulletin in the early 1990's that recommended not selling the fish, which is found in the Gulf of Mexico, the South Pacific and tropical waters around the world. Early last year, the alert was canceled because the agency, unlike the Japanese government, decided escolar was not toxic.

Escolar (Lepidocybium flavobrunneum) and its West Coast cousin, walu (Ruvettus pretiosus), have been available across the country since the 1980's. The two fish, members of the snake mackerel family, are sometimes called white tuna. They are a by-catch of long-line fishing for tuna, which means their availability is erratic. They were once considered practically worthless.

What gives these fish their desirable taste is actually a component similar to that used to produce Olestra, the fake fat found in some snack foods: fatty substances called wax esters, in this case, gempylotoxins. Humans cannot digest these wax esters because they lack the enzymes necessary to break the large molecules into smaller, absorbable components.

Flounder, Also Fluke and Sole

Flounder is a member of the vast and rather peculiar flatfish family. Why peculiar? When the fish are born, they swim like most other fish, with their bodies perpendicular to the ocean floor and with eyes on either side of their head. But before they reach maturity, they turn and will spend the rest of their life swimming parallel to the ocean floor, like rays. At the same time, one of their eyes migrates to the opposite side of the head, alongside the other eye, so both eyes are on the same side. That side has darker skin and, from above, blends into the color of the ocean floor. The underside, or blind side, of the fish becomes white. That's the side you see in the fish market.

There are various kinds of flounder, and the nomenclature can be downright confusing. Yellowtail, winter, the most excellent witch–a fish that is delicious sautéed whole–are all known as flounders. Fluke is another name for summer flounder. Western sand dabs, petrale soles, halibut, turbot and the European brill and plaice are members of the flounder family. Gray sole and lemon sole are also flounders. But Dover sole, a true sole and a succulently meaty little fish, is another variety entirely.

Substitutes: fluke, turbot, sole, also fillets of tilapia, sea bass, catfish

ECUADORIAN CEVICHE "MARTINI"
Time: 30 minutes, plus 2 hours marinating

    1½ pounds flounder fillets in ½-inch pieces
    Juice of 3 limes
    Juice of 1 lemon
    Juice of 1 orange
    1 ripe Hass avocado, peeled and diced in ½-inch cubes
    ⅓ cup finely diced red onion
    1 cup peeled, finely diced, seeded tomatoes
    1 cup tomato juice
    ½ cup ketchup
    ½ teaspoon Tabasco, or to taste
    Salt and freshly ground black pepper to taste
    ⅓ cup coarsely chopped cilantro leaves, plus sprigs for garnish

Popcorn or roasted corn is a traditional accompaniment.

1. Place flounder in a bowl. Fold in citrus juices. Cover, and refrigerate for 2 hours.

2. Just before serving, drain off the liquid from flounder and discard. Place flounder in a mixing bowl, and add the remaining ingredients.

3. Serve in chilled martini glasses and garnish with cilantro.

Yield: 6 servings
(Rafael Palomino, Sonora,
New York City)

NEW-STYLE SASHIMI
Time: 30 minutes

2 teaspoons white sesame seeds
4 teaspoons yuzu juice, or half lemon and half lime juice
3 tablespoons Japanese soy sauce
1 pound fluke fillet, skinned
1 teaspoon finely grated garlic
1 2½-inch piece fresh ginger, peeled, in fine julienne
½ bunch chives, in 2-inch lengths
4 carrot curls, for garnish
6 tablespoons fruity extra virgin olive oil
2 teaspoons Asian, or toasted sesame oil

1. Toast sesame seeds by heating briefly in small skillet. Set aside. Combine yuzu juice and soy sauce and set aside.

2. Using a large, sharp knife, cut fish on the bias in paper-thin slices. You should have about 16 slices. Arrange slices like spokes of a wheel on a serving dish, or put 4 slices on each of 4 individual plates. Top each slice with a small dab of garlic, some ginger spears and chives. Sprinkle with sesame seeds and drizzle with yuzu-soy mixture. Garnish with carrot.

3. Just before serving, heat olive oil and sesame oil together in small skillet until very hot but not smoking. Slowly pour in thin stream over fish and serve.

Yield: 4 servings
(Nobu Matsuhisa, Matsuhisa,
Los Angeles, Calif.)

FLUKE AMATRICIANA STYLE

Time: 1 hour

3 tablespoons extra virgin olive oil

2 pounds fluke fillets

Juice of 1 lemon

Salt and freshly ground black pepper

4 ounces pancetta, diced

2 medium onions, sliced thin

2 cups finely chopped ripe plum tomatoes or chopped
   well-drained canned tomatoes

Red chili flakes to taste

2 tablespoons flat-leaf parsley leaves

1. Lightly brush a baking dish that will hold the fish in a single layer with a little of the oil. Place fish in the dish and sprinkle with lemon juice. Season with salt and pepper. Cover and refrigerate while preparing sauce.

2. Heat remaining oil in a heavy skillet. Add pancetta and sauté until lightly browned. Add onions and continue to sauté over low heat until golden.

3. Stir in tomatoes, increase heat to medium high and cook, stirring, 10 to 15 minutes, until sauce begins to thicken. Season to taste with salt and red chili flakes.

4. Remove fish from refrigerator. Preheat oven to 425 degrees.

5. Spoon sauce over the fish. Place fish in oven and bake 15 to 20 minutes, until it is just cooked through. Scatter parsley on top and serve.

Yield: 6 servings
(Florence Fabricant)

The sauce for the fish is from the spaghetti repertory. Consider doubling the sauce ingredients and serving pasta, especially a small pasta like orzo or farfalle, with some of the sauce alongside.

FLOUNDER FILLETS WITH MUSHROOMS AND TOMATOES

Time: 35 minutes

1 tablespoon butter
1 tablespoon extra virgin olive oil
⅓ pound white mushrooms in small cubes
2 teaspoons finely chopped garlic
4 ripe plum tomatoes, peeled and cut into small cubes
1 tablespoon lemon juice
2 sprigs fresh thyme or 1 teaspoon dried
Salt and freshly ground pepper to taste
6 tablespoons sesame seeds
4 flounder fillets, each about 5 ounces
2 tablespoons vegetable oil
3 tablespoons chopped parsley

1. Heat butter and olive oil in a skillet. Add mushrooms, and cook briefly over medium-high heat, shaking pan until mushrooms are lightly browned. Add garlic; cook a few seconds, then add tomatoes, lemon juice, thyme and salt and pepper to taste. Cook, stirring, for 5 minutes. Remove from heat and keep warm.

2. Spread sesame seeds on a large platter. Season fillets with salt and pepper. Lay them over sesame seeds on one side, then on the other to coat them lightly.

3. Heat vegetable oil in nonstick skillet large enough to hold fillets without crowding. Cook over high heat until fillets and seeds are lightly browned on both sides.

4. Spoon mushroom sauce onto warmed serving plates. Place fillets over sauce, sprinkle with parsley and serve.

Yield: 4 servings
(Jacques Pépin)

FLOUNDER WITH PINK GRAPEFRUIT

Time: 45 minutes

1 pink grapefruit
2 tablespoons flour
Salt and freshly ground black pepper to taste
4 flounder or gray sole fillets, each about 6 ounces
3 tablespoons unsalted butter
2 shallots, finely minced
1 tablespoon balsamic vinegar
1 tablespoon finely minced cilantro leaves

1. Peel grapefruit, removing all white pith. Hold grapefruit over a bowl and with a small, sharp knife, separate grapefruit into segments, cutting them away from the membrane that separates them. Reserve two tablespoons of the juice in the bowl. Set the segments and juice aside.

2. Season flour with salt and pepper and spread it on a plate. Dip flounder fillets into flour, dusting off any excess.

3. Heat two tablespoons butter in one or two large skillets. Sauté flounder about three minutes a side, until cooked through and lightly browned. If you cannot fit all the flounder into the pan at one time, do it in two shifts or use two pans.

4. Remove flounder from pan and put on a warm platter. Add remaining butter and the shallots to pan and sauté a few minutes. Add the grapefruit segments, grapefruit juice and balsamic vinegar and bring to a simmer. Season to taste with salt and pepper. Spoon the sauce over the fish. Sprinkle with cilantro and serve.

Yield: 4 servings
(Florence Fabricant)

Prepare this dish in winter, when pink grapefruit are at their peak and meaty blackback or witch flounders are also in season. If you can obtain fresh Dover sole fillets, they are excellent in this recipe, as are sand dabs and petrale sole.

BAKED ROMAN-JEWISH TIMBALE

Time: 45 minutes

The Jewish cooking of Rome, which can be experienced in the restaurants of the former Jewish ghetto, the Portico d'Ottavia, is considered by some to be based on the city's most ancient culinary traditions. This dish is an example.

1½ pounds chicory or frisée, cored
5 tablespoons extra virgin olive oil
½ cup fine, dry unseasoned bread crumbs
1 clove garlic, minced
1½ pounds thin fillets of grey or lemon sole
Salt and freshly ground black pepper to taste

1. Rinse chicory well, chop leaves coarsely and set aside.

2. Preheat oven to 350 degrees. Smear a tablespoon of olive oil around bottom and sides of a 2-quart casserole. Sprinkle bottom and sides with about ¼ cup of the bread crumbs. Combine garlic with chicory. Spread a third of the greens in bottom of casserole. Top with half the fish fillets, arranged like spokes of a wheel. Sprinkle salt, lots of pepper and a tablespoon of bread crumbs over fish, then drizzle a tablespoon of olive oil on top. Continue with another layer of half the remaining chicory, the remaining fish and more salt, pepper, half the remaining bread crumbs and oil. Top casserole with remaining chicory; sprinkle with salt, pepper, and remaining crumbs and olive oil.

3. Using a spatula, press top layer gently to tamp it down in casserole. Place in oven and bake 20 minutes. Then, raise the heat to 425 degrees, press top layer again gently and continue baking an additional 10 minutes.

4. Remove from oven and serve hot or at room temperature.

Yield: 8 servings as a first course
(Paola di Mauro)

SAUTÉED LEMON SOLE WITH FRESH TOMATO AND GINGER SAUCE

Time: 45 minutes

1 tablespoon extra virgin olive oil
2 tablespoons chopped shallots
1 teaspoon finely chopped garlic
4 ripe tomatoes, about 1 pound, peeled, seeded and diced

2 tablespoons grated fresh ginger

1 teaspoon ground cumin

Salt and freshly ground black pepper to taste

4 tablespoons unsalted butter

4 skinless fillets of lemon sole, about 1 pound

4 tablespoons milk

½ cup flour

2 tablespoons vegetable oil

1 tablespoon lemon juice

4 sprigs basil or flat leaf parsley

1. Heat olive oil in a saucepan, add shallots and garlic. Cook briefly. Do not brown. Add tomatoes, ginger, cumin, and salt and pepper to taste. Bring to a boil and simmer 5 minutes.

2. Place tomato mixture in a blender. Add 1 tablespoon butter and blend quickly to a fine texture. Check seasoning; transfer to a small saucepan and keep warm.

3. Meanwhile, sprinkle fillets with salt and pepper to taste. Pour milk into a shallow bowl; put flour on a dish. Dip fillets in milk, then dredge each with flour, patting so flour adheres and shaking to remove excess.

4. Heat vegetable oil in a large nonstick skillet over medium-high heat. Place as many fillets in the pan as will fit in one layer without crowding.

5. Brown fillets thoroughly on one side; turn, and brown on other side. Cooking will take about 2 minutes on each side, depending on the thickness of fillets. Do not overcook.

6. Divide tomato mixture equally among four warm serving plates. Place fillets over tomatoes and keep warm.

7. While the pan is still warm, wipe it out with a paper towel and return it to medium-high heat. Add remaining butter and cook until hazelnut brown. Add lemon juice and pour mixture equally over each serving. Top with basil or parsley.

Yield: 4 servings
(Pierre Franey)

MUSTARD-MARINATED SOLE

Time: 30 minutes

*Dover sole
fillets can also
be used.*

> 4 tablespoons red wine vinegar
> 1 tablespoon grainy mustard
> 4 gray sole fillets, about 1½ pounds total
> 6 tablespoons extra virgin olive oil
> 2 tablespoons finely minced shallots
> ¼ cup flour
> Salt and freshly ground black pepper
> 1 tablespoons finely chopped flat-leaf parsley

1. Beat vinegar and mustard together. Brush fish with 1½ tablespoons of this mixture and allow to sit for 15 minutes.

2. Heat 4 tablespoons of the oil in a large skillet. Add shallots and sauté over medium heat until golden. Stir in remaining vinegar mixture, remove from pan and set aside.

3. Dust fish with flour to coat. Add remaining oil to pan and heat. Add fish to pan and sauté until lightly browned, about 3 minutes per side. Pour reserved vinegar, oil and shallot mixture over fish. Season with salt and pepper. Transfer to serving platter, sprinkle with parsley and serve.

Yield: 4 servings
(Florence Fabricant)

BRAISED LEMON SOLE WITH WATERCRESS

Time: 15 minutes

*If you can
obtain fresh
Dover sole,
this is a recipe
that will suit
it beautifully.*

> 1 tablespoon butter
> ½ cup plus 1 tablespoon extra virgin olive oil
> 1½ pounds skinless lemon sole fillets (2 large fillets)
> Sea or kosher salt
> ¼ cup red wine vinegar
> ½ cup fish broth (recipe page 321) or chicken broth
> 1 bunch watercress, about 1 pound, heavy stems removed,
>   leaves coarsely chopped

1. Place a large nonstick sauté pan over medium-high heat for 1 to 2 minutes. Add butter and 1 tablespoon olive oil. Meanwhile, season sole on both sides with salt. When butter stops foaming and begins to brown, lay sole skinned side down in pan, and sauté until it begins to brown on edges. Carefully transfer fillets to a plate. Take pan off heat; cool for a minute.

2. Meanwhile, whisk together remaining oil, vinegar and broth. Slip fish back into pan, and pour over enough oil-broth mixture to come up just around the edges of the fish. Bring to a simmer (barely bubbling around sides of fish), while continually spooning broth over top of fish. Braise until just cooked through, 3 to 4 minutes.

3. Remove fish to a serving platter. Reduce pan juices for a minute; add watercress to pan and let wilt, 20 to 30 seconds. Spoon watercress and juices over fish. Serve.

***Yield: 4 servings**
(Tom Colicchio, Craft,
New York City)*

Grouper

Also called black grouper, this fish, which is usually harvested in the Caribbean, is from the same family as black sea bass. But groupers tend to run larger. The flesh is snowy white and meaty.

Substitutes: sea bass, tilefish, blackfish, red snapper

GROUPER WITH HERBS AND GARLIC
Time: 25 minutes

½ **bunch cilantro**
½ **bunch flat-leaf parsley**
2 large cloves garlic
¼ **teaspoon ground cumin**
⅛ **to** ¼ **teaspoon red chili flakes**
2 tablespoons lemon juice
1½ **tablespoons extra virgin olive oil**
10 ounces grouper fillet, cut in 2 portions

1. Preheat broiler. Cover broiler pan with aluminum foil.

2. Wash, dry and coarsely chop cilantro and parsley. Mince cilantro, parsley and garlic in food processor.

3. Add cumin, red chili flakes, lemon juice and 1 tablespoon olive oil, and process until well blended.

4. Rinse and dry fish. Brush remaining oil on foil. Place fish in a single layer on foil, and spread herb mixture evenly over fish.

5. Broil fish four inches from heat, about 8 minutes, or until just cooked through.

Yield: 2 servings
(Marian Burros)

GROUPER WITH CAPERS

Time: 15 minutes

1½-pound grouper fillet
2 tablespoons extra virgin olive oil
Coarse sea salt and freshly ground black pepper
1 tablespoon fresh thyme leaves
2 tablespoons capers, rinsed and drained
Thyme sprigs to garnish
Juice of ½ lemon

1. Preheat oven to 400 degrees. Brush grouper with the olive oil, and season with salt and pepper. Heat a nonstick skillet and sear grouper on one side so that it is lightly browned.

2. Place fish, browned side up, in baking dish. Sprinkle with thyme and capers. Bake 6 to 8 minutes, or until done. Garnish with thyme sprigs, drizzle with lemon juice and serve.

Yield: 4 servings
(Florence Fabricant)

GROUPER WITH ZA'ATAR AND TOMATO

Time: 45 minutes

2 tablespoons extra virgin olive oil
4 large cloves garlic, sliced
1¼ cups finely diced onion
10 large plum tomatoes, coarsely chopped
1½ tablespoons za'atar (sold in Middle Eastern
    food shops)
¼ teaspoon salt
¼ teaspoon black pepper
¼ cup lemon juice
4 6-ounce grouper fillets
Salt and pepper to taste

Za'atar is a Middle Eastern spice blend, predominately sumac, roasted sesame seeds and thyme. It is sold in spice stores and Middle Eastern shops.

1. In medium nonstick skillet, heat one tablespoon olive oil. Sauté garlic and onion until soft. Add tomatoes and cook 10 to 15 minutes, until soft but still chunky. Stir in za'atar, salt, pepper and 1½ tablespoons lemon juice. Cook one minute. Keep warm.

2. Sprinkle fish with salt and pepper. Heat 1 tablespoon olive oil in large nonstick skillet. Sauté fish over high heat 3 to 4 minutes on each side.

3. Spoon sauce on 4 plates and top with fish. Sprinkle with remaining lemon juice.

Yield: 4 servings
(Rozanne Gold)

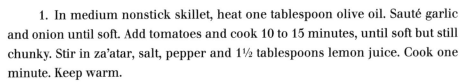

Haddock

Haddock is a member of the cod family, and when the fish is small (less than two pounds), it's often sold as scrod. Haddock, or scrod, is also sold smoked, as finnan haddie.

Substitute: cod, hake

HADDOCK WITH MUSHROOMS
Time: 30 minutes

Small chanterelles can be used in place of plain white mushrooms. But be sure to scrape the outer layer off the stems of the chanterelles.

2 tablespoons extra virgin olive oil
2 tablespoons finely chopped shallots
1 clove garlic, minced
½ pound white mushrooms, sliced
2 pounds haddock or scrod fillets
Salt and freshly ground black pepper
1 cup dry white wine
2 tablespoons white wine vinegar
4 tablespoons softened butter
2 tablespoons finely chopped flat-leaf parsley

1. Preheat oven to 400 degrees.

2. In a large ovenproof skillet, heat olive oil and sauté shallots and garlic until soft but not brown. Add mushrooms and sauté until they begin to soften. Arrange scrod on the mushrooms and shallots in a single layer. Season with salt and pepper, add wine, place in the oven and bake about 8 minutes, until the fish has just turned opaque in the middle. Do not overcook.

3. Transfer fish and mushrooms to a warm serving platter and cover to keep warm.

4. Add vinegar to the skillet and cook rapidly until the liquid in the pan just coats the bottom. Swirl in the butter with a whisk, cooking gently until the sauce begins to thicken. Stir in the parsley, season with salt and pepper, pour over the fish and serve.

Yield: 4 servings
(Pierre Franey)

Hake

A member of the cod family, hake, called merluza in Spain, where it is a kitchen staple, is relatively underutilized in America. It's a meaty fish that has the same broad, silky flake as cod, but it is only worthwhile when it is very fresh. Hake is also related to whiting, though hake fillets are usually fairly large and thick, while the whiting in American markets tend to be smaller.

Substitutes: cod, scrod, whiting, halibut

BLACKENED HAKE FILLETS WITH ROASTED RED PEPPER SAUCE

Time: 40 minutes

In place of roasted red bell peppers, jarred Spanish piquillo peppers can be used. The wine of choice to serve with this Iberian-inspired dish is a red Rioja.

4 roasted red bell peppers, skinned and seeded
6 slices bacon, diced
3 shallots, minced
1 cup dry white wine
2 tablespoons chopped tarragon leaves
4 tablespoons cold unsalted butter, diced
Salt, cayenne and freshly ground black pepper
4 tablespoons paprika
4 teaspoons onion powder
1 tablespoon garlic powder
1 tablespoon dried thyme
1 tablespoon dried oregano
3 pounds hake fillets, 1½ inches thick, cut into
    12 to 16 pieces
6 tablespoons clarified butter

1. To make the sauce, puree the peppers in a food mill. Cook the bacon in a skillet on medium heat for 2 minutes. Add shallots, lower heat to medium low and cook until softened, about 5 minutes more.

2. Add the wine to the skillet and bring to a boil over high heat, scraping the bottom and sides of the pan and simmering the mixture until the liquid is reduced by half. Stir in the pepper puree, remove from heat and add 1 tablespoon tarragon leaves. Whisk in the butter and season sauce with salt, cayenne and black pepper. Keep warm.

3. Place a large, heavy cast-iron skillet over high heat for 10 minutes. Combine paprika, 1 teaspoon salt, onion powder, garlic powder, thyme, oregano, ½ teaspoon cayenne and ¼ teaspoon black pepper on a plate. Dip fish pieces in clarified butter and then coat with the spice mix. Working in batches, place coated fish in hot skillet and sear for 4 to 6 minutes on each side. (Be prepared for smoke.) Serve immediately, topped with the warm red pepper sauce and garnished with remaining tarragon.

Yield: 6 to 8 servings
(Tim McNulty)

Halibut

Halibut is a flatfish, like flounder (page 55), but runs considerably larger. Most halibut is caught in Alaska, and if you're buying Alaskan halibut, it's important to determine that it is fresh, not frozen. Even then, Alaskan halibut can be coarser and less elegantly flavored than the smaller Atlantic halibut. Though fillets and steaks are thick and meaty, halibut is actually a fish with a delicate texture that is better steamed, roasted or baked than seared in the sauté pan.

Substitutes: for fillets: fluke, flounder, turbot; for steaks: wild striped bass, cod

HALIBUT TIRADITO
Time: 15 minutes

> 12 ounces sashimi-quality halibut
> 1½ teaspoons Chinese or Thai chili paste
> ½ teaspoon salt
> 1 tablespoon fresh or bottled yuzu juice or a mixture of 1½
>   teaspoons grapefruit juice and 1½ teaspoons orange juice
> 1 tablespoon lemon juice
> 2 tablespoons cilantro leaves

1. Slice halibut as thinly as possible into long strips. Place strips on a large serving plate, radiating from the center to look like flower petals.

2. Brush chili paste on fish, and season with salt. Sprinkle with yuzu juice and lemon juice. Garnish with cilantro leaves, and serve immediately.

Yield: 4 servings
(Nobu Matsuhisa, Nobu,
New York City)

Tiradito is a kind of South American sashimi.

BROILED HALIBUT WITH MISO GLAZE

Time: 45 minutes

This recipe is a close relative to the now-classic black cod with miso glaze.

1 teaspoon grated ginger
2 tablespoons mirin
3 tablespoons mellow white miso
1¾-pound halibut fillet with skin, cut into four pieces
Vegetable oil for brushing pan
Steamed sticky rice
Sautéed bok choy

1. In small bowl, combine ginger, mirin and miso, and mix until smooth. Rub on flesh side of fish pieces. Marinate 30 minutes.

2. Heat broiler. Brush broiling pan with oil. Lay fish in pan, skin side down, and broil for 7 to 9 minutes, until flesh flakes and glaze bubbles and browns. Serve with steamed sticky rice and sautéed greens.

Yield: 4 servings
(Nina Simonds)

STEAMED HALIBUT IN BORSCHT WITH WARM CHIVE-HORSERADISH SAUCE

Time: 1¼ hours

2 tablespoons extra virgin olive oil or corn oil
1 medium onion, julienned
1 cup julienned fennel bulb
2 tablespoons sliced garlic
2 sprigs thyme
2 sprigs flat-leaf parsley
1 cup chopped savoy cabbage, plus 3 of the darker outer leaves, finely julienned
1 quart well-seasoned chicken or vegetable stock
4 cups peeled and julienned fresh beets (about 1½ bunches)
Salt and freshly ground white pepper to taste
1 cup crème fraîche, sour cream or mayonnaise
¼ cup bottled white horseradish

½ teaspoon sugar

1 tablespoon minced chives

8 halibut steaks or fillets, each 4 to 6 ounces, or 8 portions
   chilled gefilte fish (recipe page 316)

1. Heat oil in a heavy 3-quart saucepan. Add onions and fennel, and cook slowly about 5 minutes, until softened. Tie garlic, thyme, parsley and chopped cabbage in a double thickness of cheesecloth, and add it to saucepan along with stock and beets. Simmer 15 minutes. Season to taste with salt and pepper. Remove from heat. Discard cheesecloth and its contents. To serve the dish chilled, refrigerate beet mixture at least 4 hours or overnight.

2. Bring 3 cups water to a boil in a small saucepan. Add julienned cabbage leaves, cook just until bright green, then drain. Set leaves aside, covered, to keep warm; for a cold dish, refrigerate.

3. Mix crème fraîche, sour cream or mayonnaise with horseradish, sugar and chives. If using mayonnaise, thin it beforehand with 2 tablespoons water. This sauce can be gently warmed in a small saucepan or chilled to serve cold.

4. To serve, steam halibut until fully cooked outside and just warm inside, 6 to 8 minutes. Keep warm. Reheat beet mixture, spoon into warmed shallow soup plates, scatter with julienned cabbage and top with fish. Or spoon chilled beet mixture into shallow soup plates, add cabbage, and top with gefilte fish. Serve horseradish sauce, warm or chilled, on the side.

Yield: 8 servings

(Eric Ripert, Le Bernardin, New York City)

HALIBUT WITH TOMATO CREAM
Time: 30 minutes

4 medium-size halibut steaks, 8 ounces each

3 tablespoons unsalted butter

½ cup finely chopped onion

2 cloves garlic, minced

½ cup heavy cream

2 tablespoons dry white wine

3 medium-size tomatoes, peeled, seeded and finely chopped

1 tablespoon finely chopped chives

Salt and freshly ground black pepper

The simple but lush sauce in this recipe would be suitable for almost any sautéed or poached white-fleshed fish.

1. Pat halibut steaks dry. Heat 2 tablespoons butter in a large, heavy skillet, preferably nonstick. Add halibut and sauté over medium-high heat until the fish is lightly browned but not quite cooked through, about 3 minutes on each side.

2. Transfer fish to a warm serving platter and cover with foil.

3. Add the remaining butter to the skillet, then add the onion and garlic and sauté until tender. Add cream and wine and cook for a few minutes, until the mixture begins to thicken. Stir in the tomatoes, sauté over high heat a minute or so, just until tomatoes soften, then add the chives. Season with salt and pepper.

4. Return the fish and any fish juices to the pan. Baste fish briefly with sauce, arrange on serving platter. Spoon some of the sauce over each fish steak and serve.

Yield: 4 servings
(Florence Fabricant)

Herring

Fresh herring, an important European catch, is a rarity in American markets. In late spring some fresh or lightly marinated herring from Holland and Scandinavia becomes available. It can be used in this recipe, as can marinated maatjes fillets, usually sold in shops that carry smoked fish.

Substitute: white anchovies

HERRING SANDWICHES

Time: 15 minutes

> 2 Boston lettuce leaves
> 6 slices rye cocktail bread
> 3 tablespoons sour cream
> 4 ounces herring in wine sauce (available in
>   8-ounce jars)
> 1 ounce thinly sliced red onion
> 2 tablespoons chopped chives

1. Break each lettuce leaf into three pieces and arrange on bread. Spread each slice of bread with a little sour cream. Top each leaf with 1 teaspoon of the sour cream and 1 or 2 pieces of the herring.

2. Top with the red onion and chives. Arrange on a serving plate.

Yield: 6 open-face sandwiches

(Jacques Pépin)

John Dory

John Dory is a roundish fish with a characteristic dark spot behind the gills. It's also called St. Peter's fish and is supposedly the source of the biblical legend. It's more popular in Europe than in America but is an excellent, mild, white-fleshed variety. It is often farmed.

Substitutes: red snapper, fluke, pompano, tilapia

JOHN DORY IN CILANTRO-CURRY CHUTNEY

Time: 1 hour

>½ cup unsalted shelled pistachios
>1 tablespoon finely minced fresh ginger
>1 tablespoon minced cilantro leaves
>1 tablespoon minced mint leaves
>½ cup plain yogurt
>2 teaspoons curry powder
>2 tablespoons lime juice
>Salt and freshly ground black pepper to taste
>4 John Dory fillets, about 1½ pounds total
>1 tablespoon extra virgin olive oil
>Cilantro sprigs and lime wedges for garnish

1. Lightly toast pistachios by heating in skillet, stirring, 2 to 3 minutes. Grind in food processor, blender or spice mill. Combine with ginger, cilantro, mint, yogurt, curry powder, lime juice, salt and pepper.

2. Put fish in glass or ceramic dish in single layer. Spread spice mixture over, cover and set aside at room temperature for 20 minutes.

3. Preheat oven to 450 degrees. Brush baking dish with oil. Put fish with yogurt and spice coating in baking dish and bake about 15 minutes, until cooked through. Serve garnished with cilantro and lime.

Yield: 4 servings
(Florence Fabricant)

Mackerel

Forget Its Reputation: Mackerel Has a Multitude of Virtues

By MARK BITTMAN

Mackerel is a symbol of stinkiness, widely considered to be too strong-flavored, too oily, too fishy. Its high fat content means that its quality deteriorates rapidly once the fish is out of the water. The English realized this 300 years ago, when they made an exception to their blue laws and allowed mackerel to be hawked on Sunday, because fish caught on Saturday would be nearly worthless by Monday.

When its quality is high, however, mackerel is delicious. It is not only flavorful and moist but also so sweet that it almost has to be cooked with acidic flavorings such as lemon, tomato or vinegar. With its iridescent, blue-green, silvery skin and vertical stripes, mackerel is one of the most attractive fish in the ocean. Besides, it is versatile, plentiful and downright cheap.

And mackerel fat is healthful. According to the Department of Agriculture, no fish is higher in omega-3 fatty acids, which are thought to lower cholesterol and strengthen the immune system.

A nice Atlantic mackerel, sometimes called Boston or Northern mackerel, will usually weigh less than two pounds and frequently less than one. It should look alive, as if it could swim right off the ice. It should smell sweet, too. Spanish mackerel are equally fine.

Once home, mackerel must be kept ice-cold: Either bury it in ice in the vegetable compartment of the refrigerator, or sandwich it between two ice packs. And cook it soon.

Traditionally, the English smoked mackerel, the Japanese and French pickled it, and the Greeks dried it in the breeze. All these treatments are ways to preserve a fragile fish that is still caught by the ton. But there is no need to resort to complicated methods of preparation; it is delicious grilled, roasted, poached or broiled. 🐚

Substitutes: bluefish, sardines, rouget

MACKEREL IN WHITE WINE

Time: 30 minutes, plus overnight refrigeration

This French appetizer classic can also be made with fresh sardines.

2½ cups dry white wine
3 tablespoons red wine vinegar
1 bunch thyme
1 carrot, sliced
1 large Spanish onion, peeled and thinly sliced
1½ teaspoons unflavored powdered gelatin
6 mackerel fillets, 6 to 8 ounces each
Salt and freshly ground black pepper
6 bay leaves
6 thin slices lemon

1. In an enameled or other nonreactive saucepan, combine wine, vinegar and thyme. Place over high heat, bring to a boil, and cook for 5 minutes. Add carrot and onion, and simmer for another 3 minutes. Remove from heat and stir in gelatin until it dissolves. Pour through a strainer into a heat-proof bowl, and set aside.

2. Place mackerel fillets skin side up in a flameproof baking dish. Pour hot wine mixture on top, and season with salt and pepper. Place a bay leaf decoratively on each fillet, anchoring one end with a slice of lemon.

3. Place baking dish over high heat to bring wine mixture to a full boil. Immediately remove pan from heat. Cover with aluminum foil, and cool to room temperature. Refrigerate pan overnight.

4. To serve, place a fillet on each of six serving plates with some of the jellied sauce. If desired, serve with frisée salad or potato salad.

Yield: 6 servings
(Jean-Michel Bergougnoux,
L'Absinthe, New York City)

ROAST MACKEREL WITH ONIONS AND LEMON

Time: 30 minutes

¼ cup unsalted butter
1 large onion, chopped
1 teaspoon minced garlic
1 medium-size shallot, minced
½ cup minced fresh herbs: parsley, tarragon, chives, thyme
**   and chervil**
4 mackerel, about ¾ pound each, cleaned and left whole
Salt and freshly ground black pepper to taste
2 lemons, cut into thin slices
Juice of ½ lemon

1. Preheat oven to 450 degrees.

2. Melt 1 tablespoon of the butter in a medium-size skillet or saucepan over medium heat. Add onion and cook slowly, stirring occasionally, until softened but not browned, about 10 to 15 minutes.

3. Mix together the garlic, shallot and herbs, and stuff the cavities of the fish with this mixture. Sprinkle the fish with salt and pepper. Melt the remaining butter.

4. Lay the onions and a few of the lemon slices on the bottom of a baking dish large enough to hold the fish. Place the fish on top, drizzle with the melted butter and lemon juice, and top with the remaining lemon slices.

5. Roast, uncovered, until done, about 15 minutes (the interior cavity of the mackerel will have the barest trace of pink). Serve immediately, spooning the pan juices over the fish.

Yield: 4 servings
(Mark Bittman)

SAUTÉED MACKEREL WITH GARLIC AND ROSEMARY

Time: 30 minutes

This recipe requires opening that expensive bottle of aged balsamic vinegar. Everyday balsamic vinegar will not do.

3 cloves garlic, peeled
1 lemon
3 tablespoons extra virgin olive oil
2 mackerel, about ¾ pound each, cleaned and left whole
Flour for dredging
2 sprigs rosemary
Salt and freshly ground black pepper to taste
½ cup red wine
1 teaspoon aged balsamic vinegar

1. Crush one of the garlic cloves. Mince the other 2 garlic cloves. Cut 3 slices from the lemon; squeeze the juice from the rest of the lemon. Set minced garlic and lemon slices aside.

2. Preheat oven to its lowest setting.

3. Heat a 12-inch, nonstick skillet over medium heat for 3 or 4 minutes. Add the olive oil.

4. Dredge the mackerel lightly in flour. When the oil is hot, place the fish in the skillet. Add crushed garlic and one of the sprigs of rosemary. Cook the mackerel at the highest heat it can take without burning. Sprinkle the fish with salt and pepper, turn it when it has browned on one side and then season the other side. Cook until the belly cavity has just the barest trace of pink remaining. Remove it to a platter and place in the oven.

5. Remove the garlic and rosemary from the skillet and discard. Add wine and balsamic vinegar to the skillet. Stir with a wooden spoon over medium-high heat. Add the minced garlic and the remaining sprig of rosemary, and stir.

6. Decorate the fish with the lemon slices. Remove the rosemary from the skillet and place it atop the lemon. Add the lemon juice to the sauce, along with any liquid that has accumulated around the mackerel; stir once, pour over the fish and serve.

Yield: 2 servings
(Mark Bittman)

MACKEREL FILLETS IN SOY SAUCE

Time: 30 minutes

1 cup long-grain rice
½ cup soy sauce
⅓ cup dry sherry
2 tablespoons rice or white wine vinegar
6 thin slices peeled fresh ginger
3 or 4 crushed cloves garlic
4 mackerel fillets, about 1 pound total, skin on

1. Place rice in a saucepan, add 1½ cups water, bring to a boil, lower heat and cook, covered, 15 minutes. When rice is done, remove from heat and set aside, covered, 10 minutes.

2. While rice is cooking, mix together all the remaining ingredients except the fish in a 12-inch skillet with a cover. Add ½ cup water, bring to a boil, and simmer uncovered over medium heat for about 5 minutes.

3. Add the fish, skin side down; cover, and simmer 7 to 10 minutes, or until the fish is cooked through (the thinnest end of the smallest fillet should just flake when prodded with a fork or knife, and the fish should all be opaque).

4. To serve, mound some rice on each of 4 plates and spoon a fillet and some sauce onto each.

Yield: 4 servings
(Mark Bittman)

As with many mackerel dishes, red wine would suit this one.

Mahimahi

Mahimahi is a fish in the dolphin family. It's no relation to dolphin the mammal, but until the Hawaiian name *mahimahi* came into fairly universal use, there was considerable confusion about it. When told that the fish was dolphin, many assumed it was the mammal and that they might be eating Flipper. Now, the name dolphin is rarely used for the fish. It's an appealing, meaty, white-fleshed fish that has a tough skin.

Substitutes: grouper, halibut, tilefish, wild striped bass, yellowtail

CUMIN-CRUSTED MAHIMAHI
WITH LIME-CHILI SAUCE

Time: 25 minutes

> **4 8-ounce mahimahi steaks**
> **¼ cup toasted cumin seeds**
> **Salt and freshly ground black pepper**
> **2 limes**
> **2 to 3 teaspoons red chili flakes**
> **¼ cup finely chopped cilantro**
> **3 tablespoons extra virgin olive oil**
> **1 teaspoon minced garlic**
> **1 tablespoon molasses**
> **2 tablespoons vegetable oil**

1. Rub the fish on all sides with cumin, and sprinkle generously with salt and pepper. Set aside.

2. Peel limes and separate into segments with a sharp paring knife, making sure to remove all membranes between the sections. In a small bowl, combine limes, chili, cilantro, olive oil, garlic and molasses. Mix well. Set aside.

3. In a large sauté pan over medium-high heat, heat vegetable oil until hot but not smoking. Add mahimahi steaks and sauté for 3 to 5 minutes a side, or until the fish is barely translucent at the center.

4. Remove fish from the pan. Peel off skin. Stir the lime-chili mixture, spoon a portion over each fish steak and serve.

*Yield: **4 servings***
(John Willoughby and
Chris Schlesinger)

MAHIMAHI IN LOBSTER SAUCE
WITH MACADAMIA NUTS

Time: 1½ hours

¼ cup macadamia nuts, roughly chopped

Shell from 1 cooked lobster, broken into pieces (no meat)

¼ pound sliced bacon, cut into 2-inch lengths

1 small carrot, peeled, roughly chopped

1 small onion, peeled, roughly chopped

1 stalk celery, roughly chopped

¼ cup chopped basil leaves

2 tablespoons minced thyme leaves

5 whole black peppercorns

½ cup tomato paste

4 cups heavy cream

Salt and white pepper

1 tablespoon vegetable oil

4 7-ounce skinless mahimahi fillets

Hawaiian macadamia nuts are an appropriate addition to a recipe for a fish that goes by its Hawaiian name.

1. Preheat oven to 350 degrees. Toast macadamia nuts on a baking sheet until golden brown, about 10 minutes. Set aside. Increase oven temperature to 375 degrees. Place lobster shell pieces on a baking sheet and bake 20 minutes. Set aside.

2. Place a large flameproof casserole over medium-low heat. Sauté bacon until soft. Add carrot, onion, celery, basil, thyme and peppercorns. Sauté until vegetables have softened, about 10 minutes. Add lobster shells, tomato paste and heavy cream. Stir well, and simmer until reduced by half, about 45 minutes.

3. Place a very fine strainer (or one lined with cheesecloth) over a 2 to 3-quart saucepan. Pour in lobster sauce; discard shells and vegetables. Gently heat sauce. Season with salt and white pepper to taste, and keep warm.

4. Place a large nonstick skillet over medium-high heat. Add vegetable oil. When hot, add fish fillets. Sear on both sides, about 1 minute a side for medium rare or longer to cook more thoroughly. Immediately transfer to four warm plates, and drizzle lobster sauce on and around each fillet. Garnish with macadamia nuts.

Yield: 4 servings
(Roy Yamaguachi, Roy's,
Honolulu, Hawaii)

Monkfish

Ugly is the word for this fish, also called goosefish. At one time fishermen threw the monkfish back. But French chefs, who call it lotte, started using it and now its popularity is beginning to threaten the viability of the fishery. Only the tail of the fish is eaten; the huge head and belly are discarded. But monkfish tails, which consist of two thick fillets on either side of a sturdy bone, have an almost lobsterlike consistency and can be roasted, baked, sliced and sautéed, grilled or added to fish stews. Small monkfish tails can be roasted on the bone.

Substitutes: blackfish, tilefish, lobster

BRAISED MONKFISH WITH POTATOES AND LEEKS

Time: 1 hour

> 1 tablespoon extra virgin olive oil
> 2 ounces slab bacon, diced
> 3 tablespoons finely chopped shallots
> 2 bunches leeks (white part only), rinsed, trimmed
>   and chopped
> 1 tablespoon minced fresh chives
> ⅔ cup dry white wine
> ¾ pound small new potatoes, scrubbed
> Salt
> 1⅓ pounds monkfish
> Freshly ground black pepper
> Juice of ½ lemon

1. Heat oil in a heavy 3-quart casserole. Add bacon and sauté until it starts to brown. Add shallots and leeks and sauté over low heat until softened but not brown. Stir in half the chives. Add half the wine, scraping the bottom of the pan. Cover and cook over low heat until the leeks are very tender, about 25 minutes. Remove from heat.

2. While the leeks are cooking, slice the potatoes in half, put them in a

saucepan and cover with salted water. Bring to a boil and simmer until tender, about 15 minutes. Drain potatoes and stir them into the casserole. Cover the casserole and set aside until about 10 minutes before serving time.

3. Cut the monkfish into uniform pieces about 1 inch by 2 inches and 1 inch thick. Season with salt and pepper.

4. Shortly before serving, add the remaining wine to the casserole and reheat until it simmers. Put the pieces of monkfish on top of the leeks and potatoes, cover the casserole and cook over low heat just until the fish is cooked through, about 10 minutes.

5. Add the lemon juice, season with salt and pepper if needed, dust with remaining chives and serve.

Yield: 4 servings
(Florence Fabricant)

CHA CA
Time: 20 minutes, plus 2 hours marinating

3 pounds monkfish
4 large shallots
3 large cloves garlic
½ small onion
1 tablespoon ground turmeric
2 tablespoons plus ¼ cup canola oil
¼ teaspoon freshly ground white pepper
1 bunch scallions, white part removed and green
    sliced into tiny rings
1½ bunches dill, minced
6 cups cooked Vietnamese rice noodles
1 small bunch mint, leaves only
1 small bunch basil, leaves only
½ cup dry-roasted, unsalted peanuts
Nuoc mam (bottled fish sauce)

1. Cut monkfish into slices ½-inch thick.

2. With the food processor running, add the shallots, garlic and onion, processing until the ingredients are smooth. Add turmeric, 2 tablespoons oil and pepper, and continue processing until mixture is a fairly smooth paste.

A 100-year-old restaurant in Hanoi, called Cha Ca La Vong, serves only this dish. Small charcoal burners are placed on the table, along with the noodles, herbs and condiments, and the customers cook the fish themselves. It might be time to take out that fondue pot!

MONKFISH   83

3. Mix monkfish slices with the turmeric mixture and allow to marinate, covered, in the refrigerator for at least two hours or overnight.

4. When ready to cook, either prepare a charcoal fire or use a top-of-stove grill. Arrange fish pieces on a greased 2-piece wire grill to make them easy to flip. Grill only long enough to brown a little on both sides.

5. Meanwhile, heat the remaining ¼ cup of oil in a pan that can be taken to the table. Add ⅔ of the scallions and of the dill. When the fish is ready, arrange it on the scallions and dill and top with remaining scallions and dill. Cook the fish in the oil at the table until done. For each serving, put some rice noodles in a bowl and top them with the monkfish, then sprinkle with torn mint, basil leaves, peanuts and nuoc mam.

Yield: 6 servings

(Cha Ca La Vong, Hanoi, Vietnam)

MEDALLIONS OF MONKFISH WITH LENTILS

Time: 1 hour

Recommending French lentils is not snobbery. They're smaller and have a nuttier flavor. Most come from Le Puy in south-central France.

4 ounces lentils, preferably French

2 tablespoons chopped bacon

2 tablespoons finely minced onion

2 tablespoons finely minced carrot

2 tablespoons finely minced celery

1 clove garlic, minced

2 cups well-flavored chicken stock

1 whole clove

1 sprig thyme

1 bay leaf

1½ pounds monkfish

Salt and freshly ground pepper to taste

3 tablespoons unsalted butter

1 teaspoon lemon juice

½ teaspoon Dijon mustard

2 tablespoons extra virgin olive oil

1 teaspoon chopped parsley

1. Place the lentils in a bowl, cover with water to a depth of one inch and soak for one hour. Drain, rinse twice and set aside.

2. Preheat oven to 300 degrees.

3. Heat bacon in a heavy saucepan. Add onion, carrot and celery and sauté until tender. Stir in garlic. Add the lentils and chicken stock. Tie the clove, thyme and bay leaf together with a piece of string and add to saucepan. Bring to a simmer. Cover and place in the oven for about 20 minutes, until the lentils are just tender. All the liquid will not have been absorbed. Remove the bundle of herbs and set the lentils aside. The recipe can be prepared in advance up until this point.

4. Cut the monkfish into medallions about 1 inch thick. You should have 12 to 15 medallions. Season with salt and pepper.

5. Shortly before serving, reheat the lentils and beat in the butter a bit at a time. Season with lemon juice, mustard and salt and pepper to taste.

6. Heat the olive oil in a heavy skillet. Cook the medallions over medium-low heat for about 3 minutes on each side, until they are just cooked through.

7. Spoon some of the lentils in the center of each of 4 warmed plates. Arrange the medallions of fish on top and spoon more of the sauce from the lentils around them. Garnish with parsley and serve.

Yield: 4 servings

(Thomas Keller, Rakel, New York City)

HERB-MARINATED GRILLED MONKFISH WITH SHERRY VINAIGRETTE

Time: 2½ hours, including marinating

4 4-to-6-ounce portions monkfish, all membranes removed
1½ tablespoons plus ⅓ cup extra virgin olive oil
6 tablespoons coarsely chopped mixed fresh herbs: summer
savory, tarragon, sage, parsley
1 teaspoon pure maple syrup
¼ cup sherry vinegar
3 tablespoons finely chopped shallots
3 tablespoons finely diced red bell pepper
Kosher or sea salt
Freshly ground black pepper
Freshly ground white pepper

1. In a large mixing bowl, combine the monkfish fillets with 1½ table-spoons of the olive oil and the herbs. Rub the fish well with this mixture so the herbs stick to the fish. Cover and marinate, refrigerated, for at least 2 hours.

2. While the fish is marinating, in a medium mixing bowl combine the maple syrup and vinegar. Add ½ cup of olive oil, shallots, red bell pepper, and salt and black pepper to taste. Refrigerate until serving (may be prepared a day ahead of time, with improvement in flavor).

3. Prepare a hot grill. Sprinkle the fish with salt and white pepper. Place on hot grill, and cook for about 3 minutes. Turn, and grill until the fish is opaque, about 3 to 4 more minutes. Transfer to a platter and allow to rest for 1 minute. To serve, slice the fillets diagonally, and arrange on individual plates. Spoon the vinaigrette over and around the fish. Serve.

Yield: *4 servings*

(Sophie Parker, Chez Sophie, Malta, N.Y.)

MATELOTE OF MONKFISH
Time: 1 hour

The red wine sauce for this fish (steps 1, 3, 4 and 6) would suit many varieties of fish fillets, especially when there's a menu with red wine.

3 ounces tiny pearl onions
1½ pounds monkfish
2 tablespoons fine, dry bread crumbs
2 ounces slab bacon, diced
½ cup finely chopped red onion
1 tablespoon minced tarragon leaves
1 cup dry red wine, or more, to taste
½ cup fish broth (recipe page 321)
1 tablespoon tomato paste
Salt and freshly ground black pepper
1 tablespoon soft unsalted butter
Sprigs of tarragon for garnish

1. Bring a small pot of water to a boil, add the onions and cook for 2 min-utes. Drain onions and run under cold water. Peel onions and set aside.

2. Cut the monkfish into slices about ¾ inch thick. Pat dry on paper towel and lightly dust on one side with the bread crumbs.

3. Place bacon in a heavy skillet large enough to hold the monkfish in a single layer. Cook bacon over medium heat, stirring, until it is crisp and golden brown. Remove to a bowl, draining as much fat as possible back into the skillet.

4. Heat bacon fat over medium heat, add pearl onions and toss briefly in the bacon fat until they begin to turn golden. Remove and add them to the bowl with the cooked bacon.

5. Place the monkfish in the skillet crumb-side down and sear the fish on one side only over medium-high heat until it is attractively browned. Remove fish from the skillet and set it aside on a platter, crumb side up, covered loosely with foil or parchment.

6. Place the red onion in the skillet and cook over low heat until it is soft but not brown. Stir in the tarragon, wine and fish broth. Increase the heat and cook the sauce until it is reduced by half. Stir in the tomato paste and cook a few minutes longer, until the sauce has thickened to the consistency of heavy cream. Season to taste with salt and pepper.

7. Just before serving reheat the sauce over medium heat and adjust the seasonings. Add a little more wine if desired. Swirl in the soft butter. Add the bacon and pearl onions to the sauce, along with any juices in the bowl. Then carefully place the slices of monkfish in the skillet in a single layer, browned side up. Cook about 5 minutes, until the monkfish is just cooked through.

8. Divide the monkfish slices among 4 warmed dinner plates. Carefully spoon some of the sauce with the pearl onions and bacon around, not over, the fish. Garnish each serving with a sprig of tarragon.

Yield: 4 servings
(Florence Fabricant)

MONKFISH LIVER WITH RED WINE SAUCE

Time: 1 hour

*Monkfish
liver, a
Japanese
delicacy,
resembles
foie gras.*

3 large shallots, thinly sliced

4 cloves garlic, sliced

A 5-inch piece fresh ginger, peeled and thinly
    sliced

Zest of 1 orange

1 teaspoon coriander seeds

2 teaspoons fennel seeds

1 teaspoon cardamom seeds

1 tablespoon black peppercorns

2 tablespoons clarified butter

3 cups ruby port

1½ cups fish broth (recipe page 321)

1 teaspoon honey

1 teaspoon lemon juice

1 teaspoon balsamic vinegar

Salt and freshly ground black pepper

8 ounces monkfish liver

½ cup arborio rice

½ cup flour

1 egg, beaten

1. Place shallots, garlic, ginger, orange zest and spices in a 2-quart saucepan. Add 2 teaspons of the butter, cover and cook over medium heat until shallots are transluscent.

2. Add port and fish broth and stir, scraping pan to deglaze. Cook over medium heat until liquid is reduced to about 1 cup. Strain. Return sauce to pan, add honey, lemon juice and vinegar and simmer until sauce is the consistency of heavy cream. Season to taste with salt and pepper. Set aside.

3. Rinse liver, removing any membrane and blood spots. Place in a bowl, add ice water to cover and add enough salt so the water tastes quite salty. Set aside 10 minutes.

4. Meanwhile, grind rice in a blender until the consistency of flour. Drain and dry the liver, dip in flour and then in egg, then in ground rice.

5. Heat a heavy skillet. Add remaining butter. Sauté liver over high heat until it is golden brown, about 2 minutes on each side. Remove from pan. Cut liver in four pieces.

6. Reheat sauce. Arrange each piece of liver on a small plate, spoon sauce around and serve.

Yield: 4 servings
(Sony Club, New York City)

Pollack

Pollack, a lean, white-fleshed fish with a fairly large flake, is a type of cod that's more popular in Europe than in America. The fish should not be undercooked or it will be tough, but care should be taken to avoid overcooking lest it dry out. Let the doorbell ring.

Substitutes: cod, hake, halibut.

BREADED AND BROILED POLLACK
Time: 15 minutes

> 5 cloves garlic, peeled
> 6 slices white bread, preferably 1 or 2 days old
> ½ cup minced scallions
> ½ teaspoon freshly ground black pepper
> 1½ teaspoons salt
> 6 tablespoons extra virgin olive oil
> 6 pollack steaks, 1 inch thick, each about 6 ounces
> 1 lemon, cut into 6 wedges

A creamy potato gratin deserves to be served alongside.

1. Preheat broiler.

2. Turn on food processor. Add garlic through feed tube and process until minced. Add bread slices and process into crumbs. You should have 4 cups.

3. Transfer garlic and bread crumbs to a bowl and mix in scallions, pep-

per and salt. Add the oil and rub the mixture gently between your hands to moisten the bread crumbs with oil. The mixture should be loose.

4. Arrange pollack steaks side by side on a nonstick baking sheet. Cover with half the crumbs, patting crumbs lightly over the surface of the fish. Place under broiler about 5 inches from the heat and cook about 3½ minutes, until the crumbs are nicely browned.

5. Gently turn fish with a spatula and pat the remaining seasoned bread crumbs lightly over their surface. Return to broiler for another 3½ minutes. The crumbs should be thoroughly browned and the fish just cooked through. Cooking time will vary depending on the thickness of the fillets and heat of broiler; check to see if they are cooked by cutting into one. If more cooking is needed, leave fish in broiler with heat turned off another 3 to 4 minutes.

6. Serve immediately with wedges of lemon.

Yield: 6 servings
(Jacques Pépin)

Pompano

Bait and Switch I
By MOLLY O'NEILL

The slim, silvery fish with the distinctive forked tail is impossible to mistake. Pompano is plump and smooth, its snowy flesh tasting faintly oily, somewhere between a lean whitefish and a dark, fatty one. Its neither-here-nor-there quality makes it prized above all others in the jack family that plies southern waters. While a pompano can weigh up to three pounds, it is most widely available at half that size. But when other members of the family grow large, they're too strong-tasting. Plate-size pompano is suitable for baking, roasting or grilling whole.

Substitutes: porgy, croaker, John Dory

SALT-BAKED WHOLE POMPANO WITH PARSLEY OIL

Time: 1 hour, plus macerating

> 2 cups flat-leaf parsley leaves, lightly packed
> ¾ cup extra virgin olive oil
> 1 whole pompano, about 2 pounds, cleaned and scaled,
>   gills removed
> Freshly ground black pepper
> 2 large sprigs rosemary
> 1 clove garlic, peeled and smashed
> 8 cups (3 pounds) kosher salt or coarse sea salt
> 2 large egg whites
> Lemon slices for garnish

1. Have a bowl of ice water ready. Bring a saucepan with 3 cups water to a boil and add parsley. Cook just until the leaves turn bright green, about 30 seconds. Immediately drain and plunge the leaves into ice water to stop the cooking.

2. Drain the leaves again and wring out as much water as possible. Transfer parsley to a blender and add olive oil. Blend until pureed. Transfer to a bowl and refrigerate for at least 1 hour and up to 1 day. Strain oil through a fine-mesh sieve, pressing on the solids to extract as much oil as possible. Discard solids and refrigerate oil.

3. Preheat oven to 400 degrees.

4. Rinse and pat the pompano dry and season inside and out with pepper. Place the rosemary and garlic inside the cavity. Place salt in a large bowl. Whisk the egg whites with ¼ cup water and pour over the salt. Using your hands, distribute the liquid evenly through the salt.

5. Choose a baking dish just slightly larger than the fish and pour a half-inch layer of salt mixture into the bottom. Place the fish on it and pour the remainder of the salt over and around fish, making sure that a good layer covers the fish on all sides. Place in oven and bake 35 minutes.

6. Remove fish from the oven. Wrap the head of a hammer or mallet in cloth and use the flat side to break the salt. Pull the salt away to expose the fish and gently lift it from the salt, brushing away any salt that adheres to the skin. Place the fish on a platter and peel back and discard the skin. Pour parsley oil over the fish, surround with lemon slices and serve.

Yield: 2 servings
(Molly O'Neill)

POMPANO BROILED WITH
LEMON, CINNAMON AND MINT

Time: 1 hour, 20 minutes

The cinnamon
in this recipe
gives the fish
a touch of
exotic flavor.
With the mint,
lemon and
cumin it
suggests
Morocco.

4 8-ounce pompano fillets
2 tablespoons extra virgin olive oil
Juice of ½ lemon
1 clove garlic, minced
1 teaspoon ground cinnamon
1 teaspoon ground cumin
Salt and freshly ground black pepper to taste
2 tablespoons roughly chopped mint leaves
1 lemon, quartered

1. Place fillets in a shallow baking dish large enough to hold them in a single layer.

2. In a small bowl, thoroughly mix the oil, lemon juice, garlic, cinnamon, cumin, and salt and pepper to taste. Pour this mixture over the fish, and refrigerate, covered, for 1 hour, turning once.

3. Remove the fish from the marinade and transfer to a foil-lined broiling pan. Preheat broiler.

4. Broil fillets 5 to 6 minutes, without turning, until fish is opaque all the way through. Remove from broiler, dust with mint, garnish with lemon wedges and serve.

Yield: 4 servings
(Moira Hodgson)

Porgy

Though porgies are sold mostly in ethnic markets in America, the porgy family is vast, and outside this country the fish are known mostly as bream. Where porgies are sold, they tend to be relatively inexpensive, on the small side, and have a fair amount of bone to sweet, meaty flesh.

Substitutes: croaker, pompano, dorade

ROASTED PORGY WITH WARM TOMATO DRESSING

Time: 45 minutes

> ⅓ cup extra virgin olive oil
> 2 whole porgies, about 1¼ pounds each, gutted
> Salt and freshly ground black pepper
> 1 large clove garlic, sliced
> 3 large sprigs fresh thyme or ¾ teaspoon dried
> 1 small onion, chopped fine
> 3 ripe plum tomatoes, chopped fine

1. Preheat oven to 500 degrees. Spread 2 tablespoons of the oil in a shallow baking dish large enough to hold fish.

2. Pat the fish dry on paper towels. Roll in the oil in dish to coat on both sides. Season inside and out with salt and pepper. Tuck a few slices of the garlic and 2 sprigs fresh or ½ teaspoon dried thyme in the cavity of the fish.

3. Roast fish uncovered about 20 minutes, until the flesh can be lifted from the bone with the point of a knife and has turned opaque. Transfer fish to a serving platter.

4. Heat remaining olive oil in a small saucepan until quite hot. Drop in remaining garlic and remove from heat. Add onion, tomatoes and remaining thyme. Stir. Season sauce with salt and pepper to taste.

5. Remove the skin from the top of the fish, lift off the top fillet and serve. Turn the fish over and remove skin and bottom fillet in the same manner. Spoon the warm sauce over each portion.

Yield: 2 servings

(Florence Fabricant)

Puffer

Northern puffers, or blowfish, are available in markets on the mid-Atlantic and New England coasts from time to time. This fish must be carefully cleaned because the skin and entrails can be toxic. Only the tail meat, often called sea squab, is sold, a small, meaty and exceptionally delicious fillet with a single center bone. It can be prepared in recipes that call for jumbo shrimp or langoustines. Puffers from southern seas, notably the Caribbean, should not be eaten. The tiger puffer, or fugu, is a risky delicacy in Japan. Recently, cleaned fugu, tested by the Japanese government and certified to be free of toxins, has been served, in season, in Japanese sushi bars in America.

Substitutes: jumbo shrimp, tiger shrimp, langoustines

SAUTÉED PUFFER WITH SUMMER TOMATOES AND BASIL
Time: 20 minutes

> 12 to 16 puffers, about 2 pounds
> Salt and freshly ground black pepper
> 1 cup flour
> 2 tablespoons extra virgin olive oil
> 2 tablespoons unsalted butter
> 4 teaspoons lemon juice
> 1½ cups diced ripe tomatoes (about 2 medium)
> Tabasco
> 4 to 5 basil leaves

1. Thoroughly dry puffer with paper towels and season to taste with salt and pepper. Spread flour in a large, shallow dish. Dredge fish in flour, pat off excess, and set aside.

2. Place a large nonstick skillet over high heat and add olive oil. When oil is hot, add puffers in a single layer. Brown until the underside is lightly golden, about 2 minutes. Turn and sauté until the second side is golden and flesh is opaque, about 2 minutes more. Use a spatula if needed to press fish lightly so

they do not curl. Transfer fish to heated dinner plates or a serving platter and keep warm.

3. Return skillet to medium heat and add butter, stirring with a wooden spoon. As soon as butter turns a medium nut-brown, stir in the lemon juice. Add tomatoes and warm briefly about 15 seconds. Remove the pan from heat, add 4 or 5 drops of Tabasco, and salt and pepper to taste.

4. To serve, spoon tomatoes over fish. Tear basil leaves into bite-size pieces and scatter over tomatoes. Serve immediately.

Yield: 4 servings
(Leslie Revsin)

Red Snapper

Bait and Switch II
By MOLLY O'NEILL

Even before Florida had the razzle-dazzle of Disney, the Sunshine State was no stranger to flimflam. Florida's most prized fishes, pompano and red snapper, have long been maligned by cheeky impostors. Not that bad fish is necessarily being foisted on an unsuspecting public. Indeed, yellowtail snapper (not to be confused with yellowtail flounder or the Pacific yellowtail, also called hamachi) is, to some, a far superior fish than red snapper, more assertively meaty and firm, yet still versatile and delicate. Many Floridians actually prefer lane snapper, mutton snapper or even mangrove snapper to their red-skinned cousin. And then there's onaga, or long-tail snapper, a newly popular and increasingly available Hawaiian fish. When it comes to red snapper, you are paying for a esthetics—the visual feast of red skin against snow-white flesh. There are more than a dozen varieties of snapper, and it pays to buy a whole fish so you know just what you are getting. 🐚

Substitutes: sea bass, sea trout, yellowtail

RED SNAPPER BAKED IN CHERMOULA

Time: 1 hour

Chermoula is a typical Moroccan seasoning, usually paired with fish.

1 tablespoon minced cilantro leaves
1 tablespoon minced flat-leaf parsley leaves
2 cloves garlic, minced
¼ teaspoon hot Hungarian paprika
2 teaspoons ground cumin
1 teaspoon ground coriander
¼ teaspoon cinnamon
Salt and freshly ground black pepper
1 small green bell pepper, cored, seeded and slivered
1 medium onion, peeled and coarsely chopped
2 pounds red snapper fillets
8 ripe plum tomatoes
1 jalapeño chili, seeded and chopped
⅓ cup extra virgin olive oil
1 lemon, cut in 6 wedges

1. Combine cilantro, parsley, garlic, paprika, cumin, coriander, cinnamon, salt and pepper. Rub fish with this mixture. Scatter green pepper and onion in glass or ceramic baking dish big enough to hold fish in a single layer. Put fish atop vegetables, cover with plastic wrap and set aside at room temperature for 30 minutes.

2. Preheat oven to 450 degrees. Put rack in highest position.

3. Slice four of the tomatoes thin and puree the rest. Scatter tomato slices and jalapeño over fish. Mix pureed tomatoes with olive oil and season to taste with salt and pepper. Pour over fish. Cover loosely with foil.

4. Place in oven and bake about 15 minutes, until fish is just cooked through. Serve at once with lemon wedges.

Yield: 4 to 6 servings
(Florence Fabricant)

RED SNAPPER WITH EGGPLANT AND TOMATO

Time: 1 hour

6 tablespoons, approximately, extra virgin olive oil

1 large onion, peeled and diced

2 large tomatoes, peeled, seeded and diced

2 teaspoons fresh thyme leaves

1 bay leaf

1 clove garlic, peeled and crushed

2 tablespoons red-wine vinegar

2 teaspoons honey

Salt and freshly ground pepper to taste

1 eggplant, about 1 pound, peeled and cut into rounds
¼ inch thick

1½ pounds red snapper fillets, with skin, cut into 8
uniform pieces

1. In a large saucepan, place 1 tablespoon of the olive oil and the onion, cover the pan, and sweat onion over low heat about 10 minutes. Add the tomatoes, thyme, bay leaf, garlic, 1 tablespoon of the vinegar, the honey and 1 additional tablespoon of the oil. Simmer, uncovered, over medium heat for 15 minutes, until much of the liquid has evaporated. Discard bay leaf and season to taste with salt and pepper. Puree in a food processor, then pass through a fine sieve back into saucepan.

2. Heat 2 more tablespoons of the oil in a large nonstick pan, and fry some of the eggplant until the rounds are golden brown on both sides. Repeat until all the eggplant has been cooked, adding more oil, if needed, for each new batch. Drain on paper towels. Season with salt and pepper. Place on a plate.

3. Add remaining tablespoon of vinegar to the pan, and stir for 1 minute over high heat to deglaze the pan. Spoon the liquid over the eggplant.

4. Clean the nonstick pan. Add remaining 2 tablespoons oil. Salt and pepper fillets on both sides. Place in pan, and sauté over medium heat 2 to 3 minutes on each side.

5. Reheat tomato sauce to warm. Place sauce in the middle of each plate, top with several rounds of the eggplant and with 2 fish fillets, skin side up. Serve warm.

Yield: 4 servings

(Pierre Troisgros, Troisgros, Roanne, France)

RED SNAPPER WITH WHITE ASPARAGUS AND ASPARAGUS JUS

Time: 30 minutes

> **Kosher salt**
> **18 thick asparagus spears, preferably white, ends snapped, peeled**
> **5 tablespoons extra virgin olive oil**
> **1 tablespoon sherry vinegar**
> **6 red snapper fillets, about 6 ounces each**
> **Chervil sprigs, for garnish**

1. In a large pot, combine 3 quarts water and 2 tablespoons salt. Bring to a boil. Add asparagus, and cook until tender, 5 to 7 minutes. Drain asparagus, reserving 1½ cups cooking liquid.

2. Place the reserved asparagus liquid in a small pan and bring to a boil. Reduce the liquid to ⅓ cup. Remove the liquid from the heat, and whisk in 3 tablespoons of the olive oil, and then the vinegar. Season to taste with salt, and set aside.

3. Heat oven to 400 degrees. Season the snapper fillets on both sides with salt to taste. Place a large nonstick, ovenproof sauté pan over medium-high heat. Heat the remaining 2 tablespoons of olive oil, and add snapper fillets, skin side down. Sauté until skin is crispy and brown, 3 to 4 minutes. Transfer pan to oven, and bake until fillets are cooked through, about 2 minutes. Remove from oven, and keep warm.

4. With an immersion blender or a whisk, blend sauce with asparagus liquid until foamy. Place a fillet skin side up on each of 6 plates. Lay 3 asparagus spears next to each fillet, and spoon a little sauce over the asparagus. Garnish each fillet with a sprig of chervil. Serve immediately.

Yield: 6 servings
(Marco Arbeit, Auberge St.-Laurent,
Sierentz, France)

YELLOWTAIL SNAPPER GRILLED IN FENNEL

Time: 1¼ hours

1 head garlic, cloves peeled
2 shallots
1 tablespoon fresh thyme leaves
½ cup extra virgin olive oil
3 lemons
2 whole yellowtail snappers, each about 2¼ pounds, cleaned
Salt and freshly ground black pepper
4 to 6 heads fennel with branches and fronds untrimmed
1 tablespoon unsalted butter
½ cup heavy cream
1 cup Parmigiano Reggiano shavings

Many markets trim the long stems and fronds from the fennel bulbs. But you need them for this recipe, so ask for untrimmed fennel.

1. Place garlic cloves in saucepan, cover with water and simmer 15 minutes, until tender. Drain. Mash by hand or puree by machine in small food processor (the quantity is too small to use full-size processor). Finely mince 1 shallot, mix with garlic, add half the thyme and, by hand or machine, beat in 3 tablespoons olive oil and juice of ½ lemon.

2. Cut 4 deep slashes in each side of each fish. Rub fish inside and out with some of the remaining oil and juice of ½ lemon. Season with salt and pepper. Fill slashes with garlic paste and spread any remaining inside fish. Slice remaining shallot and put slices in cavities of fish. Slice one lemon and put slices in cavities.

3. Cut off fennel bulbs. Spread half the fennel stems and fronds on work surface. Remove a few sprigs of fennel for garnish and set aside. Place fish on bed of fennel and cover each fish with remaining fennel to wrap completely. Tie fennel around fish in 3 places with butcher's cord. Drizzle with remaining olive oil.

4. Preheat grill, preferably charcoal. Preheat oven to 425 degrees. Butter a shallow 4-cup baking dish.

5. Slice off bottom half inch from fennel bulbs. Slice each bulb vertically, in ½-inch-thick slices. Place in saucepan, cover with water and bring to a boil. Cook 3 minutes, drain and refresh by placing in bowl of ice water. Drain and pat dry. Arrange fennel slices, partly overlapping, in baking dish. Scatter with remaining thyme. Dot with butter, drizzle with cream and scatter cheese on top.

6. Place fish on grill and grill 10 to 15 minutes on each side, until tip of knife inserted in thickest part slips out easily and feels very warm when touched to your chin or the inside of your wrist. Remove fish from grill.

7. While fish is grilling, place dish with fennel in oven and bake about 15 minutes, until browned on top.

8. To serve, snip off strings around fish and remove fennel. Remove lemon and shallot slices from inside fish. Fillet fish and arrange on platter or individual dinner plates and garnish with remaining lemon cut in wedges and reserved fennel sprigs. Serve baked fennel alongside.

Yield: 4 to 6 servings

(Mark Militello, Mark's Las Olas, Fort Lauderdale, Fla.)

ONAGA BAKED IN THYME AND ROSEMARY ROCK SALT CRUST

Time: 1¼ hours

Salt-baking is usually done with a whole fish so the skin of the fish can serve as a protective layer between the flesh and the salt. But this crust is mostly flour, so the salting does not pose a problem for the fillets.

1 pound coarse sea salt

2 pounds all-purpose flour

1 tablespoon dried rosemary

1 tablespoon dried thyme

5 large egg whites

9 tablespoons extra virgin olive oil

1 pound spinach leaves

6 garlic cloves, finely chopped

Salt and fresh black pepper

2 to 3 large leaves romaine lettuce

2 onaga (long-tail snapper) fillets, about 6 ounces each, with skin

2 shallots, peeled and finely chopped

1 tomato, peeled, seeded and diced

½ cup white wine

1 sprig tarragon, finely chopped

1 sprig chervil, finely chopped

2 tablespoons finely chopped scallions

1. In a large mixer fitted with a dough hook, combine salt, flour, rosemary and thyme. Mix at medium speed, adding 1 egg white at a time, until mix-

ture is blended and moistened. Slowly add 1 cup water, to form a stiff dough. If necessary, add 1 to 2 tablespoons more water. On a lightly floured surface, roll out dough to a rectangle about 10 by 14 inches, large enough to enclose fish completely.

2. Place a large skillet over medium heat, and add 3 tablespoons olive oil. Add spinach and half the garlic. Sauté until spinach is wilted. Remove from heat and season with salt and pepper. Cool.

3. Preheat oven to 375 degrees. Place romaine lettuce over one-half of dough. Top with spinach. Place fillets, skin side up, side by side on spinach. Fold dough over to enclose. Seal edges, and shape dough like a fish. Transfer to baking sheet, and bake until dough is lightly browned and fish is aromatic, about 35 minutes. Meanwhile, prepare sauce.

4. Place a medium saucepan over medium-low heat, and add 3 table-spoons olive oil. Add shallots, remaining garlic, and sauté until softened but not browned. Add tomato and white wine, and reduce by half. Add tarragon, chervil, scallions and remaining 3 tablespoons olive oil. Season with salt and pepper to taste.

5. To serve, transfer baked fish in crust to a serving platter. At table, cut crust lengthwise, removing only top layer; do not allow salt crystals to fall onto fish. Remove skin from fish. Place a fillet on each of two plates, and top with a serving of spinach. Pour sauce around fish, and serve.

Yield: 2 servings

(George Mavrothalassitis, Chef Mavro, Honolulu)

❧

Rouget

The American name for rouget is red mullet, a far less attractive-sounding fish. Or how about the unappetizing fact that this assertive, tasty little fish is a member of the goatfish family? No wonder the people who write signs in the fish markets and menus in restaurants prefer *rouget*. The silver-and-red fish has darkish, somewhat oily flesh, is usually imported from the Mediterranean and must be very fresh.

Substitutes: sardines, smelts

ROUGET ESCABECHE

Time: ½ hour, plus at least 3 hours marinating

⅓ cup flour
Salt and freshly ground black pepper
6 rouget, filleted and split
2 tablespoons extra virgin olive oil
Juice of 2 lemons
1 cup finely chopped leeks
2 large garlic cloves, sliced
6 ripe plum tomatoes, sliced about ¼ inch thick
2 tablespoons capers
½ cup pitted Kalamata olives
1 tablespoon sherry vinegar
12 large basil leaves, slivered

1. Season flour with salt and pepper and spread it on a plate. Dip fillets in flour to coat lightly.

2. Heat the oil in a heavy, nonstick skillet over medium-high heat. Cook fish a couple of minutes on each side until lightly browned. Transfer to a shallow serving dish that will hold them in a single layer. Drizzle with all but one tablespoon of the lemon juice.

3. Lower heat and add the leeks and garlic to the skillet. Cook over medium-low heat until tender. Stir in tomatoes and continue to cook about 5 minutes longer, just until tomatoes have softened. Remove from heat and stir in the capers and olives. Spread this mixture evenly over the fish, sprinkle with remaining lemon juice and vinegar and scatter basil leaves on top.

4. Cover and set aside at room temperature up to 3 hours before serving, or refrigerate for 6 hours, then bring to room temperature.

Yield: 6 servings
(Molly O'Neill)

Sablefish

The Fish That Swam Uptown
By MARIAN BURROS

Sablefish is the Cinderella of the seafood world. But unlike Cinderella, who was transformed in a day, it took sablefish three-quarters of a century to move from the teeming Lower East Side of New York, where it sold for 70 cents a pound, smoked, and was usually carried home wrapped in butcher paper, to today's grand temples of gastronomy. On its circuitous journey uptown, sablefish, the stuff of Jewish delis, has assumed a fashionable new name and been cloaked in elegant new garments. It has become the darling of the culinistas.

The nom de cuisine of paprika-covered smoked sable is black cod, but long before this buttery, silken fish, with its pristine white flesh, appeared, fresh, in rarefied dining rooms, it was a delicacy in Japan, which still consumes about 95 percent of the American catch, mostly from Alaska. Fresh black cod has long been popular in Seattle, and the Makah Indians were fishing it centuries ago, but no serious chef paid attention to it. Miso-glazed black cod changed all that. The marinade, a traditional Japanese mixture of mirin, sake, miso and sugar, gives the fish a sharp, sweet flavor dear to the American palate. It was only a matter of time before miso cod was on menus across the country.

A Scandinavian connection may explain how sablefish became black cod. Many Norwegians, for whom cod is a staple, settled in the Pacific Northwest, and black cod, which is two feet long and can weigh up to 40 pounds but is generally less than 10 pounds today, looks a little like cod, though unrelated. A fish called aiglefin is similar and came from the Norwegian fjords.

Black cod, whose true name is skilfish, a member of the Anoplopoma fimbria family, owes its richness to where it lives, in the deepest waters of Alaska and the Bering Sea and the Pacific Ocean down to California, and what it eats, the likes of crabs and squid. Pound for pound it is the most valuable fish in Alaska. The best fish are caught on long lines, in the summer and fall, when the fish feed heavily and build up oil reserves. 🐚

Substitutes: salmon, cod, shad, tuna

BLACK COD WITH MISO

Time: 20 minutes, plus one day's marinating

1 cup miso
1 cup sake
1 cup mirin
1 cup brown sugar
4 6-ounce Alaskan black cod fillets, with skin
1 tablespoon soy sauce
1½ teaspoons Asian, or toasted sesame oil
2 scallions, green part only, chopped

1. Combine miso, sake, mirin and sugar; set aside ½ cup. Marinate fish in remaining mixture in refrigerator for 24 hours.

2. Preheat broiler. Cover broiler pan with foil. Remove fish from marinade and place on pan, skin side up, 4 to 6 inches from heat. Broil until fish is caramelized, 8 to 10 minutes.

3. Meanwhile, whisk soy sauce and sesame oil together. Place marinade in a saucepan and bring to a boil. When fish is cooked, spoon warm marinade over fish and then drizzle with soy-sesame mixture. Garnish with chopped scallions.

Yield: 4 servings
(Ruby Foo's, New York City)

Salmon

Wild Alaskan Salmon: The Glory Days Are Here; Copper River Salmon Reign Supreme
By TIMOTHY EGAN

SEATTLE: The Gulf of Alaska was tossing up waves of 20 feet or more and the winds roared to 40 miles an hour, but the storm did not deter the fleet in pursuit of Copper River salmon on their first run of the season.

In Seattle, New York, Tokyo and Los Angeles anxious chefs clicked on to Web sites and called fishermen on cell phones. Forget the weather. The chefs wanted to know how the fish looked. A seafood buyer for a supermarket chain in Seattle had the salmon hoisted directly from the boat into a rented helicopter to take it to a waiting jet in the Alaskan port of Cordova. Then, he airlifted it 1,500 miles south to Seattle. He displayed his 500 pounds of Copper River king salmon at 5 A.M.–10 hours after they were yanked from the Alaskan seas.

Why all the fuss? After all, the world is full of farm-raised Atlantic salmon, available year-round. And there is certainly no shortage of Alaskan wild salmon. But Copper River fish are different. A string of restaurants and fish vendors from Puget Sound to Long Island Sound, from Miami to Los Angeles, swear that there is no other fish that gets people quite like this first wild salmon of the season.

The best-tasting of these fish, connoisseurs say, are the early-running ones, which are available until mid-June. Copper River salmon are rich in oil, firm in flesh, almost nutty in taste. They are high in omega-3 fatty acids, which have been shown to have certain health benefits. They are hardy, having bulked up for the river journey of nearly 300 miles to icy headwaters in the Wrangell Mountains.

As fish sex lives go, that of Copper River salmon is noble but prosaic: After a few years at sea, they dodge ice chunks and sharp-eyed eagles and fight the gravitational torrent of the river to find a little home in the gravel hundreds of miles upstream, near the very place of their birth. There, they spawn and die. Fishermen catch them just before they head upstream.

The Copper River Delta, at 700,000 acres, is the largest wetland on the Pacific coast of North America. More than 235 species of birds–from trumpeter swans to bald eagles to horned puffins–nest in the delta. The marine waters are home to killer whales, Steller's sea lions, sea otters. Onshore, moose, grizzly bears and wolves are abundant.

And then there are the salmon. Five species of wild Pacific salmon—the small pinks, the bigger sockeyes or reds, the medium-size coho or silver, the late-running chums, and the majestic kings or chinook—are caught off Alaska's shore. The two prized Copper River fish are the reds and the kings. ✿

The Catch of the Moment: White Salmon
By AMANDA HESSER

White king salmon was once a curiosity, if not a nuisance. When fishermen in the Pacific Northwest pulled it up, it went in the pile headed for the cannery or the smokehouse. The demand for wild king salmon from waters from Seattle to Alaska, after all, is for a large, meaty fish with bright red flesh.

White king salmon is unmistakable. Its flesh is as white as bone. That it has extraordinary flavor didn't matter. It wasn't red, or even pink. It could have remained unknown, except that something else occurred: Novelty became a big commodity in cuisine.

The former misfit fish is now known as ivory king salmon. And instead of being destined for the cannery or the smokehouse, it is bound for fine restaurants and markets.

It would be unfair, however, to say that novelty was the only reason for its success. This is much more than salmon without pigment. It is different from the red in taste, in texture and in many other subtle qualities. It has a softer flesh, buttery and silky, less meaty and somehow less salmony. It tastes at once sweet, like a freshwater fish, and deeply of the sea. It is clearly salmon, but with flavors reminiscent of perch and Chilean sea bass. Compared with farmed salmon and even red king salmon, which tend to be oily and assertive, white king salmon's delicacy is incomparable.

Only about 6 to 8 percent of a king salmon catch is white, and there is no way to know until a fish is gutted whether it has white or red flesh. And whites have seasons that come and go with the predictability of wind. Preservation efforts limit the king salmon catch, so the fisheries are open only in certain weeks, determined month to month.

White king salmon turns up only sporadically in fish markets. Of the five species of salmon in the Pacific—silver, chum, pink, sockeye and king—king is the only type with a white variety. There are indications that the white color is inherited and simply a mutation. Two red king salmon, for instance, can produce a white.

An easy way to cook the fish is to poach it with just enough fish broth and butter to cover the bottom of a shallow pan. As it simmers, you can spoon the pan juices over the fish, or gently turn it. The fish cooks in just a few minutes. White king salmon also sautés beautifully. Slow roasting in a low oven guarantees that the fish won't overcook from one minute to the next; you can monitor it carefully. It also allows you to enjoy the fish in a pure way. It does not color, so there are no caramelized edges, and it is rare in the center, so it is very much like sashimi.

Because the fish is oily, it needs some kind of acidity. But a fish as fine and rare as white king salmon is best unencumbered by strong flavors. Its taste of sea and krill and the Pacific should be as unmistakable as its color. 🐚

Eating Well; Is Salmon Organic? Not Yet
By MARIAN BURROS

Calling Alaskan salmon organic has little to do with the philosophy of organic agriculture.

In the past, Alaska has promoted its wild salmon as superior to farmed in flavor and quality. But few people know the difference between wild and farmed salmon and have no idea which kind they are eating. By 2001, farmed salmon accounted for 60 percent of the world's market and have seriously depressed the price of wild salmon. Like commercial chickens, farmed fish live in not particularly sanitary conditions. They are fed dye pellets to give them the pink color that occurs naturally in free-swimming salmon. They eat manufactured food that may contain genetically modified ingredients. They are treated with antibiotics because of fish lice. And their waste material can pollute a natural habitat.

All Atlantic salmon is the same species, Salmo salar, regardless of whether it is wild or farm-raised. It is even being cultivated in the Pacific waters off Chile and British Columbia, as well as in the North Atlantic and Scandinavia. Farm-raised Atlantic salmon with the distinctive striations of white fat are generally richer than the Western salmon, the Oncorhynchus species, pulled from the natural habitat.

There is a great deal of difference between salmon that spend a great portion of their lives in deep, cold waters and those raised on a farm. Wild fish are not subject to any kind of runoff from farmlands, pesticides, to the growth of viruses in tanks or ponds. They really are disease free. Wild salmon or *saumon sauvage,* which we consider superior, comes from the cold, deep ocean waters. Technically, you might call them organic, but how can you certify wild fish? ◆

Substitutes: for steaks: halibut, wild striped bass; for fillets: arctic char, sea bass, wild striped bass; for whole fish: arctic char, wild striped bass

SALMON CONSOMMÉ
Time: 1¾ hours

For a richer soup, use fish broth or dashi (recipes page 321–322) in place of water.

> 4 very fresh salmon heads, gills removed
> 1 celery stalk, roughly chopped
> 1 large onion, roughly chopped
> 1 carrot, roughly chopped
> 2 teaspoons black peppercorns
> 1 teaspoon kosher salt, or to taste
> 4 sprigs thyme
> 1 carrot, julienned and blanched, for garnish
> 10 sprigs cilantro, for garnish

1. In a large soup pot, place salmon heads and 6 cups cold water or enough to cover ingredients. Bring to a boil and skim for several minutes. Add celery, onion, chopped carrot, peppercorns, salt and thyme. Lower heat and simmer for 1½ hours.

2. Strain soup through a colander lined with cheesecloth and discard the contents of colander. Divide the garnishes among the serving bowls, and top with hot soup. Serve immediately.

Yield: 4 servings
(Carol Lawson)

COLD SALMON WITH CAVIAR AND MUSTARD SEED SAUCE

Time: 15 minutes, plus chilling

2 ½-pound pieces salmon fillet, skinned

2 teaspoons extra virgin olive oil

Salt to taste

Freshly ground black pepper to taste

¼ cup mayonnaise

1 tablespoon coarse-grained Dijon mustard

¼ teaspoon lemon juice

4 teaspoons sevruga caviar

1 kirby cucumber, peeled and thinly sliced

4 teaspoons chopped chives

Salmon or trout roe or American sturgeon caviar can be used instead of sevruga caviar.

1. Slice each piece of salmon in half horizontally, making 4 thin paillards. Heat olive oil in a large nonstick skillet over medium-high heat. Add salmon to the skillet in batches, and cook so that it is seared on both sides but rare in the center, about 15 seconds a side. Season with salt and pepper and refrigerate until cold.

2. Meanwhile, stir together mayonnaise, mustard, lemon juice, and salt and pepper to taste. To serve, coat 4 plates with the mustard sauce. Place 1 piece of salmon on each plate and top with 1 teaspoon caviar. Fan a few of the cucumber slices on one side of salmon, and sprinkle the chives over the cucumbers and around the edge of the plate.

Yield: 4 servings
(Hubert Keller, Fleur De Lys,
San Francisco)

GRILLED CURED SALMON

Time: 20 minutes

The first part of this recipe actually makes a kind of spicy gravlax, which can be served without grilling. To serve uncooked, the fish can be cured up to 12 hours.

1 tablespoon whole coriander seeds
1 tablespoon Sichuan peppercorns
1 dried cascabel chili
½ cup turbinado or light brown sugar
¼ cup sea salt
½ teaspoon freshly ground black pepper
4 pieces skinless, boneless salmon fillet, preferably Pacific, about 1¾ pounds total

1. In a small skillet over high heat, toast coriander and peppercorns until fragrant, about 2 minutes. Transfer to a plate to cool. Place cascabel chili in pan and toast on all sides until skin blisters, about 5 minutes. Let cool, then tear into small pieces.

2. Combine toasted coriander seeds, peppercorns and cascabel chili in a spice grinder or mortar. Grind to a fine powder. Combine powder with sugar, salt and ground black pepper in a medium mixing bowl. Sprinkle half this cure mixture onto a baking sheet lined with parchment or waxed paper. Shape cure into a flat mound that matches shape and size of salmon fillets. Place salmon on top and cover with remaining cure. Cover with a small piece of parchment or waxed pepper, then wrap with plastic and refrigerate for 2 hours.

3. Scrape spices off salmon with knife. Preheat a grill or broiler. Grill or broil salmon, turning once, for a total of 5 to 7 minutes, or until slightly translucent in center.

Yield: 4 servings
(Michel Nischan, Heartbeat,
New York City)

LEMONGRASS GRAVLAX WITH HONEY-LEMON MAYONNAISE

Time: 20 minutes, plus 48 hours marinating

2 tablespoons salt, plus extra for mayonnaise

2 tablespoons sugar

2 tablespoons crushed black peppercorns

¾ pound skinless, boneless salmon fillet, cut into two
    equal-size pieces

2 tablespoons minced fresh lemongrass bulb

½ cup mayonnaise

2 tablespoons honey

Grated zest of 1 lemon

Freshly ground black pepper to taste

Run your hand lightly over the fish to check for little pin bones. They can be pulled out with tweezers or small pliers.

1. In a large bowl, mix salt, sugar and crushed pepper. Coat both sides of each fillet with mixture. Spread a third of the lemongrass in the bottom of a shallow dish, place a fillet in the dish, and spread with another third of the lemongrass. Place other fillet on top and spread with the remaining lemongrass. Cover tightly with plastic wrap and rest a 3- or 4-pound weight on fish. Refrigerate.

2. After 24 hours, remove weight and plastic wrap and baste with accumulated liquid. Turn fish over. Replace plastic wrap and weight, and refrigerate for an additional 24 hours.

3. Meanwhile, in a small bowl, mix mayonnaise, honey, lemon zest and pepper. Season with salt to taste. Refrigerate.

4. To serve, remove lemongrass, and slice salmon thinly on the bias with a sharp knife. Serve with honey-lemon mayonnaise and, if desired, toast and lemon wedges. The fish can remain unsliced in the refrigerator for up to 1 week.

*Yield: 40 hors d'oeuvres
or 8 first-course servings*
(Carol Lawson)

SALMON AND BEET TARTARE

Time: 2½ hours

4 medium beets, washed and trimmed
1½ teaspoons finely chopped chives
1½ teaspoons minced tarragon
1 teaspoon Dijon mustard
3 teaspoons finely chopped shallots
6 teaspoons lemon juice
3 drops Tabasco sauce
2½ tablespoons extra virgin olive oil
Salt and freshly ground black pepper
8 ounces skinned salmon fillet, cut into small dice
1½ teaspoons finely chopped parsley
Pea shoots or radish sprouts for garnish, optional

1. Preheat oven to 400 degrees. Place beets in a small roasting pan with ½ cup water. Cover and cook until tender when pierced with a fork, about 1 hour. Cool, then peel and cut into fine dice.

2. In a bowl, combine beets with ¾ teaspoon chives, ¾ teaspoon tarragon, ½ teaspoon mustard and 1½ teaspoons shallots. Add 4½ teaspoons lemon juice, Tabasco and 1½ tablespoons olive oil. Mix well, and season with salt and pepper to taste. Cover and refrigerate.

3. In a medium mixing bowl, combine salmon, remaining chives, tarragon and shallots. Add parsley and remaining mustard and lemon. Add remaining oil, and season to taste. Mix well, cover and refrigerate until ready to serve.

4. To assemble, place ¼ of the beet tartare in the bottom of a 3-inch ring mold on a salad-size plate. Top with an even layer of ¼ of the salmon tartare. Pat gently to compress. Remove ring molds and garnish with pea shoots or radish sprouts if desired. Repeat with three more plates.

Yield: 4 servings
(Dave Pasternack, Esca,
New York City)

GRILLED COPPER RIVER KING SALMON FILLET WITH PINOT NOIR SAUCE

Time: 1 hour

1 head garlic

3 tablespoons, approximately, extra virgin olive oil

1 cup pinot noir

1 cup fish broth (recipe page 321), or bottled clam juice

4 teaspoons chopped shallots

2 sprigs thyme, leaves separated from stems

¼ cup heavy cream

8 tablespoons salted butter, cut into 1-inch pieces

8 tablespoons unsalted butter, cut into 1-inch pieces

6 6-ounce king salmon fillets, preferably Copper River

Copper River salmon is not essential, nor is king salmon. But the salmon should be Pacific. Try the recipe with sockeye salmon from Alaska or Washington.

1. To roast garlic, preheat oven to 350 degrees. Brush garlic with ½ tablespoon oil and wrap in foil. Roast until cloves are soft when pierced, about 45 minutes. Cool. Mash 2 cloves and set aside. Reserve rest of garlic for another use.

2. While garlic is roasting, in a heavy saucepan combine pinot noir, fish broth, shallots and thyme stems. Place over high heat, and reduce until just more than a glaze, 7 to 10 minutes. Add cream and reduce by half. Reduce heat to low and whisk in salted and unsalted butter, one piece at a time, until thoroughly incorporated. Do not boil or sauce will separate.

3. Immediately pour sauce through a fine strainer or cheesecloth and discard solids. Add 1½ teaspoons thyme leaves and mashed cloves of roasted garlic. Mix well, and keep warm until serving, preferably by putting in a wide-mouthed thermos.

4. Preheat grill, preferably charcoal, until very hot. A heavy-duty grill pan on top of a stove can also be used. Brush flesh side of fillets with olive oil and place salmon, flesh side down, on the grill. Allow the bars of the grill to sear fish (it will take only a few seconds), then use spatulas to give fillets a quarter turn; this sears crisscross lines on the flesh.

5. Brush skin side of fillets with olive oil. Turn fillets and grill just until the center begins to look less translucent, about 6 to 8 minutes depending on the thickness of the fish. Serve with pinot noir sauce.

Yield: 6 servings

(Charles Ramseyer, Ray's Boat House,
Seattle, Wash.)

POACHED SALMON IN RAVIGOTE SAUCE

Time: 30 minutes

    1 cup plum tomatoes, seeded and cut into ¼-inch pieces
    2 tablespoons drained capers, optional
    4 scallions, trimmed and chopped (½ cup)
    ½ cup chopped onion, rinsed in a sieve under cool water
        and drained
    2 tablespoons crushed and chopped garlic
    ½ cup coarsely chopped flat-leaf parsley
    1 teaspoon salt
    ½ teaspoon freshly ground black pepper
    6 tablespoons extra virgin olive oil
    3 tablespoons lemon juice
    6 salmon steaks, all bones, sinews and skin removed (5 ounces
        each when cleaned), each 1¼ to 1½ inches thick

1. Mix all ingredients except salmon in a small bowl and set aside at room temperature.

2. Tie each steak with butcher's cord around its circumference so it holds its shape.

3. In a stainless steel saucepan large enough to hold salmon, bring 4 cups water to a boil. Place salmon steaks in the pan and bring water back to a boil over high heat, about 2 minutes. Immediately remove from heat and let salmon steep 5 minutes, until fish is slightly underdone in the center.

4. Remove steaks from pan with a large spatula or skimmer, drain well, and place a steak on each of 6 warm plates. Remove cord: Sponge up any liquid that collects around steaks on plates with paper towels. Spoon sauce over and around steaks. Serve immediately.

Yield: 6 servings
(Jacques Pépin)

SALMON ADOBADO

Time: 1 hour

10 dried chilies, preferably a mixture, including chipotle, ancho and guajillo
3 tablespoons chopped garlic
¼ cup chopped scallion, white part only
⅓ cup red wine vinegar
½ teaspoon dried oregano, preferably Mexican
½ teaspoon dried thyme
6 bay leaves, crumbled
2 tablespoons extra virgin olive oil
Salt to taste
4 slices salmon fillet with skin, each about 7 ounces
1 lime, quartered

1. Heat a grill or large cast–iron skillet. Place all the chilies on the grill or in the skillet, and heat, turning once or twice, to toast. Do not allow them to burn. Remove chilies, split them in half and discard stems. Remove and reserve seeds for another use.

2. Return split chilis to the grill or skillet, and lightly toast the insides. Cut chilies in small pieces and place in a blender, with garlic, scallion, vinegar, ⅓ cup water, oregano, thyme and bay leaves. Process until well blended.

3. Heat oil in the skillet, add chili mixture and cook, stirring, about 5 minutes. Remove from heat and allow to cool 10 to 15 minutes. Season lightly with salt if desired.

4. Place salmon in a shallow bowl and coat with chili mixture. Allow to marinate at room temperature 20 to 30 minutes.

5. Preheat a grill or broiler. Grill or broil salmon, skin side first, close to the source of heat, until the outside is browned and fish is barely cooked on the inside, 3 to 4 minutes on each side. Serve with lime wedges.

Yield: 4 servings
(Isadora restaurant, Mexico City)

SALMON CAKES WITH YOGURT-CHIPOTLE SAUCE

Time: 30 minutes

The cakes can be served slightly underdone in the middle, so they're still juicy.

1 or 2 canned chipotle chilies, to taste, drained and seeded

1 cup plain yogurt

Salt

1 pound skinless, boneless salmon fillets

1 tablespoon safflower oil

½ large onion, chopped

1 teaspoon fresh thyme leaves

½ red bell pepper, seeded and chopped

4 large eggs

1 cup mayonnaise

1 teaspoon freshly ground black pepper

1½ cups bread crumbs

1. Place chilies and half the yogurt in a blender and puree. Fold in remaining yogurt, and add salt to taste. Refrigerate.

2. Bring a large pot of water to a simmer, place salmon in it for 3 or 4 minutes, drain and cool. Break into chunks.

3. In a frying pan over low heat, combine safflower oil, onion and thyme. Sauté until onion is translucent, about 5 minutes. Add red pepper, and cook for 1 more minute. Cool.

4. In a large bowl combine salmon, onion mixture, eggs, mayonnaise, salt, pepper and 1 cup bread crumbs.

5. Preheat oven to 450 degrees.

6. Shape patties according to size desired: about 1 tablespoon for hors d'oeuvres, 3 tablespoons for first-course servings, 6 tablespoons for main-course servings. Coat patties with bread crumbs and place on a baking sheet. Bake medium-size patties about 5 minutes. Turn over, and bake 2 more minutes or until lightly browned. Adjust baking time for other sizes as needed. Serve with yogurt-chipotle sauce.

Yield: 40 hors d'oeuvres, 12 first-course servings
or 6 main-course servings

(Jacques Pépin)

SALMON WITH SORREL SAUCE

Time: 30 minutes

1⅓ pounds center-cut salmon fillet, skinned and boned

2 shallots, peeled and minced

½ cup fish broth (recipe page 321), or bottled clam juice

1 cup Sancerre or other dry white wine

1 tablespoon dry vermouth

1¼ cups heavy cream

3 ounces sorrel leaves, trimmed of tough veins

1 teaspoon lemon juice, or more to taste

Salt and freshly ground black pepper

1 tablespoon unsalted butter

This is a classic recipe from the Michelin three-star restaurant in Roanne, France. It can also be prepared with shad.

1. Cut salmon into 4 pieces of equal size, then cut each into thirds, for a total of 12 slices. Place each piece between wax paper, and flatten gently with a mallet until it is of even thickness. Set aside.

2. In a medium saucepan, combine shallots, fish broth, white wine and vermouth. Place over medium heat and simmer until reduced to a glaze on bottom of pan. Add cream, and continue to simmer until sauce thickens, about 5 minutes. Tear sorrel leaves into large pieces and add to pan. Add lemon juice and salt and pepper to taste. Remove from heat and keep warm.

3. In a nonstick sauté pan, melt butter over medium heat. Season the darker-colored sides of the salmon with salt and pepper to taste, and place in pan seasoned side up. Sear about 25 seconds, turn and sear again about 15 seconds; fillets should be rare in center.

4. To serve, spread sorrel sauce equally among four large, warm plates. Place three overlapping slices on each plate. Serve immediately.

Yield: 4 servings
(Pierre Troisgros, Troisgros,
Roanne, France)

SLOW-COOKED WHITE KING SALMON WITH WATERCRESS BROTH

Time: 40 minutes

The low-temperature cooking results in fish that has an almost custardy consistency.

4 tablespoons butter at room temperature
1 pound watercress, trimmed and washed
Fleur de sel or another fine sea salt
1½ teaspoons rice vinegar
3 tablespoons canola oil
2 tablespoons crème fraîche
8 3-ounce pieces king salmon, preferably white,
  skin removed

1. Preheat oven to 225 degrees. In a large sauté pan over medium heat, melt 2 tablespoons butter. Add watercress and salt to taste. Toss until watercress has wilted, about 3 minutes. Transfer to a blender and puree a few seconds. With blender at low speed, gradually add rice vinegar and canola oil, scraping down sides of container as necessary.

2. Strain mixture into a small saucepan, pressing out as much liquid as possible with back of spoon. Place over medium-low heat, and whisk in crème fraîche. Adjust seasonings, and keep warm.

3. Rub 2 remaining tablespoons butter on both sides of salmon pieces. Season lightly with salt. Place on a rack in a shallow roasting pan about an inch apart. Bake, turning every few minutes, 8 to 12 minutes, or until surfaces of fish are opaque; centers remain rare.

4. Place a salmon fillet on each of 8 shallow soup plates for a first-course serving, or 2 fillets on 4 plates for a main course. Spoon watercress broth around fish and serve.

Yield: 8 first-course or
4 main-course servings
(Amanda Hesser)

SAUTÉED WHITE KING SALMON WITH SUCCOTASH

Time: 45 minutes

> 4 **ears corn, husked**
>
> **Sea salt**
>
> 4 **ounces green beans, trimmed**
>
> 6 **ounces sugar snap peas**
>
> 4 **5-ounce fillets white king salmon with skin**
>
> **Freshly ground black pepper**
>
> 6 **tablespoons butter**
>
> 1 **tablespoon peanut oil**
>
> 2 **tablespoons chives, minced**
>
> 4 **lemon wedges**

1. Bring a large pot of water to a boil. Add corn, turn off heat and let sit 5 minutes. Remove corn and cool. Cut kernels from cobs into medium saucepan, scraping off and including as much milky liquid as possible. Set aside.

2. Return water to a boil and season with salt. Add green beans and cook until tender and slightly crisp, about 3 minutes. Remove with slotted spoon and cool. Bring water back to a boil and add snap peas. Cook until tender but slightly crisp, about 3 minutes. Drain and cool. Halve green beans, and slice snap peas diagonally into ½-inch pieces. Add to corn.

3. Generously season salmon fillets on both sides with salt and pepper. In a large nonstick pan over medium-high heat, melt 2 tablespoons butter with the oil. When bubbles subside, add fillets skin-side down. Cook until brown and crisp, about 4 minutes. Turn once and brown other side 3 minutes; fish should be slightly rare in center.

4. Add remaining butter to corn mixture, place pan over medium heat and stir until thoroughly warmed. Add salt to taste, and stir in chives.

5. To serve, make a bed of corn mixture on each of 4 plates and place a fillet on top, skin side up. Garnish with a lemon wedge.

Yield: 4 servings
(Amanda Hesser)

Sardines

Sardines are imported from Europe. They're not in the market every day, so when you see them, it pays to buy them and serve them. The only trick is buying them fresh. They have to be shiny silver, with bright eyes, their bellies unbroken. Have them gutted, or do that yourself. You don't have to worry about scales because sardines lose their scales as soon as they come out of the water.

Substitutes: rouget, mackerel

GRILLED SARDINES WITH CAPONATA

Time: 3 hours, including salting

> 1½ pounds eggplant, preferably 3 to 4 small ones
> Salt
> 2½ tablespoons extra virgin olive oil
> 1 clove garlic, sliced
> ½ cup minced onion
> 1 bay leaf
> 1 tablespoon capers, preferably salted,
>   rinsed and dried
> 15 pitted Gaeta or Kalamata olives
> 1 tablespoon golden raisins
> 2 tablespoons pine nuts
> 2 tablespoons dark brown sugar
> ⅓ cup balsamic vinegar
> Freshly ground black pepper
> 12 fresh sardines, gutted
> 2 lemons, in wedges

1. Remove green stems and cut eggplants in 1-inch dice. Salt generously, toss and spread to drain at least 2 hours on a rack placed over a baking sheet with sides.

2. Squeeze eggplant dry with your hands, discarding juices. Heat 1½

tablespoons olive oil in heavy skillet, add eggplant and sauté over high heat until lightly browned. Transfer to a colander to drain.

3. Add garlic and ½ tablespoon oil to skillet. Sauté over medium heat until golden. Add onion and bay leaf and sauté until onion is transluscent. Add capers, olives, raisins, pine nuts, brown sugar and vinegar. Stir, then add drained eggplant. Sauté, stirring until mixture is thick and liquid has evaporated. Remove from heat, season to taste with pepper and adjust salt, taking care not to oversalt because capers and olives are salty. Set aside.

4. Preheat grill. Dry sardines and brush with 1 tablespoon olive oil. Sear on very hot grill, preferably charcoal, until lightly browned.

5. Place caponata in center of large serving dish. Surround with sardines. Using a sharp knife, cut a shallow slit lengthwise in each sardine and pour in remaining olive oil. Garnish platter with lemon and serve.

Yield: 4 servings
(Dave Pasternack, Esca, New York City)

BROILED SARDINES WITH GREEN OLIVE RELISH

Time: 30 minutes

½ **cup pitted, brine-cured green olives**
1 **teaspoon minced garlic**
½ **medium red onion, peeled and diced**
¼ **cup roughly chopped flat-leaf parsley leaves**
¼ **cup extra virgin olive oil**
¼ **cup lemon juice**
Salt and freshly ground black pepper
8 **sardines, boned and butterflied**
3 **tablespoons extra virgin olive oil**
2 **teaspoons ground cumin**

1. In a bowl, combine olives, garlic, red onion, parsley, olive oil, lemon juice and salt and pepper to taste. Mix well, and set aside.

2. Preheat broiler or grill. Rub flesh side of fish lightly with oil and sprinkle with cumin and salt and pepper to taste.

3. Place the fish in a broiler pan, and broil until the flesh is completely opaque throughout, about 5 minutes. If desired, fish can be grilled, turning once.

4. Place fish on warm serving platter, spoon on relish and serve.

Yield: 4 servings
(Florence Fabricant)

Sea Bass

Sea bass, often called black sea bass, is found mostly in the North Atlantic, in American waters off the coasts of New England, New York and as far south as the Carolinas. It's also harvested in Europe. Increasingly, farmed European sea bass, or branzino, are arriving in American markets. But the farmed variety, despite its Italian allure, is less flavorful than the wild fish. Most chefs will attest that wild sea bass is one of the finest fishes in the market. Sea bass range from about two to five pounds, have succulent, snowy flesh and can be roasted whole, grilled, steamed or baked. The fillets are suited to myriad preparations.

Substitutes: red snapper, mahimahi, grouper

CURRY-DUSTED SEA BASS WITH CHIVE OIL
Time: 30 minutes

Searing the fillets on the skin, then turning them and finishing the fish in the oven, yields attractive, crispy skin when served.

1½ tablespoons curry powder
1½ pounds sea bass fillet, with skin
Coarse salt and freshly ground pepper
2 tablespoons peanut or vegetable oil
1 bunch chives
½ cup extra virgin olive oil
1 lemon, quartered

1. Preheat oven to 450 degrees. Lightly sprinkle curry powder all over fish. Season to taste with salt and pepper.

2. Heat peanut oil in a nonstick, ovenproof skillet. Sear fish on skin over high heat, about 1 minute, turn and sear another minute. Transfer to oven and bake 10 to 15 minutes until barely opaque in the center.

3. Meanwhile, rinse chives and reserve a few stalks for decorating fish. Coarsely chop the rest and transfer to a blender with the olive oil. Puree. Season with salt and pepper to taste.

4. Transfer fish to a serving platter. Spoon chive oil around and decorate with lemon quarters and remaining chives.

Yield: 4 servings
(Moira Hodgson)

SEA BASS WITH PESTO
Time: 45 minutes

2½ cups loosely packed basil leaves
½ cup loosely packed flat-leaf parsley
12 cloves garlic, smashed and peeled
½ cup extra virgin olive oil
½ teaspoon kosher salt
2-pound sea bass, cleaned

The pesto in this recipe is simple, without the usual nuts and cheese. It can be made in a mortar.

1. To make the pesto, place basil, parsley, garlic and 2 tablespoons olive oil in a food processor. Process until finely chopped. With the machine running, slowly pour in remaining olive oil. Scrape down sides of bowl, add salt and process until smooth.

2. Preheat oven to 400 degrees.

3. Using a sharp knife, cut four 2-inch slits across each side of fish. Place the fish in a 14-by-9-by-2-inch oval dish. It is fine for the tail to hang over the edge of the dish. Rub about half of the pesto all over fish, into the slits and inside the cavity.

4. Bake fish about 25 minutes, until cooked through. Serve with remaining pesto.

Yield: 2 main-course servings
(Florence Fabricant)

HERB-GRILLED BLACK SEA BASS
WITH MINT VINAIGRETTE

Time: 40 minutes

> 2 black sea bass, each about 1½ pounds, cleaned
> 1 cup extra virgin olive oil
> Coarse salt and freshly ground black pepper
> 1 lemon, sliced thin
> 3 bunches mint
> 3 tablespoons red wine vinegar
> 1 clove garlic, minced

1. Wash fish inside and out, and blot dry. Make 3 slashes in thick part of sides of each fish. Generously rub fish inside and out with 2 tablespoons olive oil, and generously season with salt and pepper. Place a few lemon slices and mint sprigs in cavity of each fish. Chop up ¼ mint leaves. Reserve remaining mint. Place fish in a baking dish and let marinate.

2. Place vinegar in a mixing bowl and add salt and pepper to taste. Whisk until salt has dissolved. Whisk in ½ cup olive oil in a thin steam, followed by garlic and chopped mint.

3. Preheat grill.

4. Arrange fish on oiled grate and grill over a medium fire, preferably hardwood charcoal, until just cooked, 10 to 15 minutes per side. Baste fish with remaining olive oil as it grills, using a bunch of mint as a basting brush. Using a long spatula, move fish to side of grill. Lay remaining mint on grill over hottest part of fire with stems at right angles to grate. Place fish on mint a few minutes to absorb the flavor.

5. Transfer fish and mint to a platter. Stir vinaigrette with a fork, removing and discarding garlic clove. Fillet fish at the table and serve with vinaigrette spooned over it.

Yield: 4 servings
(Frank DeCarlo, Peasant,
New York City)

SICHUAN-STYLE POACHED SEA BASS WITH HOT BEAN SAUCE

Time: 30 minutes

1 whole sea bass (1½ to 2 pounds), cleaned

6 cups fish broth (recipe page 321), or chicken stock

2 tablespoons vegetable oil

1 tablespoon minced ginger

1½ cups finely chopped scallions

1 tablespoon bottled Chinese chili paste with garlic

1 tablespoon Chinese chili-bean paste

6 tablespoons sweet rice wine, preferably Shaoxing

1½ teaspoons sugar

½ teaspoon salt

Sea bass is popular in Chinese cooking, and this recipe is a classic.

1. Using a sharp knife, make 3 deep, parallel cuts about 2 inches apart in each side of fish.

2. Bring broth to a boil in a large wok or sauté pan. Leave the heat at high and add fish. When the liquid returns to a boil, lower the heat to simmer. Cook about 6 minutes or until the fish is barely cooked through. Gently remove fish to a strainer or colander over a large bowl. Reserve any liquids that drip into the bowl.

3. Place clean wok or skillet large enough to hold fish over high heat. When it is hot, add vegetable oil, ginger and scallions. Cook, stirring, for 10 seconds, then add chili paste, bean paste and sweet rice wine. Cook, stirring, for 20 seconds, then add reserved poaching liquid, along with sugar and salt. Bring sauce to a boil.

4. Place fish in the boiling sauce and spoon some sauce over it. Baste fish with the sauce for 2 minutes. Remove from heat.

5. Carefully transfer fish to a platter. Check sauce for seasoning, pour over fish and serve.

Yield: 2 to 4 servings
(Michael Tong, Shun Lee Palace,
New York City)

Sea Trout

Sea trout is a marketing name for weakfish, an Atlantic variety in the family of fish called drums. It is usually sold only in markets near where it is caught. It's a somewhat fragile fish, with a soft texture, and must be very fresh.

Substitutes: sea bass, red snapper.

SEA TROUT WITH PINE NUTS AND CILANTRO

Time: 30 minutes

This recipe can also be made with whole fish. A three-pound sea trout will serve four. Simply spread the pureed mixture inside the fish and bake or grill the whole fish. Sprinkle each serving with the toasted pine nuts.

> 6 tablespoons extra virgin olive oil
> 1 cup pine nuts
> 2 pounds sea trout fillets
> ¼ cup lime juice
> 4 cloves garlic
> ¼ cup cilantro leaves
> 2 tablespoons flat-leaf parsley leaves
> Salt and freshly ground black pepper to taste
> ½ teaspoon chili powder

1. Preheat oven to 350 degrees.
2. Place 3 tablespoons of the olive oil in a baking dish large enough to hold fish fish fillets in a single layer. Add ½ cup pine nuts, toss, spread out nuts and place in oven and toast about 5 minutes until browned. Remove nuts.
3. Place fish in baking dish.
4. Place remaining nuts along with remaining olive oil, lime juice, garlic, cilantro, parsley, salt, pepper and chili powder in a blender or food processor and puree to make a pestolike sauce that has a little texture. Spread mixture over fish.
5. Bake 8 to 12 minutes, depending on the thickness of the fish. Sprinkle with toasted pine nuts and serve.

Yield: 4 to 6 servings
(Florence Fabricant)

Shad

Shad is a harbinger of spring. The fish work their way up the Atlantic coast, from Florida, starting in February, and reach the mid-Atlantic states by April. A member of the herring family, shad is a rich-tasting fish with an elaborate bone structure that's tricky to fillet, so it is best to purchase it already filleted. The rich roe is found in the female, but the male fish has a nuttier flavor.

Substitutes: sablefish, eel, salmon, arctic char

SHAD WITH PINEAPPLE-RHUBARB SALSA
Time: 30 minutes

2 tablespoons vegetable oil
½ cup finely diced onion
1 pound fresh rhubarb, finely diced
½ cup pineapple juice
½ cup sugar
1 cup finely chopped fresh pineapple
1 teaspoon finely minced, seeded jalapeño chili
Salt and freshly ground black pepper to taste
1 large shad fillet, about 1½ pounds

1. Preheat broiler.

2. Heat 1 tablespoon oil in a skillet, add onion and sauté over medium heat until softened and golden brown. Stir in rhubarb, pineapple juice and sugar and cook over medium-low heat, stirring often, until the rhubarb is tender, about 10 minutes. Remove from heat and fold in pineapple and jalapeño. Season to taste with salt and pepper and set aside.

3. Brush shad with remaining oil and season with salt and pepper. Broil shad under high heat until lightly browned and just cooked through, 6 to 8 minutes. Do not turn the fish.

4. Place shad on a serving platter and spoon rhubarb salsa in a band running the length of the fillet, then serve.

The rhubarb, with its acidity, is a perfect foil for shad; it's also a spring crop, so it makes for a good seasonal complement.

Yield: 4 servings
(Florence Fabricant)

HERBED OVEN-STEAMED SHAD

Time: 5½ hours

Though shad
is notoriously
bony, this
technique of
cooking the
fish until the
bones literally
dissolve was
discovered by
Craig
Caliborne and
Pierre Franey
in a seafood
brochure they
came upon in
Maryland.
They tested
the recipe and
found that it
worked
admirably
and that
indeed the
bones, even
the large
backbone,
melted to be
soft enough to
eat. It's
important for
the pan to
have a tight-
fitting lid.

1 4-pound shad, cleaned, head removed, but not filleted
Salt and freshly ground black pepper
1 cup dry white wine
2 celery ribs, coarsely chopped
1 small onion, chopped
2 bay leaves
Lemon-basil beurre blanc (recipe, page 331)

1. Preheat oven to 300 degrees.

2. Rinse shad and dry on paper towels. Season inside and out with salt and pepper. Place fish on a rack in a roasting pan or fish poacher with a cover. Add 4 to 5 cups water and the wine so liquid is just below the fish. Add celery, onion and bay leaves.

3. Cover tightly, bring to a simmer, transfer to the oven and steam 5 hours, basting every 30 minutes or so and adding additional water if level drops too low and threatens to scorch.

4. Remove fish from pan. To serve, slice crosswise through the bones. Spoon on warm butter sauce.

Yield: 6 servings
(Craig Claiborne and
Pierre Franey)

SHAD ROE POACHED IN BUTTER

Time: 20 minutes

1 pair shad roe
Salt and freshly ground black pepper
4 tablespoons unsalted butter
1 tablespoon finely chopped parsley
Lemon wedges

1. Trim excess membranes from shad roe. Do not split the pair of roe, though it may separate as it cooks. Puncture the roe in several places with a pin. Season with salt and pepper.

2. Melt butter in a small skillet or a casserole with a tight-fitting lid. Add roe, cover and let cook over gentle heat about 3 minutes. Use a spatula to turn roe carefully. Cover and let simmer about 6 minutes on the second side.

3. If roe has not split, divide it carefully. Transfer pieces to 2 hot serving plates. Spoon a little of the melted butter over each, sprinkle with parsley and serve with lemon wedges.

Yield: 2 servings
(Craig Claiborne and
Pierre Franey)

At one time it was thought that shad roe should be cooked longer, for 30 minutes. But shorter cooking makes for better flavor and texture.

Shark

Mako is one of the few sharks that has commercial value as a food fish. Dog-fish, a small shark, was once the staple of fish and chips in England, but these days sharks are getting scarcer, and environmentalists advise against using them for food at all. Recent research has shown, however, that the mako is the only shark with a population that appears to remain stable.

Substitutes: swordfish, albacore tuna

GRILLED SHARK WITH SALSA

Time: 1½ hours, including marinating

¼ cup fresh lime juice
8 tablespoons extra virgin olive oil
2 tablespoons minced sun-dried tomatoes
1 teaspoon ground cumin
Hot-pepper sauce to taste
2½ pounds mako shark steaks, 1 inch thick
1 medium tomato, chopped
1 sweet red pepper, seeded and finely chopped
1 small onion, finely chopped
½ jalapeño chili, seeded and minced
1 small clove garlic, minced
2 scallions, finely chopped
1 teaspoon sherry vinegar
2 tablespoons chopped cilantro leaves
Salt and freshly ground black pepper

1. Combine the lime juice, 3 tablespoons of the olive oil, 1 tablespoon of the sun-dried tomatoes and the cumin in a shallow dish. Season to taste with pepper sauce. Add fish, turn the pieces to coat with the marinade, and allow to marinate for 1 hour.

2. Meanwhile, combine remaining ingredients to make the salsa. Set aside.

FISH A TO Z   130

3. Preheat a grill or broiler. Grill or broil fish, turning once, about 4 minutes perside, until just cooked through, or to desired degree of doneness, basting with the marinade. Serve fish topped with salsa.

Yield: 4 to 6 servings
(Florence Fabricant)

Skate

Mild in Taste, Elegant in Look, Skate Joins the A-List
By ELAINE LOUIE

Skate is actually related to the ray and is found year-round and worldwide–in the Gulf of Maine, as well as the Pacific, the Atlantic, the Mediterranean and the Arctic Ocean. On American tables, skate was a culinary gift of the French, underappreciated until French restaurants led the way.

The fish's flat, diamond shape yields two edible wings. Fan-shaped, with a ribbed texture, skate fillets look like pearlescent angel wings, pristinely white with occasional tinges of pink.

What a customer sees at a fish market is a skinned and cleaned wing, usually on the cartilage. Whether to cook skate on or off the cartilage is a question of flavor, just like cooking meat on the bone. Chefs sometimes cook the fish on the cartilage, then serve it as a fillet. Or, for the sake of efficiency, they will cook it already filleted. (Home cooks may prefer it filleted; to remove it from the cartilage after it is cooked is tricky and often causes the wing to fall apart.)

Substitutes: none

SKATE AND SPINACH SALAD

Time: 40 minutes

2 pounds skate wing fillets

1 cup dry white wine, or more if needed

1 pound fresh spinach, well rinsed and dried,
  stems removed

¼ pound bacon

2 tablespoons finely chopped chives

2 tablespoons extra virgin olive oil

1 teaspoon Dijon mustard

4 tablespoons red wine vinegar

Freshly ground black pepper

1. Place skate in one or two skillets that will hold fillets in a single layer, add wine, bring to a simmer and poach gently for 8 minutes. Remove from heat and set aside in poaching liquid.

2. Place spinach leaves in a bowl.

3. Fry bacon until golden. Remove from the pan and drain on paper towels. Crumble bacon into ½-inch pieces and mix with chives. Add olive oil to the bacon fat in the pan.

4. Beat mustard and vinegar together and whisk into bacon fat mixture. Toss spinach will all but 3 tablespoons of this dressing. Arrange spinach salad on each of 6 plates.

5. Drain fish and divide it into 6 equal portions. Place a warm fish filet on each bed of spinach. Spoon remaining dressing over each filet, then sprinkle with crumbled bacon and chives. Season with pepper and serve.

Yield: 6 servings
(Rebecca Charles, Pearl Oyster Bar,
New York City)

SKATE WITH BLACK BUTTER

Time: 25 minutes

4 skate wing fillets
½ cup white vinegar
1 teaspoon crushed black peppercorns
2 bay leaves
2 thyme sprigs
Salt and freshly ground black pepper
¼ pound butter, clarified
4 tablespoons drained capers
1 tablespoon red wine vinegar
2 tablespoons finely chopped parsley

1. Place skate wings in a skillet that will hold them in a single layer, or use two skillets if necessary. Add water to cover, the vinegar, peppercorns, bay leaves and thyme. Bring to a simmer and turn off heat. Allow to cool 10 minutes.

2. Drain fish well and transfer to a hot serving platter. Season with salt and pepper.

3. Place butter in a skillet and cook over high heat, swirling pan as it cooks until it becomes dark brown. Add capers and red wine vinegar. Swirl skillet to blend, pour sauce over skate, sprinkle with parsley and serve.

Yield: 4 servings
(Craig Claiborne and
Pierre Franey)

Though called "black butter" or "beurre noir," the butter in the sauce for this dish is never quite blackened. To allow it to become dark brown it's important to use clarified butter, otherwise it will become bitter. With butter that has not been clarified, the butter should be no more than a nut brown color.

Smelts

Sleek, silver smelts are found in both salt and fresh water and are usually caught in winter and spring. The fish are exceptionally rich-tasting and best quickly sautéed or grilled. The bones are soft and edible, but also easily lifted out of the cooked fish.

Substitutes: sardines, rouget, whitebait, small whiting

GRILLED SMELTS, VENETIAN STYLE

Time: 1 hour, 40 minutes

> 12 smelts, about 6 ounces each, cleaned, butterflied,
>   heads removed
> Juice of 1 lemon
> ½ tablespoon finely minced flat-leaf parsley
> 1 clove garlic, minced
> ½ teaspoon thyme leaves
> Salt and freshly ground black pepper
> 3 tablespoons dry bread crumbs
> 2 tablespoons extra virgin olive oil
> 1 lemon, quartered

1. Spread butterflied smelts flat on a work surface, skin side down. Sprinkle the flesh with lemon juice.

2. Combine parsley, garlic, thyme, salt and pepper to taste and 1 tablespoon of the bread crumbs in a bowl. Mix in 1 tablespoon of the olive oil. Spread mixture on smelts.

3. Close up the fish to sandwich the stuffing and arrange fish on a platter. Cover with plastic wrap. Place a plate or cutting board on top to weight fish down slightly. Refrigerate 1 hour.

4. Preheat grill or broiler until very hot.

5. Rub skin of the fish with remaining olive oil and lightly dust fish with the remaining bread crumbs.

6. Grill or broil fish close to the source of heat until lightly browned,

about 4 minutes. Turn to grill second side. Alternatively, the fish can be seared in a nonstick pan over medium-high heat.

7. Serve with lemon wedges.

Yield: 4 to 6 servings
(Scott Bryan, Veritas, New York City)

CORNMEAL-CRUSTED SMELTS WITH CORN DRESSING

Time: 45 minutes

½ cup fresh, canned or frozen corn kernels
¼ cup finely chopped red bell pepper
½ jalapeño chili, seeded and minced
¼ cup finely chopped onion
1 teaspoon dill seed
1½ tablespoons sugar
4 tablespoons cider vinegar
18 smelts, cleaned, gutted and headless
1 cup skim milk
1 cup stone-ground yellow cornmeal
Salt and cayenne pepper to taste
3 tablespoons butter or vegetable oil
1 cup mayonnaise
1 tablespoon Dijon mustard
Lemon wedges

This dish can also be prepared with catfish fillets.

1. Combine corn, bell pepper, jalapeño, onion, dill seed, sugar, vinegar and ¼ cup water in a small nonreactive saucepan. Bring to a simmer and cook gently for 30 minutes. Set aside to cool.

2. Rinse smelts and pat dry. Place in a bowl and add milk. Season cornmeal with salt and cayenne pepper to taste and place in a shallow dish.

3. When the corn mixture has finished cooking, heat the oil in a large nonstick skillet. Roll smelts in cornmeal mixture to coat, place in skillet and cook over medium-high heat about 2 minutes on each side until lightly browned. Transfer to a warm platter.

4. Drain corn mixture of any excess liquid, then fold in mayonnaise. Stir in mustard and season to taste with salt and pepper.

5. Serve fish garnished with lemon wedges with the sauce on the side.

Yield: 6 servings

(Molly O'Neill)

Striped Bass

A Catch to Make a Chef's Heart Leap

By AMANDA HESSER

Wild striped bass has long been the prize of sport fishermen, a moneymaker for commercial fishermen and the darling of chefs. But just a decade or so ago, you couldn't have found a wild striped bass at any market. Low stocks of the fish and the presence of toxic substances in local spawning waters had led to a ban on commercial fishing for the bass. It was a low point for one of the most revered fish in the Atlantic, and a depressing time for its followers.

Then, with the same brutish vigor it uses to wrestle a fisherman on the line, the wild striped bass came back. Its resurgence is so strong that in 1996 more wild striped bass were spawned in the Chesapeake Bay than in any other year since records were first kept in 1954. And right now, both fishermen and cooks are more optimistic about the prospects for the fish than they have been in decades.

If it were not for conservationists, stocks of the fish could have been wiped out. Through the 1970's, wild striped bass were harvested with almost no restrictions. But now, free-for-all days are over: Strict size limitations, which vary by state (18 inches and up), are being enforced, along with quotas.

While it was gone, a farmed variety of the wild striped bass–which is called, simply, striped bass, while the real thing is always designated *wild*–tried to pick up the slack but without much success. The farmed bass is much smaller, usually less than three pounds, and is actually a hybrid, a combination of white and striped bass that lacks the muscular flesh and rich flavor of the wild fish.

Plenty of restaurants serve the farmed version, and fish markets sell it hoping that customers won't notice the difference. But the farmed version is about as close to the wild as a dog is to a wolf.

The real thing, which is sometimes called a striper, linesider or rockfish, is unmistakable. It is not just a large fish, but also a beefy one, marked with strong black stripes that seem carefully stitched on, stretching from behind its gills to its tail.

You can taste its story in its succulent flesh: It takes on the sweetness of the fresh river waters where it is spawned, salinity from the ocean and meatiness from muscling its way down the Eastern coastline. It's a fish to poach or roast whole, to sear on the skin, fillet, and bake, or to slice into steaks and grill. ❦

Substitutes: for fillets: salmon, halibut, sea bass; for steaks: halibut, salmon; for whole fish: large salmon

ALGERIAN SPICED STRIPED BASS TAGINE

Time: 2¾ hours, plus 2 hours marinating

7 tablespoons extra virgin olive oil
½ cup, packed, cilantro, heavy stems removed
4 cloves garlic
1 3-inch piece ginger, peeled and chopped
2 teaspoons ground cumin
1 teaspoon ground coriander
½ teaspoon anise seeds
¼ teaspoon cayenne pepper
Salt
Juice of 1 lemon
2 pounds wild striped bass fillets, with skin
Freshly ground black pepper
4 ripe plum tomatoes, halved lengthwise
1 medium onion, diced
1 red bell pepper, seeded and diced
1 green bell pepper, seeded and diced
2 cups diced eggplant
¼ cup pitted black Moroccan oil-cured olives
Cilantro leaves for garnish

A tagine is a terra-cotta baking dish with a conical cover that is used in North Africa. Because the inside of the cover is not glazed like the rest of the dish, steam that rises during cooking is absorbed into the clay, resulting in a rich concentration of juices.

1. Place 4 tablespoons olive oil in blender with cilantro, garlic, ginger, cumin, coriander, anise, cayenne pepper, ¼ teaspoon salt and lemon juice. Process until smooth.

2. Cut fish in 4 or 6 portions. Season with salt and pepper. Place, skin side down, in dish, and coat with blended mixture. Marinate 2 hours.

3. Meanwhile, heat oven to 300 degrees. Place tomato halves in tagine or baking dish. Brush with 1 tablespoon olive oil, season with salt and bake uncovered 1½ hours, then chop coarsely.

4. Heat remaining oil in skillet. Add onions and peppers and sauté about 5 minutes. Add eggplant and sauté 5 minutes longer. Add baked tomatoes and olives. Season to taste.

5. Place mixture in tagine or in baking dish, or leave in skillet if it is ovenproof and has a cover. Place fish on top of vegetables, skin side down. Cover tagine, baking dish or skillet. Place in oven 20 to 30 minutes, or simmer on top of stove over low heat, about 15 minutes. Garnish with cilantro and serve.

Yield: 4 to 6 servings
(Joseph Savino, Peccavi, New York City)

STRIPED BASS IN GRAPE LEAVES
Time: 1½ hours

1 16-ounce jar grape leaves
1 lemon to yield 1 tablespoon lemon zest, with juice
    squeezed out and reserved
1 cup instant couscous
4 red bell peppers
¾ cup extra virgin olive oil
1 tablespoon chopped garlic
1 tablespoon chopped cilantro leaves
1 tablespoon chopped mint
1 tablespoon chopped flat-leaf parsley
2 large scallions, chopped on diagonal (½ cup)
Zest from ½ orange, minced, juice squeezed out and reserved
Salt and freshly ground white pepper to taste
1 2-pound wild striped bass fillet
¾ cup dry white wine

2 bay leaves

3 tablespoons chopped shallots

½ cup pitted Kalamata olives

¼ cup red wine vinegar

1 sprig rosemary, leaves chopped

4 ounces feta cheese

1. Preheat oven to 375 degrees.

2. Blanch grape leaves in boiling water with half the lemon juice. Remove and drain.

3. Place couscous in a bowl. Pour 1 cup boiling water over it. Set aside, covered, for 5 minutes. Stir and break up any lumps with your fingers.

4. Meanwhile, char peppers over a flame or under a broiler. When they are warm enough to handle, run under cold water and remove the blackened skin with a paring knife. Halve, and scrape out seeds and ribs. Cut each pepper half into 2 large triangles.

5. Heat 1 tablespoon olive oil and garlic in a sauté pan over medium heat. Place peppers, skin side down, in the pan, and cook gently 15 minutes, or until tender. Set aside.

6. Combine lemon zest, cilantro, mint, parsley, scallions and orange zest and add to couscous. Add 1 tablespoon olive oil and salt to taste.

7. Spread out a sheet of foil large enough to enclose the fish. Lightly oil it. Arrange grape leaves, vein side up, on foil in 1 layer, overlapping slightly to form a single sheet large enough to encase fish. Spoon couscous down the center of grape leaves. Salt and pepper fillet. Lay fillet, skin side up, over couscous. Gently encase fillet and couscous with grape leaves. Enclose in foil.

8. Brush 2 tablespoons olive oil in a roasting pan large enough to hold fish. Gently place fish in the pan. Pour wine over fish and add 2 bay leaves to the pan. Cook 25 minutes.

9. While fish is baking, make vinaigrette by combining shallots, olives, vinegar, rosemary, orange juice and remaining lemon juice in a bowl. Whisk in remaining ½ cup olive oil. Season to taste.

10. Remove fish to a platter and remove foil. Let rest 5 minutes. To serve, cut 8 portions crosswise with a sharp knife. Arrange each portion in the center of a plate. Garnish with pepper triangles. Spoon vinaigrette over and crumble some feta cheese over the top.

Yield: 8 servings

(Susan Spicer, Bayona, New Orleans, La.)

SAUTÉED STRIPED BASS WITH WILD MUSHROOMS

Time: 45 minutes

> 3 large baking potatoes, peeled and sliced crosswise
>   ⅛-inch thick
> 6 tablespoons vegetable oil, approximately
> Salt
> 3 cups coarsely sliced porcini or stemless shiitake mushrooms
>   (about 1 pound)
> 1 cup coarsely sliced chanterelles (about ⅓ pound)
> Freshly ground pepper to taste
> 4 tablespoons finely chopped shallots
> 1 teaspoon finely chopped garlic
> 4 tablespoons finely chopped flat-leaf parsley
> 24 ounces striped bass fillets, with skin removed, in 4 pieces
> ¼ cup flour for dredging
> 4 tablespoons unsalted butter
> 1 tablespoon lemon juice
> 4 tablespoons chopped chives

1. Rinse potato slices under cold running water, drain well and pat dry.

2. Heat 2 tablespoons oil in a large, nonstick skillet over high heat. Add potatoes, salt to taste, and cook until lightly browned on both sides. Remove from skillet; keep warm.

3. Add a little more oil to the pan if necessary and add the porcini and chanterelles. Salt and pepper to taste. Cook over high heat until the mushrooms wilt. Add the shallots, garlic and parsley. Cook for about a minute, stirring gently. Set aside and keep warm.

4. Dredge fish in flour and shake off the excess. Season with salt and pepper. Set aside.

5. In another large, nonstick skillet over medium heat, add 4 remaining tablespoons vegetable oil. Add fillets. Cook until lightly browned, about 3 or 4 minutes. Reduce the heat to medium, gently flip fish and cook 3 to 4 minutes more, or until done. Do not overcook. Remove and keep warm.

6. Divide potatoes evenly over 4 plates in a ring pattern. Place fish over the center and put mushroom mixture over fish.

7. In a saucepan over medium-high heat, melt butter, and cook, swirling

occasionally, until lightly browned. Add lemon juice, then pour lemon butter equally over each serving. Sprinkle with chives and serve.

Yield: 4 servings
(Jean-Jacques Rachou, La Côte Basque,
New York City)

WHOLE ROASTED STRIPED BASS
Time: 30 to 40 minutes, plus resting

1 large whole striped bass, 6 to 8 pounds, cleaned and
   gutted, head removed if necessary
2 tablespoons extra virgin olive oil
Salt and freshly ground black pepper
1 large bunch rosemary
Several large sprigs cilantro for garnish
1½ to 2 cups romesco sauce (recipe page 328)

1. You will need an oven with an opening of about 30 inches to accommodate a whole fish larger than 6 pounds with the head on. You will also need a very large pan to hold the fish. You can improvise by using a standard 17-inch baking sheet, wrapping it in several thicknesses of heavy-duty foil and extending the foil beyond the ends of the baking sheet to create a surface that will fit the fish. Turn up the edges of the foil to catch pan juices.

2. Preheat oven to 500 degrees.

3. Rub fish inside and out with the olive oil. Season the cavity of the fish with salt and pepper and stuff it with rosemary.

4. Place fish on the prepared pan, place it in the oven and roast 5 minutes per pound. Remove fish from the oven. Cover the fish loosely with a tent of foil and allow it to rest at least 15 minutes. It can rest for up to 1 hour and then be served at room temperature. Alternatively, after the resting period, the fish can be returned to the oven set at the lowest possible temperature (140 to 150 degrees) and kept warm without overcooking for up to 1 hour.

5. At serving time, transfer fish to a platter and garnish with the cilantro.

6. To serve, peel off the top layer of skin, then, using a large fork and a spatula, carefully lift sections of the fish off the bone. When all the exposed

This high-temperature roasting technique for a big whole fish may seem surprisingly fast. But it's all that is needed. And as with roasted meats and poultry, the resting time out of the oven is critical. The fish continues to cook in its retained heat while the flesh achieves a silken meatiness and holds its juices.

flesh has been removed from the bone, lift off the skeleton in one piece to expose the flesh underneath. Serve portions of it, lifting it off the skin. Pass romesco sauce alongside.

Yield: 6 to 10 servings
(Florence Fabricant)

Sturgeon

In Russia, sturgeon is a by-product of caviar manufacture. But these days in California, small sturgeon, too immature for caviar production, are being farmed as food fish. Sturgeon is a succulent fish that is underappreciated. It should be cooked until just done; overcooking will dry it out.

Substitutes: swordfish, albacore tuna, cobia

STURGEON SALTIMBOCCA
Time: 30 minutes

> 1 pound fresh sturgeon, in 8 thin slices
> 16 leaves fresh sage
> 8 slices prosciutto, about 2 ounces
> Flour
> Salt and freshly ground black pepper
> 2 tablespoons unsalted butter
> 2 tablespoons extra virgin olive oil
> ⅓ cup dry white wine

1. Pat sturgeon slices dry. Top each with 2 sage leaves, then place a slice of proscuitto over the sage, folded if necessary to fit the slice of fish. Secure with a toothpick inserted at an angle. Dredge lightly with flour on both sides and season to taste with salt and pepper.

2. Heat butter and oil in a large, heavy skillet. Add fish and sauté over

high heat, about 3 minutes on each side, until lightly browned. Remove from pan and set aside on a warm platter.

3. Add wine to the skillet, swirl and bring to a simmer. Pour a little of the sauce over each piece of fish and serve at once.

Yield: 4 servings
(Florence Fabricant)

STURGEON MIGNONS IN HAZELNUT SAUCE

Time: 30 minutes

½ **cup all-purpose flour**
1 **teaspoon dry mustard**
Salt and freshly ground black pepper
2 **pounds fresh sturgeon cut in 12 medallions** ½-**inch thick**
4 **tablespoons unsalted butter**
2 **tablespoons hazelnut oil**
1 **tablespoon finely minced shallots**
1 **tablespoon drained small capers**
2 **tablespoons coarsely chopped hazelnuts**
2 **tablespoons extra virgin olive oil**
1 **tablespoon lemon juice**
1 **tablespoon minced flat-leaf parsley**

Be sure your nut oil is fresh. It is best kept in the refrigerator to prevent it from turning rancid.

1. Mix flour, mustard, salt and pepper. Dip medallions in seasoned flour on one side only and arrange on a plate, floured side up.

2. Melt butter in small skillet. Add hazelnut oil and shallots and cook over medium heat until butter and shallots have browned, about 6 minutes; do not allow butter to blacken. Stir in capers and hazelnuts. Season with salt and pepper and set aside.

3. Heat olive oil in large skillet over high heat. Add fish, floured side down, and sauté until golden, about 30 seconds. Turn medallions, cook another 30 seconds, then transfer to six warm dinner plates. Briefly reheat hazelnut sauce, add lemon juice and parsley and spoon over each medallion. Serve.

Yield: 6 servings
(Florence Fabricant)

Swordfish

Eating Well; Serving No Swordfish?
By MARIAN BURROS

For several years, Americans have been warned not to eat swordfish more than once a week because of the potential for mercury poisoning. Then, they had a reason not to eat swordfish at all: population levels were in serious decline. Conservationists feared that within a decade, there might not be a commercial swordfish industry at all.

So many swordfish were being caught that many did not grow to full size. In the early part of the century, the average weight of a swordfish when caught was around 300 pounds; by 1960 it was 266 pounds; and by 1999 it was 90 pounds. International regulations prohibit fishermen from keeping any swordfish weighing less than 33 pounds.

Most people who buy swordfish at the fish counter probably never stopped to think about why the steaks kept getting smaller and smaller.

But the efforts of conservationists and responsible chefs and retailers may be paying off. The swordfish catch has started to show signs of revival.

Substitutes: tuna, shark, cobia, sturgeon

GRILLED SWORDFISH STEAKS WITH ASIAN BARBECUE SAUCE
Time: 30 minutes

½ cup Chinese plum sauce
¼ cup Chinese hoisin sauce
1 teaspoon Chinese chili paste with garlic
Grated zest of 1 orange
½ cup fresh orange juice
4 tablespoons chopped cilantro
2 teaspoons minced fresh ginger

1 teaspoon Asian, or toasted sesame oil
20 ounces swordfish steaks, in 4 equal pieces,
   skin removed
½ cup chicken stock
2 cups loosely packed spicy greens (such as mizuna,
   red mustard, arugula and tatsoi)
4 scallions, including 2 inches of the green part, sliced thin
1 tablespoon peanut oil
1 teaspoon mixed black and white sesame seeds
Cilantro sprigs for garnish

1. Preheat grill.

2. Combine plum sauce, hoisin sauce, chili paste, orange zest, orange juice, 2 tablespoons of chopped cilantro, 1 teaspoon minced ginger and sesame oil. Brush some of this mixture lightly on the swordfish steaks and set aside.

3. Heat chicken stock with remaining ginger in a heavy saucepan. Add greens; cover and steam just until they wilt, about 1 minute. Remove from heat and stir in scallions and remaining chopped cilantro. Set aside.

4. Brush grill with peanut oil. Grill swordfish steaks 2 to 3 minutes on each side, brushing with additional sauce mixture. Alternatively, fish can be broiled.

5. Remove greens from the saucepan, drain well and place in the center of 4 shallow bowls. Place a swordfish steak on top of each. Add remaining sauce mixture to the liquid in the saucepan and quickly bring to a simmer. Drizzle around greens and swordfish. Sprinkle with sesame seeds, garnish with cilantro sprigs and serve.

Yield: 4 servings
(Elka Gilmore, Kokachin,
New York City)

GRILLED SWORDFISH WITH PARSLEY-LEMON-CAPER SAUCE

Time: 25 minutes

1½ large bunches flat-leaf parsley
Juice of 1 lemon
Grated zest from 2 lemons
1 tablespoon Dijon mustard
1 cup diced red onion
2 tablespoons capers
⅓ cup chopped cornichons
8 anchovy fillets in oil, drained and patted dry
½ cup extra virgin olive oil
6 swordfish steaks, 1 inch thick
Salt and freshly ground black pepper

1. Preheat grill or broiler.

2. In a food processor, combine parsley, lemon juice and zest, mustard, onion, capers, cornichons and anchovies. Process until coarsely chopped. Add ⅓ cup olive oil and process briefly.

3. Rub swordfish with remaining olive oil, season lightly with salt and pepper, and grill or broil, turning once, to desired degree of doneness, about 4 minutes on each side. Serve with parsley-lemon-caper sauce.

Yield: 6 servings
(Lansdowne, London)

LACQUERED SWORDFISH WITH SCALLIONS

Time: 40 minutes

1 tablespoon sesame seeds
3 tablespoons peanut oil
1 teaspoon Asian, or toasted sesame oil
1 1-inch piece fresh ginger, peeled and finely slivered
2 large bunches scallions (white and 3 inches green part only),
    halved crosswise and quartered lengthwise

2 teaspoons plus ¼ cup soy sauce
¼ cup turbinado sugar
½ teaspoon freshly ground black pepper
4 swordfish steaks, 1 inch thick, skinned

1. Stir sesame seeds in a heavy, small, dry skillet over medium heat until brown. Place in a small dish and set aside. Heat 1 tablespoon peanut oil, the sesame oil and ginger in the skillet over medium-high heat. Add scallions and stir-fry about 1 minute. Add 1 tablespoon water and 2 teaspoons soy sauce and stir-fry about 1 minute more. Set aside.

2. Mix sugar and pepper in a large soup plate. Dip one side of each swordfish steak in mixture. Heat remaining peanut oil in 1 very large or 2 smaller nonstick skillets over medium-high heat (you will need more oil if using 2 skillets). Add swordfish, coated side down, and cook until the bottom is browned and caramelized, about 3 minutes. Pour ¼ cup soy sauce in the skillet(s), cover and cook until fish is glazed and just opaque throughout, about 1 to 2 minutes.

3. Reheat the scallion sauce by stirring over medium-high heat. Place 1 swordfish steak on each of 4 plates, top with scallion sauce and sprinkle with reserved sesame seeds. Serve immediately.

Yield: 4 servings
(Molly O'Neill)

Tilapia

Tilapia is the most farmed fish in the world. Cichlids, as they are known scientifically, are native to Africa, and the farmed varities are the blue tilapia and the Mozambique tilapia, both of which are extensively cultivated in the United States. Israel is another important source. Other names and varieties for the fish include Nile perch, which can grow to enormous size, and St. Peter's fish. Red tilapia is a hybrid that's also widely farmed. Tilapia is usually sold in fillets and has white flesh and a bland flavor.

Substitutes: catfish, flounder

WOK-COOKED FISH AND
NAPA CABBAGE WITH CHILIES

Time: 45 minutes

The mild flavor of tilapia is given a vibrant personality in this Sichuan dish using chili paste and Sichuan peppercorns. Sichuan peppercorns, the rust-colored dried berries of the prickly ash tree (called sansho in Japan), are not a true pepper and have a smoky pungency. They are a component of Chinese five-spice blend.

1 egg white, beaten

2 tablespoons cornstarch

1 teaspoon sugar

Salt

1 pound tilapia fillets, cut in 2-inch squares

1 tablespoon Sichuan peppercorns

2 cups peanut oil

2 tablespoons minced fresh ginger

2 cloves garlic, minced

6 cups Napa cabbage in 2-inch pieces

1 leek, white part only, coarsely chopped

½ cup chicken stock

2 tablespoons soy sauce

2 teaspoons chili paste with soybeans (sold in Chinese groceries), or to taste

½ teaspoon red chili flakes

1 scallion, white part only, trimmed and cut in thin slivers

1. Mix egg white, cornstarch, sugar and pinch of salt in a shallow bowl. Add fish pieces and turn to coat. Set aside 15 minutes.

2. Heat wok. Add Sichuan peppercorns and toast until fragrant. Remove, cool briefly, grind in mortar and pass through fine sieve.

3. Add oil to wok. When beginning to smoke, add fish, reduce heat and cook about 30 seconds, turning with tongs. Remove fish with slotted spoon, drain well on paper towels and set aside. Pour off all but 1½ tablespoons oil, reserving 2 tablespoons for Step 5.

4. Turn heat to high. Add ginger and garlic to wok, stir-frying until they start to brown, and add cabbage and leek. Stir-fry until wilted. Mix together chicken stock, soy sauce and chili paste, and add. Bring to simmer. Season to taste with salt. With slotted spoon, transfer cabbage and leek to deep serving platter. Top with fish, and spoon on cooking liquid.

5. Heat reserved oil, add pepper flakes and ground Sichuan pepper and

cook 10 seconds, until spices sizzle. Pour over fish, scatter scallion slivers on top and serve.

Yield: 4 to 6 servings
(Chao Chen, Wu Liang Ye,
New York City)

THAI FISH CAKES (TOD MUN PLA)
Time: 35 minutes

1½ pounds tilapia
1 large shallot, finely minced
1 tablespoon Thai red curry paste, or to taste
1 egg, lightly beaten
½ cup fresh green beans sliced diagonally in ⅛-inch-long pieces
⅓ cup Kaffir lime leaves (about 6 6-inch leaves), ribs removed, chopped; or substitute dried leaves soaked for 15 minutes in hot water, ribs removed, chopped, or use the zest of ½ lemon
½ teaspoon salt
2 teaspoons sugar
Sweet peanut-chili dipping sauce (recipe page 324)

1. Pulse fish in a food processor until it starts to form a ball. Combine remaining ingredients except sauce in a mixing bowl, add fish and mix well by hand.

2. Shape the mixture into patties, 3 inches in diameter and ½ inch thick, and place on a greased baking sheet.

3. Preheat broiler. Broil cakes until golden brown, 3 to 4 minutes, without turning. Serve with sweet peanut-chili dipping sauce.

Yield: 4 servings
(Mick Vann)

Tilefish

A fish from the deep ocean, usually caught off the Atlantic coast, tilefish have white flesh and densely succulent flesh that is similar to monkfish and scallops.

Substitutes: monkfish, blackfish

MADRAS FISH CURRY
Time: 45 minutes

 2 tablespoons peanut oil
 1 teaspoon cumin seeds
 2 medium onions, finely chopped
 1 red bell pepper, cored, seeded and cut in slivers
 ½ jalapeño chili, seeded and minced
 1 tablespoon minced fresh ginger
 1½ tablespoons garam masala (good quality curry powder
     may be substituted)
 1 ripe tomato, peeled, seeded and chopped
 1 cup unsweetened coconut milk
 1 tablespoon fresh lime juice
 ¾ cup fish broth (recipe page 321)
 Salt and freshly ground black pepper to taste
 1 pound tilefish, in 2-inch pieces
 1 tablespoon clarified butter, optional
 2 tablespoons finely chopped cilantro

1. Heat oil in a large, shallow saucepan or sauté pan. Add cumin seeds and, when they become fragrant, add onions, bell pepper, jalapeño and ginger. Cook over medium heat until onion is soft, stir in garam masala and cook another couple of minutes.

2. Stir in tomato, coconut milk, lime juice and fish broth. Simmer about 15 minutes, until thickened. Season with salt and pepper. Recipe can be prepared in advance to this point.

3. Add fish and simmer about 8 minutes, until fish is cooked through. Stir in butter, if desired, and cilanto. Check seasonings and serve.

Yield: 4 servings
(Moira Hodgson)

Trout

Trout as Wild as All Outdoors, Almost
By TIMOTHY EGAN

BUHL, IDAHO: They call this place the Magic Valley. Just past the town of Bliss, about an hour southeast of Boise, the reason for the name is evident. First comes the sound, a distant white noise, building to a roar as you approach. Then the sight: water shooting out of the canyon walls, hundreds of springs at the end of a journey from snowmelt in the Rocky Mountains, through a vast underground aquifer, bursting out to join the Snake River.

Because of these springs, the Magic Valley is to rainbow trout what the Napa Valley is to cabernet sauvignon. The valley, a 30-mile swath through a desert plateau, provides about 70 percent of the nation's farm-raised rainbow trout. In a 15-mile stretch are a dozen trout farms.

The taste of the inland Pacific Northwest does not get much better than a sweet rainbow trout, its flesh delicate yet firm, grilled over an open fire and served with a baked spud, a sweet-onion salad and a glass of local chardonnay. It is a taste from the wildest state outside Alaska, with more wilderness and more miles of white-water stream than any other in the lower 48.

Unlike catfish, which grow in ponds of varying temperatures, trout need a constant flow of oxygen-rich, cool, fresh water. More than 60 degrees is too warm. Below 50 is too cold. Perfect, for trout, is 58 degrees—the exact temperature of the water that gushes from beneath the ground and through the walls of the Snake River Canyon.

Trout fishing in America is not what it used to be. Although wild trout have never been fished commercially, they have long been the prize catch of sport fishermen. Not long ago, no self-respecting angler would return from a stream without dinner on a stick. Herbert Hoover fished in sport coat and tie, and he took his freshly gutted rod kill home to the White House. Now, catch-and-release is the prevailing etiquette. You can stroke them, pose with them, kiss them on the snout, but trout not quickly returned to their cold-water home will prompt a pang of ecoguilt among most predators with a conscience.

Still, we have our place in the food chain; the trout gene remains in American DNA. We need to eat the native fish. That's where Idaho comes in. Much of it looks exactly the way Lewis and Clark found it in the fall of 1805; then, as now, the water was the thing. After nearly starving to death, Lewis and Clark crossed the Bitterroot Range and came upon the bounty of the Clearwater drainage. It saved their lives. The Nez Percé Indians gave them a feast of salmon, trout and bulbs of the local camas plant, a cross between an onion and a tuber. "I cautioned them of the consequences of eating too much," William Clark wrote.

Nearly a hundred years ago, Basque sheepherders discovered the high alpine trout of the Sawtooth Mountains, north of Sun Valley. They cooked their catch in garlic and olive oil, which they carried in a pouch. South of Sun Valley, Ernest Hemingway fished the magnificent flat water of Silver Creek, which burbles up out of the ground and provides optimum trout habitat. It is now protected by the Nature Conservancy.

Wild trout—rainbow, brook, brown or cutthroat—are known for tender, pinkish flesh that has just enough oil to keep it moist. It can be bony.

The rap against farmed fish has always been the texture. Consumers said it was too mushy, and the flavor too bland. The very image of a fish farm calls to mind ranchers throwing pellets into manmade ponds. What's more, the fish are said to be dumb.

Europeans tend to prefer their trout with everything showing on the plate—eyes to tail fin. Americans are a bit more squeamish. In response, trout farmers at Clear Springs have been marketing, in addition to the whole trout, products that only vaguely resemble the trout that most people are used to: boneless or partly boned fillets, with the backbone and filament-thin rib cage removed, and whole fish with the backbone and rib cage removed, with or without the head.

And there is enough of the wild of the Rocky Mountains in these farm-raised rainbows to conjure a memory, to evoke a region or maybe just an afternoon on the Clearwater. And that is half the joy of eating. 🐚

Substitutes: arctic char, coho salmon, whiting

BROOK TROUT WITH BACON-SPINACH SALAD IN BACON-BALSAMIC VINAIGRETTE

Time: 1¼ hours

6 ounces double-smoked slab bacon, skin removed,
   cut in ½-inch dice
Salt
¼ cup extra virgin olive oil
¼ cup good balsamic vinegar (at least 12 years old)
¼ cup toasted pine nuts
6 ounces baby spinach, well rinsed and dried
4 8-ounce brook trout, filleted and butterflied
Freshly ground black pepper
3 tablespoons canola oil

1. Place bacon in a saucepan and cover with cold water. Add 1 teaspoon salt, bring to boil and drain. Pat dry with paper towels.

2. Heat olive oil in a medium skillet. Add bacon and cook over medium heat until crisp, about 10 minutes. Drain bacon, reserving oil, and set aside.

3. Mix bacon oil with vinegar in a small saucepan. Stir in pine nuts. Place spinach in a large bowl.

4. Preheat oven to 450 degrees. Line with foil a jelly-roll pan or similar baking sheet large enough to hold all trout.

5. Season inside of fish with salt and pepper. Season skin with salt. Heat 1 tablespoon canola oil in a heavy nonstick skillet large enough to hold 1 trout. Add trout, skin-side down, and sear over high heat a couple of minutes, until just starting to brown around edges. Place on baking sheet. Repeat with remaining trout, adding oil as needed.

6. Place baking sheet in oven and cook about 6 minutes, until fish are just cooked at the thickest part.

7. While trout are cooking, bring bacon-oil dressing just to a simmer. Pour half dressing over spinach, add diced bacon and toss. Season with salt and pepper.

8. When trout are done, place skin-side down on 4 warm dinner plates. Drizzle with remaining dressing, top each portion with spinach salad and serve.

Yield: 4 servings
(Bill Telepan, Judson Grill, New York City)

BROOK TROUT WITH PANKO STUFFING

Time: 1 hour

Panko, a coarse Japanese bread crumb, adds texture as a breading or a stuffing.

2 tablespoons extra virgin olive oil

3 ounces slab bacon, diced

1 medium onion, finely chopped

½ cup finely chopped fennel bulb

2 cloves garlic, minced

1⅓ cups panko

1 tablespoon finely chopped flat-leaf parsley

1 tablespoon finely chopped sage leaves

2 lemons, one juiced and zested, one quartered

Salt and freshly ground black pepper

4 small fresh trout, each about ¾ pound, boned but left whole

1. Heat 1 tablespoon oil in a heavy skillet, add bacon, and sauté over medium heat until it starts to brown. Add onion, fennel and garlic and continue to sauté until vegetables are golden. Stir in all but 2 tablespoons panko. Continue to sauté until panko is golden brown. Stir in parsley and sage and add lemon zest. Season to taste with salt and pepper, and remove from heat.

2. Heat oven to 400 degrees. Line a baking pan with foil, brush with ½ tablespoon of remaining oil and scatter remaining panko in pan.

3. Rinse and dry fish. Sprinkle the insides with the juice of half the zested lemon, then season with salt and pepper. Fill each fish with the bacon and panko mixture, reserving a couple of tablespoons. Fold fish over to enclose the stuffing. Skewer the sides of the opening together if you wish. Place fish in the pan, brush with remaining oil and lemon juice, and scatter the remaining panko mixture over.

4. Place in oven and bake 15 minutes.

5. Remove fish from pan and serve with quarters of remaining lemon.

Yield: 4 servings
(Florence Fabricant)

SPRING ONION PUDDING WITH HORSERADISH-STEAMED TROUT

Time: 1 hour, 10 minutes

Fresh horseradish, widely available in spring but also sold year-round in some produce markets, is best grated by hand. It should be peeled before grating.

8 scallions, trimmed and coarsely chopped

½ cup skim milk ricotta

½ cup heavy cream

¼ cup chopped chives, plus three chives cut in 1½-inch
　lengths, for garnish

3 eggs, lightly beaten

1 teaspoon salt

Freshly ground black pepper to taste

Vegetable oil spray

2 carrots, peeled and sliced

2 tablespoons grated fresh horseradish

1 small onion, peeled and chopped

6 4-ounce brook trout fillets

30 fiddlehead ferns

2 teaspoons unsalted butter

2 cups small fresh morels or chanterelles, brushed,
　soaked in water 5 minutes and drained

1. Preheat oven to 325 degrees. Place scallions, ricotta and cream in a food processor and process until smooth, stopping once to scrape sides of the bowl. Scrape mixture into a medium-size bowl and stir in chives.

2. Whisk in eggs, salt and pepper. Spray 6 6-ounce ramekins with vegetable oil. Divide mixture among the ramekins. Place in a roasting pan, and pour in enough boiling water to reach halfway up the sides of the pan. Cover with aluminum foil. Bake until puddings are set, about 30 minutes. Remove the ramekins from the pan but keep covered with foil.

3. Meanwhile, place 6 cups water, the carrots, horseradish and onion in a large pot over medium heat. Bring to a boil, reduce heat and simmer 30 minutes. Place trout fillets in a steamer basket, and place over the simmering liquid. Cover, and cook until trout is almost cooked through, about 5 minutes. Remove from heat and let stand 3 minutes. Remove trout from steamer basket.

4. Place fiddleheads in basket and steam until tender, about 4 minutes. Set aside. Melt butter in a medium skillet over medium heat. Add morels and sauté 1 minute. Lower heat, cover and cook until tender, about 2 minutes more.

5. To serve, run a sharp knife around the edge of each pudding to loosen.

Unmold each pudding onto a plate and top with 3 chive pieces. Place a trout fillet beside each pudding and garnish with fiddleheads and morels. Serve immediately.

Yield: 6 servings
(Molly O'Neill)

Tuna

Keeping a Treasure Close to Home
By RICK MARIN

MONTAUK, N.Y.: It's August and tuna season is about to begin on the East End of Long Island. The fish migrate up the East Coast, from Florida to the Carolinas to Montauk, where the Gulf Stream will nudge them as close as 70 miles offshore. About 20 long-liners will be waiting for them, with 800 hooks on each 20-mile line, putting in with their catch every few days. And for local tuna lovers, the good news is that they have a chance of eating it.

A few years ago, Japanese buyers lined the docks here and bought all the bluefin they could get: More than 90 percent of the highest-grade tuna was exported. But since then, dealers say domestic demand for fresh tuna—whether steaks or sushi—has increased.

Still, the tuna catch fluctuates.

Bluefin, the largest of the tunas, can weigh up to 1,000 pounds each, but the fishery is at risk. Bluefin are considered "depleted" and are under a recovery plan regulated by quotas.

A 900-Year-Old Ritual Stirs Waters off Sicily

By JAMES HILL

FAVIGNANA, ITALY: For more than 900 years the fishermen of this little island off Sicily have gone after bluefin tuna in the same ritualistic way. For the four weeks in spring and early summer when the huge fish migrate through these waters, the men await a signal from their leader to begin the mattanza, a highly choreographed communal hunt with prayers and songs and rigid rules that is seldom seen around Sicily anymore.

The fishermen, called tonnoretti, wait for the signal, as they have every day since late May. The island community's head fisherman and de facto leader, called the rais, watches the sea to decide if it is calm enough for them to set out in their long wooden boats.

When the weather relents, the mattanza begins: Six wooden boats head out to sea, the fishermen join in traditional song.

Over three to four hours, the boats surround a huge web of nets set up to trap the tuna as they swim past, corralling them into successively smaller holding pens until they are tightly surrounded in a final section–the camera della morte, or chamber of death. The thrashing fish are then confined closely enough to let the tonnoretti gaff them and haul them aboard.

The ritual, which one day netted 38 tuna, is the antithesis of large-scale commercial fishing. But after a stop at the fish processing plant in nearby Trapani, about 70 percent of the tuna are destined for the same place so many bluefin land today: the sushi bars and fish markets of Tokyo.

Worldwide the bluefin are in grave danger. Fortunately, there are other tuna in the sea: yellowfin, bigeye and albacore, to name a few, and even the closely related amberjack, all worthy of the cook's attention. ❧

En Route–Hawaii: The True Treasures of the Pacific
By R. W. APPLE JR.

HONOLULU: Fish is to Hawaii as beef is to Texas. Isolated in the mid-Pacific, surrounded by waters of proverbial purity, Hawaiians have caught and eaten fish of many varieties in vast quantities ever since they first arrived here from the Marquesas Islands by canoe 1,500 years ago.

Today the islanders of the 50th state–whether Japanese, Chinese, Caucasian, Hawaiian, Samoan or Filipino in origin–consume prodigious quantities of prime seafood. Per person, they eat twice as much fish as mainland Americans, and they consume more sashimi, or sliced raw fish, than anyone else except the Japanese.

They grill, steam, broil and sauté reef fish, deep-sea fish and bottom fish and use them in soups, stir-fries and stews. In recent decades, Hawaii has helped to make fresh tuna a staple on the American dinner table and has shipped increasing amounts of swordfish as the stocks in the Atlantic have dwindled. Other fish, like opah and wahoo, still relatively little known on the mainland, are likely to become increasingly available there in the next few years, and mainlanders are likely to admire them as ardently as the Hawaiians always have. There are no obvious signs that stocks are dwindling like those of cod in the Atlantic and roughy in the Pacific. One big reason is that many Hawaiian favorites are migratory, swimming within reach of local fishermen only a few months a year.

We start with the tunas. The great prizes here are the two species known as ahi: the plump yet streamlined bigeyes (Thunnus obesus), which range up to five feet long, and the sleeker, more torpedo-shaped yellowfins (Thunnus albacares). Bigeyes, which are indeed distinguishable by their big eyes, more than an inch across, congregate in Hawaiian waters in winter; yellowfins (no kin to the yellowtail), marked by a yellow dorsal fin, swarm here in summer. Both, at their best, are rich in iron and copper, giving their flesh its red hue.

With a full-bodied, almost beefy flavor and a silky texture, raw ahi is one of the world's gastronomic treasures, in the same class with Maine lobster and Dover sole and Belon oysters–especially the hyperrich belly meat that the Japanese call toro. Quickly seared so that it is slightly crisp on the outside and meltingly pink in the center, the fish displays another but no less delicious aspect of its character.

Not all Hawaiian tuna are aristocrats like bigeye and yellowfin. Local fishermen also catch tombo, or albacore, a species often used for canning, which has lean, light-pink flesh and a sweet, subtle taste, and boldly flavored aku, or skipjack, its prettily striped cousin. These smaller fish are usually broiled, but they, too, are sometimes served raw, especially aku.

The same long-line fleets that land tuna also land billfish—Pacific blue marlin, or kajiki, one of the greatest of game fishes, whose firm texture makes it ideal for broiling and grilling; striped marlin, or nairagi, the tenderest of the billfish; hebi, or shortbilled spearfish, with a springy texture and lemony taste; and dense, meaty shutome, or broadbill swordfish, much of which ends up as steaks on East Coast menus. The blue marlins are huge. There are delicate reef fish such as goatfish, and the exquisite moi, or threadfish, once reserved for the old Hawaiian nobility. Because they are within easy reach by small boat, they are also caught in large numbers by amateur fishermen and served in island homes.

Grilled, ono tastes like chicken or veal with a slight tang. Hawaiians will tell you that its alternate name, wahoo, derives from Oahu, the name of the island on which Honolulu is situated.

But nothing is quite as dramatic looking as the great, round red-and-orange opahs, known as moonfish in tribute to their profiles, and nothing is quite as beautiful as mahimahis, their bellies bright lemon yellow and lime green. ❧

Substitutes: swordfish, salmon steaks, shark, cobia

TUNA TARTARE

Time: 2½ hours

Sushi-quality tuna is extremely fresh and usually comes from the bluefin, yellowfin and bigeye varieties.

8 ounces sushi-quality tuna

2 tablespoons minced cilantro leaves

1 tablespoon minced shallot

½ teaspoon ginger, peeled and finely grated

1 teaspoon safflower oil

½ teaspoon kosher salt

6 grinds black pepper

1 teaspoon lime juice

½ small red onion, sliced paper thin

1 medium cucumber, sliced paper thin

20 large caper berries

4 slices white bread or brioche, crusts removed,
  toasted and cut in triangles

1. Dice tuna as finely as possible, or cut in 1-inch chunks and pulse in food processor. Transfer to a small bowl and add cilantro, shallot, ginger, oil, salt and pepper. Mix until the ingredients are thoroughly combined. Cover and refrigerate up to 2 hours.

2. When ready to serve, fold lime juice into tuna. Divide tuna between 4 small plates, mounding it in the center of the plates. Garnish with onion, cucumbers, caper berries and toast points. Serve immediately.

Yield: 4 servings

(Molly O'Neill)

FILET MIGNON OF TUNA

Time: 10 minutes, plus marinating

2 cups bottled teriyaki sauce

½ cup dry sherry

4 tablespoons finely chopped ginger

½ cup chopped scallions

2 cloves garlic, peeled and thinly sliced

½ teaspoon cayenne pepper

2 teaspoons freshly ground black pepper

Juice of 2 lemons

4 yellowfin tuna steaks, 8 to 10 ounces each

2 tablespoons extra virgin olive oil

¼ cup pickled ginger

1. Combine teriyaki sauce, sherry, ginger, scallions, garlic, cayenne, black pepper and lemon juice in a bowl. Add tuna. Refrigerate 3 hours, turning tuna every hour.

2. About half an hour before serving, remove tuna from marinade to a plate and let it reach room temperature. Preheat a grill or sauté pan to very hot.

3. Brush tuna with olive oil. Grill for 1 to 2 minutes on each side. The outside should be well seared and the center should be just warm and very rare.

4. Garnish each tuna steak with pickled ginger, and serve.

Yield: 4 servings
(Michael Romano, Union Square Cafe,
New York City)

PAN BAGNA WITH FRESH TUNA
Time: 3 hours, including weighting

1 pound tuna steak, about 1 inch thick

5 tablespoons extra virgin olive oil

½ teaspoon dried thyme

Freshly ground black pepper to taste

1 10-inch-round loaf Italian or country bread with crust
   that is not too heavy

1 large clove garlic, halved

1½ tablespoons white wine vinegar

1 small red onion, sliced paper thin

1 large ripe tomato, thinly sliced

8 anchovy fillets, drained

1 small roasted red bell pepper, cut in strips

12 basil leaves

12 oil-cured black olives, pitted and minced

1. Preheat a grill or a broiler.

2. Rub tuna with about ½ tablespoon olive oil and the thyme and season

Canned tuna packed in olive oil or tuna prepared according to the recipes for ventresca (pages 166) can be substituted for the fresh tuna.

with pepper. Grill or broil to medium rare, 2 to 3 minutes on each side. Set aside.

3. Halve bread horizontally and pull out the soft interior to within about an inch of the crust and discard. Rub the inside of the bread with garlic, then drizzle with remaining oil and the vinegar.

4. Arrange slices of onion and tomato on the bottom half. Top with anchovies and red pepper strips. Slice grilled tuna into ½-inch-thick strips and place them on next. Top with basil.

5. Spread the top half of loaf with minced olives and place it down on the filled bottom half. Wrap pan bagna in plastic or foil. Place it on a plate and put another plate on top. Place several heavy cans on top to weight it down. Refrigerate loaf 2 to 3 hours.

6. To serve, cut loaf in 6 or 8 wedges.

Yield: 6 to 8 servings
(Florence Fabricant)

TUNA NIÇOISE
Time: 40 minutes

Traditionally, salade Niçoise is made with canned tuna in olive oil. For this recipe using fresh, it's important not to under-cook the tuna; it should be pink in the center but not raw.

2 tablespoons red wine vinegar
1 tablespoon chopped chervil
1 tablespoon chopped arugula
1 clove garlic, minced
1 tablespoon diced onion
4 tablespoons extra virgin olive oil
Freshly ground black pepper
½ cup each green and wax beans, cooked
4 ounces fresh tuna, grilled medium and flaked
    into large pieces
8 small potatoes, cooked, peeled and sliced
4 anchovies
6 tiny cherry tomatoes
A few basil leaves
8 Niçoise olives
2 hard-cooked eggs, peeled and halved

1. Combine vinegar, chervil, arugula, garlic, onion and olive oil. Season with pepper.

2. Using your hands, mix beans, tuna and potatoes with dressing, and mound the mixture on a serving dish. Decorate with anchovies, tomatoes, basil, olives and hard-cooked eggs.

Yield: 2 servings
(Alice Waters, Chez Panisse,
Berkeley, Calif.)

TUNA AL TAROCCO

Time: 45 minutes

½ **cup blood-orange juice**
½ **teaspoon Dijon mustard**
1 **tablespoon red wine vinegar**
Kosher salt
½ **cup plus 3 tablespoons extra virgin olive oil**
1 **juice orange**
2 **scallions, thinly sliced**
½ **pound shiitake mushrooms, rinsed, stemmed and cut into**
    ¼**-inch slices**
Freshly ground black pepper to taste
1 **medium head radicchio, cored, cut into 2-inch chunks and**
    leaves separated
2 **tablespoons toasted pine nuts**
½ **cup chopped fennel fronds, or a mixture of parsley and mint**
    leaves
4 **6-to-8-ounce tuna steaks**

As with most fresh-tuna dishes, a red wine is appropriate.

1. In a small pan over high heat, bring blood-orange juice to a boil and reduce by half. Remove from heat and allow to cool.

2. In a small mixing bowl, combine reduced orange juice, mustard, vinegar and salt to taste. Whisk to blend, and slowly whisk in ½ cup olive oil until emulsified. Set aside. Grate and reserve zest from juice orange. Cut any remaining peel and pith from orange. Over a bowl, cut orange into segments, reserving segments and juices released into the bowl.

3. In a 10-to-12-inch sauté pan over high heat, heat 1 tablespoon olive oil and add scallions. Sauté until scallions are softened, 30 to 45 seconds. Add mushrooms and season with salt and pepper to taste. Sauté until mushrooms

are softened, 2 to 3 minutes. Add radicchio, orange segments and any juice. Toss to wilt, 30 to 45 seconds. Transfer to a platter, and keep warm.

4. In a small bowl, combine orange zest, pine nuts and fennel fronds. Set aside.

5. In a 12-inch sauté pan over high heat, heat remaining 2 tablespoons olive oil until smoking. Season tuna steaks with salt and pepper to taste and add to the pan. Sauté 4 to 5 minutes, turn and sauté another 2 to 3 minutes, for medium rare. Transfer to the serving platter, laying steaks on top of radicchio mixture. Sprinkle the blood-orange vinaigrette over steaks and top with orange zest mixture. Serve immediately.

Yield: 4 servings
(Mario Batali, Babbo, New York City)

PENNE WITH FENNEL AND TUNA
Time: 25 minutes

If desired, some salted, rinsed anchovy fillets can be chopped and added to this recipe.

> 1 large fennel bulb, sliced ½-inch thick
> ⅓ cup extra virgin olive oil
> 1 large onion, peeled and chopped
> 1½ tablespoons chopped garlic
> 2 6-ounce cans tuna packed in olive oil, or ½ recipe
>   ventresca tuna (recipe page 166)
> ¼ cup chopped flat-leaf parsley
> 1 teaspoon freshly ground black pepper
> 1½ teaspoons salt
> 1 pound penne, or similar pasta

1. In a large pot, bring 3 quarts of unsalted water to a boil. Add fennel, bring water back to a boil, and cook 3 minutes. Remove fennel with a slotted spoon, place in bowl of ice water and reserve cooking liquid in pot.

2. Heat olive oil in a skillet until hot but not smoking. Add onion and sauté 1 minute. Add garlic and cook 10 seconds. Add drained fennel. Drain tuna, reserving oil, and add it, breaking it into 1-inch pieces, along with parsley, pepper and salt. Combine well and transfer mixture to a bowl large enough to hold the cooked pasta.

3. Bring fennel cooking liquid back to a boil and add pasta. Return liquid to a boil and continue to boil pasta about 8 minutes, or until al dente.

4. Add ½ cup pasta cooking liquid to tuna and fennel mixture. Drain pasta and add it to the bowl, adding additional oil from tuna, if desired. Toss well and serve.

Yield: 6 servings
(Florence Fabricant)

WHITE BEAN, FENNEL AND TUNA SALAD
Time: 15 minutes

3½ cups cooked or canned cannellini or other white beans
1 6-ounce can tuna in olive oil, or 1 cup ventresca tuna
    (recipe page 166)
4 to 6 tablespoons extra virgin olive oil
Finely grated zest of 1 lemon
2 tablespoons fresh lemon juice
2 cups finely chopped fennel bulb
3 tablespoons minced fennel fronds
¼ cup minced red onion or scallions
Salt and freshly ground black pepper to taste

1. If using canned beans, drain in a colander, and rinse under cool running water. Transfer to a large, shallow serving bowl.

2. Drain tuna, reserving oil. Flake tuna with a fork and mix it with the beans. In a small bowl, add more olive oil to tuna oil to make a total of 6 tablespoons. Whisk in lemon zest and juice. Mix the dressing with beans and tuna. Mix in minced fennel bulb, fronds and onion. Season well with salt and pepper.

3. Serve at room temperature.

Yield: 4 servings
(Suzanne Hamlin)

VENTRESCA TUNA SALAD

Time: 40 minutes, plus overnight marinating

1½ pounds fresh tuna, preferably yellowfin or albacore
    belly cut

Sea salt and freshly ground black pepper

2 large cloves garlic, smashed

1 to 1¼ cups extra virgin olive oil

3 sprigs lemon thyme (or plain thyme plus 1 teaspoon
    lemon zest)

2 bay leaves

4 large salted anchovies, preferably Recca brand, or
    8 anchovies in oil

¾ pound fingerling potatoes

1 pound flat (romano) green beans, or regular fresh
    green beans, trimmed

1 small red onion, sliced paper thin

½ cup flat-leaf parsley leaves

¼ cup lovage or inner leaves from celery

¼ cup red wine vinegar, preferably Italian

1. Cut tuna in 1½-inch chunks. Season well with salt and pepper. Place in saucepan with garlic and ¾ cup to 1 cup olive oil, so tuna is just covered. Bring to a gentle simmer, and cook over low heat about 10 minutes, taking care that oil does not boil. Remove from heat, add lemon thyme or thyme and lemon zest and bay leaves, and set aside to cool to room temperature. Tuna can be used at this point but is better if allowed to marinate overnight. Transfer contents of pan to a bowl, cover, and refrigerate overnight. Bring to room temperature at least an hour before serving.

2. Soak anchovies in water for 2 hours, drain, remove bones, cut in ½-inch pieces and toss with a little olive oil. Or drain anchovies in oil, and cut in pieces.

3. Place potatoes in pot of salted water, bring to a boil and cook until tender, about 20 minutes. Drain, peel when cool enough to handle and halve lengthwise. Place in large bowl.

4. Bring 6 quarts salted water to a boil in a saucepan. Add beans, and cook until tender, 5 to 7 minutes. Drain, and place in bowl of ice water. When cool, drain well, patting dry on paper towels, and add to bowl with potatoes.

Add anchovies, onion, parsley and lovage or celery leaves. Drain tuna, reserving oil. Break in pieces, and add to bowl.

5. Beat vinegar with remaining olive oil and ¼ cup oil from tuna. Season with salt and pepper. Pour dressing over ingredients in bowl, and fold together. Season with salt and pepper, and serve.

Yield: 4 servings
(Dave Pasternack, Esca, New York City)

Turbot

Turbot is another member of the flatfish, or flounder, family. Not a native of North American waters, its range is from the Mediterranean to the Baltic Sea, but the fish is frequently imported into the United States. Turbot can be quite large, though when mature it does not reach the size of halibut. The meat is firm and succulent.

Substitutes: halibut, fluke

TURBOT POACHED IN BUTTERMILK

Time: 30 minutes

A handheld blender works extremely well to froth the sauce.

8 tablespoons unsalted butter
½ shallot, finely chopped
1½ cups cubed white mushrooms
½ tablespoon thyme leaves
½ clove garlic, finely chopped
1½ cups cubed dry crusts of rye bread
¾ cup chicken stock
Kosher salt
Freshly ground black pepper
1 tablespoon chopped chives
1 tablespoon extra virgin olive oil
1 pound spinach, stemmed, rinsed
  and dried
Pinch of sugar
4 6-ounce fillets of turbot
Cayenne pepper
3 cups buttermilk
6 sprigs dill, leaves stripped from stems
Juice of 1 lemon, to taste

1. In a medium sauté pan, melt 3 tablespoons butter over medium-low heat. Add shallot and cook until soft, about 3 minutes. Add mushrooms, thyme and garlic. Cook until soft, about 5 minutes. Add bread, and stir to combine. Add stock and simmer until bread has soaked up the liquid. Season with salt and pepper, stir in chives. Keep warm.

2. Place olive oil and 1 tablespoon butter into a large sauté pan over medium-high heat. Add spinach and toss, using tongs, to wilt the leaves. Add sugar and season to taste with salt and pepper. Set aside and keep warm.

3. Season both sides of fish with salt and cayenne pepper. In a sauté pan large enough for fish to fit in a single layer, combine fish, buttermilk and dill. Cover and place over medium heat. When buttermilk begins to simmer, cook for 2 minutes. Turn fish and cook for about another minute. Fish is done when just firm to the touch.

4. Remove fish from pan and keep warm. In a blender or with an immersion blender, whirl buttermilk with remaining 4 tablespoons butter. When it is re-emulsified, season to taste with salt, pepper and lemon juice.

5. Arrange spinach in 4 shallow bowls. Place fish on top and pour butter-milk sauce around. Top fish with a spoonful of bread mixture. Serve.

Yield: 4 servings

(Jean-Georges Vongerichten, Jo Jo, New York City)

Walleye

A Prize Catch From the Heartland
By FLORENCE FABRICANT

When it comes to fish, geography seems to dictate consumer tastes. New York's and Seattle's markets and menus are dominated by oceangoing varieties, not fish that spend their lives in rivers and lakes. In Chicago and other Great Lakes cities, freshwater fish are more in favor. Then there's walleye from the Great Lakes, sometimes called walleye pike.

Walleye is actually not a member of the pike family at all but is related to perch. Pike-perch is another of its confusing aliases, which explains why the translation of the French *sandre* is sometimes given as both "pike" and "perch." In Michigan, walleye is also known as pickerel. In the northern Midwest, it's popular at roadside fish fries. In New York, walleye is often sold as yellow pike, which is one of the classic ingredients of gefilte fish.

Walleye range in size from about 5 to 10 pounds and have a shape like salmon but with a fierce-looking jaw. They rarely have the slightly muddy taste typical of some freshwater fish. The name *walleye* refers to its wide-set eyes, which, because it forages at night, never have the clarity and brightness characteristic of the freshest fish.

Walleye can be found in rivers and lakes from New York to Montana, as far north as Hudson Bay in Canada and as far south as North Carolina. In 1812, walleye were introduced into a branch of the Susquehanna River near Elmira, N.Y., and they thrived so abundantly throughout the Middle Atlantic river system they were called Susquehanna salmon. But they were too highly prized on the plate and had, by the end of the 19th century, been overfished in this region nearly to extinction.

Substitutes: whitefish, hake, cod

SEARED WALLEYE WITH MERLOT SAUCE

Time: 1 hour

Butter with a high butterfat content, 84 to 86 percent, will yield a richer, silkier sauce than ordinary 80 percent butter.

4 cups merlot
10 finely chopped shallots
Pinch sugar
3 sprigs thyme
5 cloves garlic: 1 whole, 1 minced, 3 crushed
1 bay leaf
4 black peppercorns, crushed
Stems from 2 large bunches red Swiss chard
Salt
4 ounces slab bacon in ½-inch dice
10 tablespoons unsalted butter in ½-inch dice
1 tablespoon chopped flat-leaf parsley
Freshly ground black pepper
2½ pounds walleye fillet, in 6 portions, with skin

1. Place merlot in saucepan with shallots, sugar, 1 sprig thyme, whole garlic clove, bay leaf and crushed peppercorns. Cook over medium heat until wine has nearly evaporated and shallots are soft and moist but not brown. Set aside in saucepan.

2. Meanwhile, trim Swiss chard stems in 3-inch lengths. (Reserve leaves for another purpose.) Bring large pot of salted water to a boil, add stems and blanch 2 minutes, until tender. Drain and place in ice water.

3. Heat large skillet and add bacon. Fry until crisp. Drain excess fat and remove bacon. Add 2 tablespoons butter. When butter starts to brown, add minced garlic. Drain and add Swiss chard. Stir-fry a couple of minutes, return bacon to pan and stir in parsley. Set aside.

4. Remove garlic, thyme and bay leaf from the saucepan that contains the wine and shallots. Place pan over medium heat. Whisk in 6 tablespoons butter bit by bit, until smooth. Remove from heat, and season with salt and pepper. Set aside.

5. Lightly score skin of fish. Season with salt and pepper. Heat remaining butter in large cast-iron pan. Add remaining garlic and thyme. When butter starts to brown, add fish, skin side down, and sear until crisp, 2 to 3 minutes. Turn and sear until done, another 5 minutes or so.

6. Reheat Swiss chard mixture and place a portion in center of each of 6 plates. Place fish, skin side up, on top. Gently reheat sauce and spoon around the fish, then serve.

Yield: 6 servings
(Laurent Tourondel, Cello, New York City)

Whitebait

Along the Loire, Dedication to Fried-Fish Delicacy
By AMANDA HESSER

What are known as whitebait are the young of various kinds of fish, including anchovies, smelts and herring, often fished from streams and rivers. Any fish between two and four inches will do, but plump, round fish cook more evenly than flatfish and have more meat on their feathery young bones. Some chefs clean them, running a thin knife down their sides to slice out their stomachs. And some even cut off their heads. It can take an hour to clean enough for four people. Some cooks do not bother with any of this, just rinsing the fish, the smaller the better, then drying them, dusting them lightly with flour–the drying prevents too much flour from clinging–then frying in hot oil. They should be fried twice, just like French fries, the first time until they are barely colored, the second to brown and crisp them.

Substitute: calamari

FRITURE

Time: 30 minutes

A classic accompaniment is deep-fried curly parlsey. Fry the parsley before frying the fish.

6 cups vegetable oil

¾ cup flour

2 pounds whitebait, sperling or small smelts, cleaned (heads removed, if desired) and dried

Kosher salt to taste

1 tablespoon chopped flat-leaf parsley

1 lemon, or lemon mayonnaise (recipe page 325)

1. In a large saucepan, heat oil over medium-high heat. If using a candy thermometer, heat to 375 degrees, or test the temperature by adding a small bread cube to the oil: It should brown in 30 seconds.

2. In a plastic bag, combine flour and a handful of fish. Twist the bag closed and shake to coat fish. Remove fish from the bag, and shake off any excess flour. Add fish to hot oil, and fry until firm, about 1 minute. Remove with a slotted spoon to a plate lined with paper towels. Repeat.

3. Fry fish a second time, in batches, until crisp and brown, about 1 or 2 more minutes. Remove with a slotted spoon to a plate lined with paper towels. When all fish is fried, place in a serving bowl. Season with salt, tossing fish to season them evenly. Sprinkle with parsley. Serve hot, with lemon wedges or lemon mayonnaise.

Yield: 4 servings
(Louis Jama, Les Terrasses du
Bord de Loire, France)

Whitefish

A denizen of rivers and lakes, whitefish is one of the most important freshwater fishes. It is often smoked.

Substitutes: walleye, sablefish, hake

CREAMY WHITEFISH CHOWDER

Time: 1¼ hours

> Vegetable oil
> ½ cup finely diced salt pork or slab bacon
> 1 medium onion, thinly sliced
> 4 cups well-seasoned fish broth (recipe page 321)
> 3 tablespoons butter
> 3 tablespoons flour
> 2½ to 3 cups peeled potatoes, in ½-inch dice
> 2 cups milk
> 1½ pounds whitefish fillets, in 1-inch cubes
> ¾ pound boneless smoked whitefish, in 1-inch chunks
> 2 cups heavy cream
> Salt and freshly ground white pepper

Other varieties of hot-smoked fish, including sablefish, can be substituted.

1. Lightly oil a large flameproof casserole or soup pot and place over low heat. Add salt pork and sauté until it gives off fat and begins to brown, about 3 minutes. Add onion and sauté until salt pork is crisp and onion is translucent but not browned, 3 to 4 more minutes.

2. Add fish broth to pot and adjust heat, bringing it to a simmer. Meanwhile, in a small saucepan over low heat, melt butter and add flour, mixing well until smooth. Add a small amount of broth from the pot to the flour mixture to thin and smooth it. Then add the thinned flour mixture to the pot. Stir until well blended.

3. Add potatoes to the pot. Cover and simmer, stirring occasionally, until they are just tender, 10 to 15 minutes.

4. Slowly stir milk into chowder. Add whitefish fillet cubes, and stir gen-

tly. Cover and simmer, stirring occasionally, until fish is cooked and potatoes are tender, about 20 minutes; do not boil.

5. Just before serving chowder, stir in smoked whitefish and heavy cream. Add salt and white pepper to taste. Reheat and serve hot.

Yield: 6 to 8 servings
(Florence Fabricant)

❧

Whiting

Whiting usually run no more than two pounds and are a relatively inexpensive variety of Atlantic fish. In winter the flesh tends to be richer, fattier and more succulent. The central, almost triangular bone is easily removed.

Substitutes: hake, smelts, trout

WHITING BETWEEN TWO PLATES
Time: 45 minutes

1 piece, 6 inches long, French ficelle (thin baguette),
    halved lengthwise
2 cloves garlic, halved
4 ounces fresh baby spinach leaves
1 shallot, minced
1 teaspoon grainy mustard
1 tablespoon white wine vinegar
5 tablespoons extra virgin olive oil
Sea salt and freshly ground black pepper
2 whiting, each about 1¼ pounds, filleted and skinned
2 sprigs fresh thyme
Juice of ½ lemon

1. Lightly toast bread. Rub cut side with garlic and set aside.
2. Rinse and dry spinach and place in salad bowl. Place shallot in small

bowl, add mustard and vinegar and beat until smooth. Beat in 3 tablespoons olive oil. Season with salt and pepper and set aside.

3. Select 2 heat-proof dinner plates large enough to be placed on, not in, a large saucepan, balanced on the rim. Rub 1 plate with a garlic clove, and drizzle with half the remaining oil. You should have 2 fillets per fish; if there is only 1 fillet per fish, cut each fillet in half lengthwise. Season fillets generously with salt and pepper. Fold each in thirds like a letter. Place on plate, place thyme on top, drizzle with remaining oil and the lemon juice.

4. Bring 3 inches of water to a boil in saucepan. Invert second plate over plate with fish. Place on saucepan and cook until fish just turns opaque, 20 to 25 minutes.

5. While fish is cooking, beat shallot dressing again, pour over spinach and toss.

6. To serve, place 2 folded fillets on each plate, spoon a little cooking liquid over each and place salad and garlic toast alongside.

Yield: 2 servings

(Didier Elena, Restaurant Alain Ducasse,
New York City)

PAN-FRIED WHITING

Time: 20 minutes

> **2½ pounds whiting, gutted and left whole**
> **1 clove garlic**
> **Salt and freshly ground black pepper**
> **¼ cup flour**
> **¼ cup white cornmeal**
> **½ cup milk**
> **2 tablespoons butter**
> **Lemon wedges**
> **Curly parsley for garnish**

1. Rinse and dry the fish. Split garlic clove and lightly mash. Rub fish inside and out with garlic. Reserve what is left of the garlic. Season fish inside and out with salt and pepper.

2. Combine flour and cornmeal. Season to taste with salt and pepper.

Whiting prepared in this fashion is an excellent brunch dish, with scrambled eggs alongside.

3. Dip fish in milk, then roll in cornmeal mixture.

4. In a large, heavy skillet melt the butter over medium-high heat. Add garlic and remove it before it has had a chance to brown. Add fish to the pan and sauté until golden brown.

5. Transfer fish to a serving platter, garnish with lemon and parsley and serve.

Yield: 2 to 4 servings
(Florence Fabricant)

Yellowtail

Yellowtail is a fish name that leads to more confusion than clarity. Perhaps it's just as well that true yellowtail is frequently called hamachi, its Japanese name, because there are also a yellowtail flounder and a yellowfin tuna to contend with. Hamachi is a member of a family of meaty ocean fish called jacks and is extensivley farmed in Japan, where it is a popular fish for sushi. It is excellent to serve raw.

Substitutes: albacore tuna.

SEARED HAMACHI (YELLOWTAIL) WITH SAUTÉED SPINACH AND GINGER
Time: 25 minutes

1 tablespoon chopped fresh ginger
1 teaspoon coriander seeds
¼ cup soy sauce
1 cup mirin
Juice of 1 lime
Juice of 1 lemon
1 orange, peel and pith removed, cut into sections

2 tablespoons extra virgin olive oil

2 cloves garlic, thinly sliced

1 pound spinach, stemmed, rinsed and dried

Kosher salt and freshly ground black pepper

1½ tablespoons canola oil

4 4-ounce hamachi steaks

2 tablespoons cilantro leaves, for garnish

1. In a small nonreactive pan, combine ginger, coriander, soy sauce, mirin, lime and lemon juice. Boil over high heat to reduce by one-quarter. Off heat, add orange sections.

2. In a large sauté pan, heat olive oil over medium-high heat. Add garlic and sauté until golden brown. Add spinach and cook until wilted. Remove from heat and season to taste with salt and pepper. Set aside.

3. Place large, heavy skillet over high heat. Add canola oil. Season hamachi. When oil is very hot, add hamachi. Sear 1 to 2 minutes on all sides.

4. To serve, divide hamachi and spinach among 4 plates. Ring each piece of fish with orange sections, and spoon citrus mixture over all. Garnish with cilantro. Serve.

Yield: 4 servings
(Amanda Hesser)

GRILLED YELLOWTAIL WITH MEXICAN MARINADE

Time: 30 minutes, plus 2 hours for marinating

1½ pounds yellowtail steaks

3 tablespoons extra virgin olive oil, plus oil for grill

Juice of 2 limes

2 teaspoons ground cumin

½ teaspoon red chili flakes, or to taste

1 medium onion, finely chopped

3 scallions, finely chopped

1 jalapeño chili, seeded and minced

1½ cups chopped seeded ripe tomato

Salt to taste

3 tablespoons chopped cilantro leaves

Alternatively to grilling, the fish can be broiled.

1. Cut fish into 4 equal portions. Put in a shallow glass dish.

2. Mix 1 tablespoon oil with half the lime juice, the cumin and a pinch of red chili flakes. Spread this mixture on fish, cover and marinate 2 hours in the refrigerator.

3. Combine onion, scallions, jalapeño and tomato with remaining olive oil and remaining lime juice. Season to taste with salt and chili flakes and fold in cilantro. Set aside.

4. Preheat grill and lightly oil the grates.

5. Grill fish over hot coals or a hot gas fire, turning once, until it is seared on both sides and just cooked through, about 5 minutes on each side. Serve at once with tomato mixture alongside each portion.

Yield: 4 servings
(Florence Fabricant)

CHAPTER TWO

Shellfish A to Z

Barnacles

Truly, Deeply Trendy: The Barnacle
By **MARIAN BURROS**

To sailors, barnacles are a scourge, destructive nuisances that have to be scraped off the bottoms of their boats. There are many species of barnacles, but only two are commonly eaten: the gooseneck barnacle, a tubelike creature with very little shell, and the rock barnacle, almost all shell.

Barnacles taste familiar, and if you can get over how strange a plate of them can look, you may also come to understand why the Spanish love them so. Gooseneck barnacles, or percebes, are similar in texture to octopus or the neck of the soft-shell clam. But they are as sweet as crabmeat.

In Spain, percebes are sometimes served raw but are usually steamed briefly, heaped on serving plates and eaten much like steamers. The triangular head is covered by a pink-and-white mosaic shell, about an inch in diameter. The body is about six inches long, though it is often shorter, and is sheathed in a reddish brown, leathery skin that slips off easily after cooking. The interior of the flesh is hot pink.

This is not elegant food. Diners twist the head from the rest of the body, and the meat slips out of the rough outer skin. The twisting usually produces a squirt or two, which more than likely will make its way to those on your left and right, and even across the table.

Sometimes percebes are bathed in olive oil and garlic, and even when they are not sweet, it's hard to stop eating them prepared that way. The Spanish love their percebes not wisely but too well, especially those gathered off the coast of Galicia: they have become rare and expensive, especially at Christmastime, when they are most in demand.

The suggested cooking time varies from 30 seconds to 5 minutes.

The rock barnacle, or picoroco, which comes from Chile, is also called beak-in-the-rock. The barnacle lives inside a craggy, volcanolike shell with an opening at the top. To catch its food, the creature reaches out with its feathery feet, which look like beaks, and snares plankton as it washes over. Picorocos grow in clusters of two or three or more, side by side on rocks from the Aleutians to Chile. After they are cooked, usually by steaming, they must be separated by whacking them with the back of a knife. It's not unlike opening a coconut. It tastes like crab to some, like scallops to others.

Preparing picorocos is a lot of hard work for little reward. Each gives up a scant tablespoon of sweet, crablike meat surrounded by an equally delicious custard that tastes like cooked sea urchin. Careful handling is required to keep the sac containing the innards from being punctured and releasing an unpleasant odor.

When you get right down to it, what makes barnacles so appealing to chefs is their mystery. Sailors wouldn't agree. One man's pest is another man's delicacy. 🐚

Clams

Arriving Now, From Every Coast
By FLORENCE FABRICANT

With clams, it's cold beer, not Champagne. Oysters call for black tie, but with clams, jeans or shorts are fine. Nobody puts caviar and crème fraîche on clams.

Clams are summer food. As the weather warms, out come the clam lovers, at tables spilling onto sidewalks and on decks by the sea. Summer means buckets of nut-sweet steamers to dip in melted butter, platters of golden fried clams, juicy littlenecks, on the half shell or set to sputter open on a charcoal grill.

Today, in the market, alongside those familiar Atlantic clams, there are dark-striped Manila clams from Washington State, tiny jade-tinged hard-shelled cockles from New Zealand and bronzed deep-water mahoganies from

Maine. Razor clams, shaped like switchblades and streaked white and taupe, used to be a rare find. Even the hulking, cement-gray geoduck clam, a softball-size specimen from the Pacific with an elephantine siphon, is in markets and on menus.

Professional clammers work year-round using hydraulic dredges or a 20-foot-long implement known as a bull rake. Amateurs usually do their clamming by hand in summer, when the water is soft and warm and the surf a mere ruffle.

The hard-shell clam is also known as the northern quahog (or *Mercenaria mercenaria*, from the days when the Indians used the shells as wampum). Littlenecks (1½ inches across), topnecks (2 inches), cherrystones (2½ inches) and chowders (3½ inches) are all quahogs, at different ages and stages of tenderness.

The American appetite for clams is changing. At one time, cherrystones were the most popular clams on the half shell, but no longer. In the United States, the European taste for smaller clams has been catching on. In Venice, the razor clams are half the width of those sold here, sometimes no longer than three inches, and served grilled on the half shell with a gloss of butter.

Tellines, often deliciously steamed in France with garlic and parsley, are no bigger than a fingernail. You can spend an hour picking a portion of them out of their shells and still be hungry. Vongole verace, the similar Italian thin-shelled, oval miniatures used with pasta, are still unavailable in the United States. The closest American cooks can come are cockles and Manila clams. Manila clams were inadvertent hitchhikers from Asia with oysters brought for cultivation to the Pacific Northwest in the 1930's. They have done extremely well.

At home, any of these clams can be enjoyed simply: Just soften a generous helping of garlic and hot-red-pepper flakes in some good olive oil, add a couple of pounds of well-scrubbed clams, cover the pan to let the clams steam open. Then, fold in some freshly boiled linguine and a handful of chopped parsley. 🐚

The Fine Art of Shucking, Step by Step

A good fish market will open clams to serve raw on the half shell. The alternative is some skill with a clam knife in the kitchen. A clam knife is not as pointy as an oyster knife and has a sharper cutting edge. Never use a regular kitchen knife to open clams. To protect your hands, gloves are a good idea.

All clams, regardless of size or variety, must be purchased live. The shells of hard-shell clams will be tightly closed or, if slightly gaping, will close when touched. Soft-shell clams like steamers and razor clams cannot close completely around their protruding necks, but a thin membrane connecting the shells should be in place, and the neck should shrink if lightly touched.

Avoid clams with broken shells, and always store clams loosely wrapped or just in a bowl in the refrigerator. Never keep them in water or sealed in plastic. Unopened, they will stay fresh and alive for days.

Step 1: Hold the clam with the hinge against the base of your thumb. Start to insert the edge of the clam knife, not the tip, between the shells. Then squeeze the fingers of the hand holding the clam against the knife, forcing the blade between the shells.

Step 2: Force the knife all the way around between the shells, close to the rim, cutting through the hinge. The knife should never penetrate deeply enough to slice the clam meat.

Step 3: Twist the knife to pry the shells apart, scraping off any clam clinging to it. Pull off the top shell.

Step 4: Run the knife under the clam to release it from the shell. Do not rinse the clam.

Here is a guide to clams on the market:

LITTLENECK: The smallest Atlantic hard-shell clam has a ridged, gray to brownish shell and pale pinkish meat. Two-inch littlenecks, about the largest, are sometimes called topnecks.

CHERRYSTONE: The midsize Atlantic hard-shell clam can be eaten on the half shell and is also good chopped, seasoned, replaced in the shell and baked. Cherrystones can be put on a charcoal grill, seared until they pop open, about 10 minutes, and then brushed with lemon butter.

QUAHOG OR CHOWDER: Best opened raw, or after steaming for 10 to 15 minutes, and chopped for chowders and clam pies. An average quahog will yield half a cup of meat.

MAHOGANY: A deep-ocean hard-shell clam dredged off the Maine coast. This clam, about the size of a littleneck, has an attractive russet shell and tasty, briny meat. A trifle chewy when raw, but fine to steam or stew.

MANILA: An Asian clam about the size of a littleneck, now cultivated in the Pacific Northwest, that is best eaten cooked.

STEAMER: An oval soft-shell clam, with a thin, white-streaked shell and a slightly protruding, rubbery black neck. It is best steamed and eaten with a butter dunk. Steamers are found in tidal areas along the East Coast. Large ones from Maryland and southern New Jersey are more readily available than the small, delicious Ipswich clams from Massachusetts and Maine.

RAZOR: A long soft-shell clam similar to a steamer, but with a more fragile shell. Small razors can be eaten on the half shell, but most are too large, so they are better in ceviche or cooked in risotto or Asian recipes.

GEODUCK: Like the steamer, the geoduck (pronounced gooey duck) gapes, and its extralong, serpentine black neck, or siphon, protrudes from the shell. Geoducks can weigh five pounds, with a neck a yard long. The body meat, not the neck, is prized for sushi and ceviche.

COCKLE: The tiny cockle, imported from New Zealand, is technically not a clam but is suitable in many recipes calling for clams. Its greenish, ridged shell is almost round, and the meat tastes assertively of the sea, making it excellent in recipes with forceful seasonings like garlic and chilies.

SURF CLAMS: Big, chalk-white shells found on Atlantic beaches. They are harvested by dredging and then are chopped and processed to be sold as frozen and canned clams.

And here is another tip: instead of buying bottled clam juice, steam open a dozen littlenecks for a cup of fresh juice.

The Deep-Fried Truth About Ipswich Clams: No matter the source of the harvest, the secret to a classic seaside meal may be the mud
By NANCY HARMON JENKINS

IPSWICH, MASS.: Was it truly a potato chip entrepreneur named Lawrence Woodman—known as Chubby—who invented the Ipswich fried clam? And did it really happen on Boston's North Shore, shortly before noon on a steamy July 3 in the year 1916? Most food-invention stories are apocryphal at best and downright self-promotional at worst, but this one may just have a grain of truth.

But are Ipswich clams always, always from Ipswich? In fact, it's no secret among seafood suppliers and restaurants that most of the soft-shell clams currently sold as "Ipswich" clams—even in Ipswich—in fact come from Maine, where muddy tidal flats like those along the Damariscotta River and in Sagadahoc Bay yield a delicious harvest.

Basically, Ipswich clams are steamers, or soft-shell clams, but it's where they live that makes them special. Though all Ipswich clams are soft-shell, not all soft-shell clams are Ipswich.

The Ipswich clam flats, along with those in neighboring Essex to the south and Rowley to the north, are part of the Great Marsh, an extensive, hauntingly beautiful and biologically rich environment of salt marshes, tidal creeks and estuaries—some 17,000 acres stretching from Cape Ann north across the New Hampshire border.

At low tide, the flats can reach out a mile or more to where the sea laps the shore at Plum Island Sound. In this wet, salty, muddy environment, the soft-shell clam, Mya arenaria, thrives, at low tide burrowing into the mud to escape its predators (crabs, mostly, and seabirds), then emerging to open to the cleansing seawater when the tide turns, as it does twice in each 24-hour period, to cover the flats once again.

Or at least the clam used to thrive here. In recent years there have been far fewer clams in the Ipswich-Essex-Rowley flats than ever before in history. For a number of reasons, the population of native Ipswich clams has plummeted. There are green crabs for one thing, a nonnative species with a voracious appetite for soft-shell clams.

There have also been other pressures on the species, such as upstream pollution and runoff. It may simply be that clams, like most other wild creatures, go through natural growth cycles. Or most likely, the decline can be traced to a combination of factors.

True or apocryphal, the story of the invention of the fried Ipswich clam—Mr. Woodman, faced with a huge vat of hot oil for his potato chips and a mess of clams harvested from the mud flats of his hometown, reportedly had a eureka moment—is unabashed gospel for lovers of this regional specialty.

At its finest, an Ipswich fried clam, whatever its provenance, is a meltingly tender soft-shell clam body surrounded, belly and all, by a crumb coating that, when deep-fried (preferably in lard), becomes a salty, crunchy-crisp casing for the soft and sweetly briny clam inside. The combination is irresistible.

And the real secret to fried clams Ipswich style? Freshly shucked clams, light breading, fresh oil that is never allowed to go stale and fresh frying. ❧

Substitutes: for steaming: mussels; for baking: oysters, mussels

BAKED CLAMS OREGANATE

Time: 30 minutes

> 1½ cups bread crumbs
> ½ tablespoon minced flat-leaf parsley
> 1 small clove garlic, minced
> 1 teaspoon dried oregano, or to taste
> Salt and freshly ground black pepper to taste
> 4 tablespoons extra virgin olive oil
> ⅔ cup chicken stock
> 36 littleneck clams on half shell
> Lemon wedges for garnish

1. Heat broiler. Place rack in lowest setting, or about 12 inches from heat.

2. Combine bread crumbs, parsley, garlic, oregano and salt and pepper. Add olive oil, and toss until crumbs are evenly coated. Stir in broth, mixing to blend. Mixture will be quite damp.

3. Put a rounded teaspoon of the crumb mixture on each clam, smoothing the top. Arrange clams on baking sheet with sides, and pour in about ⅛ inch water. Broil until topping is lightly browned, about 7 minutes. Serve with lemon wedges.

Yield: 6 to 8 servings
(Frank Pellegrino Jr., Baldoria,
New York City)

SPICY PEPPERCORN CLAMS

Time: 30 minutes

2 pounds littleneck or mahogany clams, scrubbed
3 tablespoons vegetable oil
2 shallots, minced
3 cloves garlic, minced
2 tablespoons finely slivered fresh ginger
3 long red chilies, cored, seeded and sliced thin
1 teaspoon cracked black peppercorns
½ tablespoon cornstarch dissolved in ⅓ cup dry white wine
Juice of 1 lime
1 tablespoon minced cilantro leaves
½ cup jasmine rice, steamed (optional)

1. Place clams in heavy 3-quart saucepan. Add ½ cup water, cover and steam over medium heat until clams open. Remove clams to covered dish, strain liquid and reserve ½ cup.

2. Heat oil in 4-quart shallow saucepan. Add shallots, garlic and ginger, and sauté until lightly browned. Stir in chilies and peppercorns, cook for about a minute, then stir in wine mixture and ½ cup liquid from clams. Simmer until thickened. Add lime juice. Remove from heat.

3. Remove top shells of clams and discard them. Add half-shell clams to saucepan, and simmer about 3 minutes. Sprinkle with cilantro, and serve as appetizer or, with steamed jasmine rice, as main dish.

Yield: 2 to 4 servings
(Irene Khin Wong, Saffron 59, New York City)

MANILA CLAMS WITH SOFRITO AND SHERRY

Time: 40 minutes

5 tablespoons extra virgin olive oil
2 thick slices smoked bacon, about 2 ounces
2 red bell peppers, cored, seeded and coarsely diced

1 medium onion, coarsely diced

Salt and freshly ground black pepper to taste

4 sprigs thyme

3 large cloves garlic, 2 of them sliced

2 pounds Manila or mahogany clams or cockles, scrubbed

⅓ cup oloroso sherry

¾ cup clam juice

1 tablespoon sherry vinegar

2 tablespoons cilantro leaves

4 slices grilled country bread

This dish could be served as a tapa appetizer and makes enough for 8 portions.

1. Heat 2 tablespoons oil in large sauté pan. Add bacon, and fry until almost crisp. Add peppers, onion, salt and pepper. Strip thyme leaves from stems, and add. Cover, and cook over medium-low heat until peppers are tender, about 15 minutes. Transfer to food processor and pulse until coarsely pureed.

2. Heat 2 tablespoons oil in sauté pan. Add sliced garlic, and sauté until it starts to brown. Add clams and cook, stirring, one minute. Stir in sherry. Add clam juice and pepper mixture and cook, stirring, until clams have opened, about 5 minutes. Stir in remaining olive oil and vinegar, and season to taste with salt and pepper. Sprinkle with cilantro.

3. Rub bread with remaining garlic and serve alongside.

Yield: 4 servings

(Jimmy Bradley, Red Cat, New York City)

BACON-BROILED CLAMS

Time: 15 minutes, plus time for opening clams

3 dozen littleneck clams on half shell

4 scallions, trimmed and finely chopped

4 to 5 ounces smoked bacon, sliced thin (7 to 8 slices)

French bread for serving

One of the simplest of all baked-clam recipes, and still one of the best.

1. Preheat broiler. Line a 10-by-15-by-1-inch baking sheet with aluminium foil. Arrange clams on baking sheet.

2. Scatter scallions evenly over clams. Cut bacon into 36 pieces, and place

a piece on each clam. Broil close to heat just until bacon is lightly browned. Serve at once, with bread to mop up juices.

Yield: 4 to 6 servings
(Florence Fabricant)

CLAM CHOWDER

Time: 1 hour

This recipe makes the classic New England–style chowder.

2 ounces diced slab bacon
¾ cup chopped onion
2 cups diced, peeled potatoes
4 cups milk
2 cups shucked chowder or cherrystone clams, coarsely chopped, liquid reserved
½ teaspoon dried thyme
Salt and freshly ground black pepper
½ cup heavy cream or ½ cup finely chopped canned tomatoes

1. Place the bacon in a heavy saucepan and sauté until golden. Stir in the onion and continue cooking until the onion is tender. Add the potatoes and half the milk. Bring to a simmer and cook until the potatoes are tender, about 30 minutes.

2. Roughly mash the potatoes with a fork, leaving some pieces. Add the remaining milk, the clams and clam liquid and simmer about 15 minutes. Stir in the thyme and season to taste with salt and pepper.

3. Stir in the cream for a New England–style chowder, or, for a Long Island tomato chowder, add the tomatoes instead. Bring to a simmer and serve.

Yield: 4 to 6 servings
(Florence Fabricant)

IPSWICH-STYLE FRIED CLAMS

Time: 20 to 30 minutes

1 pound shucked steamer clams
1 can evaporated milk
1 cup finely ground cornmeal or masa harina
½ cup unbleached all-purpose flour
½ cup pastry or cake flour
1 teaspoon salt, or to taste
1 teaspoon ground red chili, or to taste
1 pound lard plus ½ cup canola or other vegetable oil,
    or 2 cups canola or other vegetable oil

1. Drain clams in a colander. In a large bowl, combine them with milk and set aside.

2. In another large bowl, combine cornmeal and flours with salt and red chili. Mix well with fingers.

3. In a large wok or deep frying pan, heat lard and oil over medium heat to a frying temperature of 360 to 375 degrees.

4. Take a handful of clams and hold over bowl to let excess liquid drip off. Toss clams in flour mixture, turning to coat thoroughly. One by one, drop them into hot fat, adjusting heat to keep temperature fairly constant. Let clams fry for about 1½ minutes, or until they are crisp and golden. Remove with a slotted spoon and drain on paper towels placed on a rack. Repeat with remaining clams, and serve immediately.

Yield: 4 to 6 servings
(Nancy Harmon Jenkins)

Smaller, rather than larger, steamers are best.

DOWN EAST CLAM PIE

Time: 1½ hours

Chopped cherrystone clams can be used in place of steamers.

1 pound shucked steamer clams
¼ cup minced yellow onion
¼ cup minced red bell pepper
2 tablespoons minced flat-leaf parsley
6 tablespoons unsalted butter
24 saltine crackers
¾ cup milk or half-and-half
2 large eggs, lightly beaten
Salt and freshly ground black pepper
¼ to ½ teaspoon chili powder, optional

1. Heat oven to 325 degrees. Pick over clams, and set them in a colander over a bowl to collect juices. When clams are well drained, transfer them to another bowl.

2. In a sauté pan, combine onion, red pepper and parsley with 2 tablespoons butter; cook gently over medium-low heat until vegetables are soft but not brown. Add to bowl with clams. Crumble half the saltines in your hands, and stir into clam mixture.

3. Measure amount of juice from clams and add enough milk or half-and-half to make 1 cup. Add to clam mixture along with eggs, and stir to mix well. Add salt and black pepper to taste, and chili powder, if you wish.

4. Use ½ tablespoon butter to butter bottom and sides of a 1-quart baking or soufflé dish. Turn clam mixture into dish.

5. Crumble remaining saltines a little more finely than first batch. In sauté pan, combine cracker crumbs with remaining butter; cook over medium heat just until they start to brown. Spoon crumbs over clams, and set dish in oven for 1 hour, checking after 45 minutes. If top of casserole is still pale, turn heat to 425 degrees for last 15 minutes. If it is starting to get too brown, place a sheet of aluminum foil loosely over top while casserole finishes cooking. Remove from oven and serve immediately.

Yield: 4 to 6 servings
(Nancy Harmon Jenkins)

SPAGHETTI WITH CLAMS

Time: 30 minutes

Salt
½ cup extra virgin olive oil
4 cloves garlic, peeled
3 cherry tomatoes
1½ pounds small clams, such as Manila, cockles, mahogany
   or littleneck
1 pound spaghetti
½ cup chopped flat-leaf parsley

Some red chili flakes can be strewn over the finished dish, if desired.

1. Bring a large pot of lightly salted water to a boil for pasta.

2. In a deep saucepan or casserole over medium-low heat, heat olive oil and add garlic. Sauté until light golden brown.

3. Add cherry tomatoes to pan with garlic, and cook 1 minute. Add clams, stir well and cover pot. Steam until clams have opened, about 5 minutes. Turn off heat, and keep pot covered.

4. Add spaghetti to boiling water and cook until al dente, 7 to 8 minutes. Drain well, and transfer pasta to a large skillet. Pour oil and liquid from pot of clams into skillet; keep clams in pot, holding them back with lid as you pour. Place skillet over high heat, and cook uncovered for about a minute, until liquid bubbles and spaghetti jumps in pan.

5. To serve, add parsley to skillet and mix well. Divide pasta among 4 deep serving plates, and place equal portions of clams on all. Serve immediately.

Yield: 4 servings
(Da Dora restaurant,
Naples, Italy)

STEAMERS WITH TABASCO

Time: 2 hours, including scrubbing and 1 hour soaking

4 pounds steamer clams

**8 scallions, cleaned, trimmed but with most of the greens
left on and sliced thin, about 1 cup**

2 tablespoons thinly sliced garlic

⅔ cup dry white wine

3 tablespoons extra virgin olive oil

1 to 2 teaspoons Tabasco, or to taste

1. Place the steamers in a large bowl, cover with cold water and rub them against one another vigorously to scrape off the sandy residue that clings to their shells. Lift the steamers from the water and transfer them to another bowl of cold water. Let the steamers soak for 10 minutes and then rub them against one another again. Repeat this transferring, soaking and washing procedure 4 or 5 times, discarding the sandy residue in the bottom of the bowls and rinsing them out before each use, until there is no more sand. After the final washing, let the steamers soak for 1 hour, then lift them out of the water and place them in a large cooking pot.

2. Add remaining ingredients to the pot with the steamers, cover, and bring the mixture to a boil over high heat. Lower heat slightly and cook 3 to 4 minutes, until all the steamers have opened. (The entire cooking process should not take more than 10 minutes.)

3. Remove the steamers from the pot with a slotted spoon and divide them among 6 bowls. Taste cooking liquid and add more Tabasco if desired. Pour the cooking liquid slowly over the steamers in each bowl, leaving any sandy residue behind in the bottom of the pot. Serve immediately.

Yield: 6 servings

(Jacques Pépin)

STIR-FRIED TAIWANESE CLAMS

Time: 15 minutes

2 pounds littleneck, manila or mahogany clams
1 small red bell pepper or 1 hot red pepper, or both
8 basil leaves
2 tablespoons soy sauce
3 tablespoons dry white wine
1 teaspoon minced garlic
1 teaspoon Asian, or toasted sesame oil
3 tablespoons vegetable oil
2 cups cooked white rice or 4 cups cooked Chinese
    noodles, optional

1. Clean the clams by scrubbing under cool running water with a vegetable brush. Core and seed peppers. Cut them into thin slivers, about 1 inch long.

2. In a small bowl, mix pepper pieces with the basil leaves, soy sauce, wine, garlic and sesame oil. Heat the vegetable oil in a wok or large frying pan. When hot, add the clams and fold in the pepper mixture. Cover and simmer over low heat until clams open, about 5 minutes. Serve as an appetizer, or spoon over rice or noodles to serve as a main course.

Yield: 4 servings
(Sun Man Doo, Shun Lee West,
New York City)

A spoonful of Chinese fermented black beans, rinsed, will add a nice, salty pungency to the sauce. This recipe was prepared to replicate the food in the 1994 Ang Lee film **Eat Drink Man Woman.**

Conch

True Pearls of the Caribbean
By R. W. APPLE JR.

KEY WEST, FLA.: From here to Miami and well beyond, in greasy spoons and roadhouses and proper restaurants, conch (rhymes with honk) is the mollusk of choice. Deep-fried conch fritters are on offer, and conch chowder, cracked conch (a kind of steak), conch salad, conch ceviche—even, in a few places with no shame at all, conchburgers.

When, out of habit or ambition or professional pride, a chef treats conch right, the results can be memorable, especially if the conch is a tender, new farm-raised variety. Properly prepared, the sweet conch meat, blessed with the essence of the sea, tastes like an exotic version of the New England quahog, which is why it finds its apotheosis in chowder, I suppose. Conch chowder is Islands food. Bahamian immigrants brought a taste for conch to the Keys generations ago, and it took hold so firmly that Key West natives now call themselves conchs.

Conchs (Strombus gigas) are sea snails, beautiful creatures with spiral shells, typically about eight inches long, that end in a pearly pink lip. Conchs are the oversize cousins of tiny periwinkles, which the French often eat with drinks, pulling them from their shells with pins, and of whelks, which Italian-Americans, especially in New England, call scungilli and use in seafood salads. Conchs are herbivorous and live in tropical seas; carnivorous whelks live in much colder waters. Frozen conch, imported from Nicaragua or the Bahamas, is easily available. With local stocks approaching exhaustion, commercial fishing for conch was banned in Florida in 1975 and private fishing 11 years later. The frozen product works well enough in chowder.

But fresh conch is always better. That holds especially true for dishes where the meat is used practically raw, such as conch salad and conch ceviche.

Using tagged conch, scientists are studying ways to bring the populations of the animals in the wild back to healthy levels. The work, centered at the Florida Marine Research Institute on Long Key, started more than a decade ago.

And now, pioneering conch farms amid scrub and sand flats on Providenciales in the Turks and Caicos Islands, a tiny British colony 575 miles from Miami, between the big island of Hispaniola and the Bahamas, have developed new means of raising conch from eggs in captivity and now harvest conch in the juvenile stage, when they are about the size of small to medium shrimp—and long before they become tough. That eliminates the need for tenderizing. 🐚

Substitute: squid

GRILLED CEVICHE WITH AVOCADO BUTTER

Time: 1 hour 15 minutes

> 1½ pounds fresh Bahamian conch; squid can be
>   substituted
> ½ cup lime juice
> ¼ cup extra virgin olive oil
> 2 tablespoons dry white wine
> ¼ cup minced red onion
> 1 teaspoon thyme leaves
> Salt and freshly ground black pepper
> ¼ cup minced red bell pepper
> ¼ cup minced tomato flesh
> 2 jalapeño chilies, seeded and minced
> 16 picholine olives, pitted and minced
> 2 tablespoons minced scallion
> 2 tablespoons minced cilantro leaves
> 6 leaves Bibb lettuce
> Avocado butter (recipe, page 332)

Fresh Bahamian conch is not easy to obtain. Frozen conch can be used instead, but it may not have as sweet a flavor. Squid is another option, one that is more readily available. Even slices of sea scallop would be suitable for this recipe.

1. Cut off hard narrow end of conch and discard or grind for conch cakes or chowder. Slice meat in thirds on bias and, using a meat mallet, pound each piece flat between sheets of waxed paper. For squid, remove tentacles and discard or reserve to deep-fry, cut bodies in half lengthwise and lightly score surface in criss-cross pattern with sharp knife.

2. In a medium-size bowl combine ¼ cup lime juice, 2 tablespoons olive oil, wine, half the onion, thyme and salt and pepper. Add conch and allow to marinate 30 minutes.

3. Preheat grill or stove-top grill pan.

4. Grill conch about 20 seconds on each side, until lightly seared. Mince and place in bowl.

5. Add bell pepper, tomato, jalapeños, olives, scallions, cilantro and remaining red onion. Mix. Cover and refrigerate.

6. Lightly beat remaining lime juice and 2 tablespoons olive oil together and add to seafood. Fold all ingredients together. Season to taste with salt and pepper. Set aside at room temperature until ready to serve, no more than 30 minutes.

7. Place a lettuce leaf in each of 6 martini glasses or wine goblets. Spoon in conch. Top each with dollop of avocado butter and serve.

Yield: 6 servings
(Mark Militello, Mark's Las Olas,
Fort Lauderdale, Fla.)

Crab

Last Days of Summer Are the Time of the Crab
By JOHN WILLOUGHBY AND CHRIS SCHLESINGER

Eating crab is like playing badminton: It can be a matter of some refinement or a boisterous, rowdy and altogether convivial affair. This comes about because while crabmeat has a rich, sweet, almost ethereal flavor, extracting it is a messy business best enjoyed when you are in the mood for getting down and definitely dirty.

Crab is also a food that fosters regional loyalty. On the West Coast they swear by Dungeness; Floridians lavish praise on stone crabs; Maine folks are fond of Jonahs and peekytoe, and Southeast Asians delight in the giant hairy crab. But in our opinion the best crab for eating is the Atlantic blue, which is also perhaps the best-selling variety in the United States.

The Latin name for the blue crab, Callinectus sapidus, translates as "tasty beautiful swimmer." It is, in fact, blue, with rear claws that are actually paddles to propel the crab through water, and that makes it difficult to snare. The blue crab inhabits waters from Cape Cod to Florida and down into the Gulf of Mexico and has even popped up in Greece and Egypt. But its greatest concentration is in Chesapeake Bay, where the vast expanses of shallow, warm and brackish fresh and salt water provide an ideal environment for them. Blue crab season lasts from April through October, with the greatest abundance from July through September. In the early part of the season, when the blue crabs have shed last year's shell but have not yet developed this year's larger model, they are transformed into soft-shell crabs and are cooked and eaten whole.

Whether soft-shelled or hard-shelled, crabs must be cooked while they are alive. When buying whole uncooked crabs, don't let anyone tell you they are just sleeping–if they don't raise their claws when you tap their shells lightly (use something other than your finger), don't buy them. Pick the crabs that are heavier than others of the same size, which indicates a high proportion of flavorful fat. All packaged crabmeat is cooked before it is sold and can be kept, covered tightly and refrigerated, for about three days. 🐚

The Claw and Shell Guide to Crabs From Maine to Japan
By FLORENCE FABRICANT

Only a few members of the world's vast crab family make it to the American dinner table. Crabs must be bought live, cooked or frozen. Following is a guide to most of the varieties on the market.

BLUE CRAB: This small crab weighs less than a pound and lives on the Eastern Seaboard of the United States and the Atlantic and Mediterranean coasts of Europe. It is in season year-round, but best in summer and fall. Cooked, the blue-tinged shells turn red, with meat that is rich, sweet, white and fairly soft, the biggest lump meat coming from the back fin near the claws. The claw meat is brown. The chunky texture makes it excellent for crab cakes.

DUNGENESS CRAB: A heavy, hard-shell rock crab from the Pacific Coast, usually one and a half to four pounds; it is reddish brown and turns orange when cooked. The meat, mainly from the claws, is snow-white, delicate and sweet. It is in season all year but best in late summer, fall and winter, served hot or cold in the shell or cooked in sauces, especially with Asian seasonings.

JONAH CRAB: The deep-water, Eastern Seaboard cousin of the Dungeness, it is smaller, with tender, sweet meat. Its rough shell turns red when cooked. Available year-round. Chefs use the meat in salads. Chinese restaurants cut Jonahs in big chunks, simmered in a sauce.

KING CRAB: Among the largest crabs, 10 to 25 pounds with a spiny shell, from northern Pacific waters off British Columbia, Alaska, Siberia and Japan. It can be red, blue or brown, but the red is most prized. The meat is white, streaked with coral and very succulent, excellent in salads. Legs are often served reheated, like lobster. The Japanese have always been able to buy live king crabs. But with the Japanese market faltering, shippers see that they can make American dollars by keeping king crabs alive and flying them across the continent. And they are taking better care of the frozen legs as well. Brown or golden king crab, Lithodes aequispinus, which averages five to eight pounds, is related to the more abundant red king crab, Paralithoides camtschaticus, the largest, which can weigh 20 pounds and measure six feet across. The Alaskan king crab season is staggered throughout the fall, winter and spring, depending on the fishing ground and the type of crab. The best meat is in the legs. Unlike most other crabs, king crabs have only six legs, not eight, and two claws, which are not so prized as the legs. And if all you can find are frozen legs, just remember to steam them for a few minutes, remove the shell and serve them warm.

ROCK CRAB: These medium-size crabs are colored ivory with purple spots and live year-round off Maine and along the East Coast from Labrador to the Carolinas. The meat is moist and delicate, best used simply in salads or as a garnish. Maine rock crab includes peekytoe. In just a few years, the peekytoe, which weighs less than a pound, was been transformed from a throwaway by-product of lobster fishing to a star in the culinary firmament. The crabs can be found all along the East Coast but are especially abundant Down East, in the waters off Maine from Rockland to Eastport. A crab variously known as sand crab, mud crab and rock crab was renamed peekytoe crab, perhaps from "picked" crab. Peekytoe crab is more delicate and sweeter than other Maine crab. Except for the claws, there is no lump meat.

SNOW CRAB: Often sold as a cheaper substitute for king crab, the crab varieties called snow crab (especially opilio, bairdi and tannery) are smaller, averaging two to five pounds, reddish, with long, thin legs, and moist, slightly fibrous white meat. They come all year from Pacific waters off Canada and Alaska.

SOFT-SHELL CRAB: The soft-shell crab is a blue crab that has molted, or shed its shell, in the spring and summer. The entire crab is eaten, usually sautéed or fried. All crabs molt, up to 20 times during their life; they must do so to grow. The Venetians consider Mediterranean shore crabs that have shed their carapaces, which they call moleche, a great delicacy. It took the watermen many years to make the discovery that put the soft-shell trade on a sound commercial footing. Finding a buster in a pot or along the shore is a relatively rare occurrence. They needed some means of forecasting when other crabs were about to molt, so they could take them ashore and wait for them to do their thing. Finally, some unstoried hero noticed that on the next-to-last section of the articulated swimming leg, the most translucent part of the crab, a white line that later turns pink, and finally an intense dark red, can be detected when a crab is about to shed its shell.

STONE CRAB: A cream-color, red-tinged mud crab with a very heavy shell. Only the black-tip claws are eaten, and they yield rich, dense, lobstery meat. They are found close to shore mainly in Florida, the Carolinas and Texas (available frozen year-round). Usually served in the shell, hot or cold, with a mustard sauce. The claws are a crab aficionado's definition of perfection: all meat, tender but still a little firm, succulent, plump, juicy, briny and sweet. The meat is darker and richer-tasting than that of a blue or Dungeness crab. What makes the crabs even more delectable is knowing they are available only for a few months–the season runs from mid-October to mid-May–and are really at their best close to where they are caught, on Biscayne Bay, on Florida's Gulf Coast and in the Keys. Found as far north as North Carolina and as far west as Texas, stone crabs have a shell as hard as their name, and the claws can grow to be half a crab's weight, as much as three-quarters of a pound. Canny crabbers long ago discovered that the claws regenerate. Unlike blue crabs, which perish for human pleasure, stone crabs give up only their claws. In 12 to 18 months, they will grow new ones. In Florida, stone crabs come in six sizes: medium (eight to a serving), select (seven), large (five), junior jumbo (four), jumbo (three) and colossal (two).

Past the Shell to a Flavor Nigh Ethereal– Picking a Blue Crab

1. Grasp the top shell at the front, pull it away from the body and discard it. Turn the crab over, pry off the triangular apron and discard it, along with the spongy white gills and intestines.

2. With one hand on either side of the crab, break it in half vertically along its natural cleavage.

3. Grab the legs and claws close to the shell and twist them off.

4. Use a small fork or the point of a knife to pick the bits of meat out of the body compartments, one for each leg.

5. Break off the back fin, which is the arm connected to the large claws, and pull out the meat, the biggest chunks in the crab.

6. Turn each claw on its side and hit it with a small hammer just below the

"knee"; if you are on target, you should be able to pull apart the claw and pull out a solid piece of claw-meat cartilage running down the center.

7. Pick up each leg, bite off the end that was connected to the body, and squeeze out the meat or suck it out if the leg is small.

Substitutes: for soft-shell crabs: none; for other crabmeat: shrimp and lobster

STONE CRAB, TANGERINE AND FENNEL SALAD WITH MUSTARD DRESSING

Time: 15 minutes, plus one hour marinating

> 2 tablespoons mustard seeds, preferably black
> 1 teaspoon sea salt
> 1 teaspoon freshly ground black pepper
> 1 tablespoon cider vinegar
> 3 tablespoons extra virgin olive oil
> 1 large grapefruit
> 3 tangerines, peeled, pith removed, seeded if necessary
> 1 jalapeño chili, seeded and finely chopped
> 1 red bell pepper, seeded, cored and cut into thin strips
> 1 fennel bulb, trimmed and thinly sliced
> 3 tablespoons chopped cilantro leaves
> 12 jumbo stone-crab claws, shells removed, knuckle and claw
>   meat separated
> 1 head Bibb lettuce, broken into leaves, rinsed and dried

1. Place mustard seeds in a dry skillet over medium heat, and cook until toasted and fragrant, shaking pan, 2 to 3 minutes. Transfer seeds to small bowl to cool.

2. In a large mixing bowl combine salt, pepper and vinegar, and whisk until salt is dissolved. Gradually whisk in oil.

3. Working over the bowl so you catch juices, peel and segment grape-fruit, discarding any seeds. Place in bowl with dressing, tangerine segments, jalapeño, red pepper, fennel, cilantro, crab and 1 tablespoon mustard seeds. Gently stir to coat all ingredients. Cover and refrigerate 1 hour.

4. Arrange a few lettuce leaves on each of 6 salad plates. Arrange crab mixture on lettuce. Sprinkle remaining mustard seeds over and serve at once.

Yield: 6 servings

(Allen Susser, Chef Allen, North Miami, Fla.)

MALAYSIAN-STYLE GINGER CRAB IN CHILI SAUCE

Time: 25 minutes

8 live blue crabs
1 tablespoon extra virgin olive oil
1 tablespoon Asian, or toasted sesame oil
2 tablespoons minced garlic
3 tablespoons minced ginger
2 tablespoons seeded minced fresh serrano or
   Thai chili
½ cup pineapple juice
¼ cup white vinegar
¼ cup ketchup
¼ cup soy sauce
¼ cup fresh lime juice
½ cup roughly chopped cilantro

Beware when handling live blue crabs: Their pincers mean business! Use heavy mitts or tongs to pick them up and put them into the pot. Even so, you may find that a few have their claws ripped off by rivals.

1. Fill a large, deep pot halfway with water and bring to a rolling boil. Plunge the crabs into the water and cook just until they turn bright red, or about 1 minute. Rinse the crabs under cold running water. As soon as they are cool enough to handle, use a chef's knife or cleaver to cut each in half.

2. In a large sauté pan, heat the olive oil and the sesame oil over medium heat until they are hot but not smoking. Add the garlic, ginger and chili, and sauté the mixture, stirring, for 2 minutes. Add pineapple juice, vinegar, ketchup and soy sauce, and bring to a boil. Add the crabs and cook for 6 minutes, stirring frequently.

3. Remove the mixture from the heat, stir in the lime juice and the cilantro, and then serve, along with finger bowls of water and plenty of napkins.

Yield: 4 servings

(John Willoughby and Chris Schlesinger)

SAUTÉED SOFT-SHELL CRABS
Time: 20 minutes

1 cup flour
Salt and freshly ground black pepper
8 soft-shell crabs, cleaned
¾ cup clarified butter
½ cup canola oil
3 tablespoons lemon juice
1 tablespoon chopped curly parsley

1. Heat a large cast-iron skillet over medium heat. Place flour on a plate, and season with salt and pepper. Dredge soft-shell crabs in flour, shaking off excess. When the skillet is hot, add half the butter and canola oil to a depth of about ¼ inch. Add four crabs, backside down, being careful to avoid spattering. When they brown lightly, turn, and finish cooking on the other side, until cooked through, 3 to 5 minutes total, depending on the size of the crabs. Drain on paper towels, and repeat with remaining crabs, adding more butter or oil to pan if needed.

2. In a small bowl, stir together remaining clarified butter and lemon juice. Drizzle over crabs, sprinkle with parsley, and serve immediately.

Yield: 4 servings
(Jimmy Sneed, The Frog and the Redneck, Richmond, Va.)

TEMPURA OF SOFT-SHELL CRABS
Time: 20 minutes

8 cleaned soft-shell crabs
1 cup flour
¼ teaspoon baking soda
2 ice cubes
Peanut oil for deep frying
Sea salt

1. Lay crabs backside down on a cutting board, and cut in in half lengthwise.

2. Stir about 1¼ cups water into the flour to make a smooth, thick batter. Add baking soda and ice cubes.

3. Pour two inches oil into a deep pot and heat to 375 degrees. (Test by carefully sprinkling a drop or two of water into the pot. If the oil rumbles, it's not hot enough. If it crackles, it is.)

4. Dip crab pieces, four at a time, into batter, and immediately drop into hot oil. Stir after several seconds to separate pieces, then cook until golden brown, 30 to 45 seconds. Drain on paper towels. Repeat with remaining crab pieces. Salt to taste, and serve immediately.

Yield: 4 servings

(Jimmy Sneed, The Frog and the Redneck, Richmond, Va.)

VERMICELLI WITH CRAB AND SPINACH IN SAFFRON BROTH

Time: 25 minutes

Salt
1 tablespoon vegetable oil
1 medium onion, peeled and diced
2 tablespoons minced garlic
1 cup dry white wine
¼ teaspoon saffron threads
3 cups roughly torn, well-rinsed baby spinach leaves
1 pound lump crabmeat, picked to remove cartilage
Freshly ground black pepper to taste
12 ounces dried vermicelli, angel-hair or cappellini
2 tablespoons lemon juice
¼ cup extra virgin olive oil

King crabmeat is excellent in this recipe.

1. In a large pot, bring 2 quarts salted water to a boil over high heat.

2. Meanwhile, heat the vegetable oil in a small saucepan over medium heat. Add the onion and sauté, stirring occasionally, until transparent, about 5 minutes. Add garlic and cook, stirring occasionally, for 1 minute. Add wine and saffron, reduce heat to low and simmer for 10 minutes. Add spinach and cook, stirring about a minute until spinach is wilted. Add crabmeat. Cook for 1 more minute. Season to taste with salt and pepper. Remove from heat.

3. When water boils, add pasta, stir to separate strands and cook until pasta is al dente, about 3 minutes. Drain, leaving some moisture clinging to pasta, place in a large bowl and toss with lemon juice and extra virgin olive oil.

4. Add the crab mixture to pasta, toss well, season to taste with salt and pepper, and serve.

Yield: 4 servings
(John Willoughby and Chris Schlesinger)

Crayfish

There is a legend, in Acadian folklore, about how the Catholics fleeing persecution in Canada made their way to Louisiana. Because their lobsters were on the road such a long time, they turned into crayfish. Today crayfish, a freshwater shellfish that does look like a tiny lobster, are cultivated in Louisiana and in California.

A variety of crayfish that's native to Australia, usually called yabbies, is sometimes available. They are large as crayfish go, with grayish bodies about four inches long excluding their blue-tipped claws, and like most crustaceans, they turn red when cooked. Preparations suitable for lobsters and langoustines work with yabbies.

Substitutes: langoustines, shrimp

FRIED CRAYFISH TAILS (CAJUN POPCORN) WITH HORSERADISH
Time: 30 minutes

 ¾ cup mayonnaise
 ¼ cup sour cream
 ⅛ cup prepared horseradish
 ⅛ cup Creole or coarse-grained mustard

1 cup Louisiana hot sauce

¼ cup lemon juice

1 pound cooked crayfish tailmeat, thawed if frozen

Peanut oil for frying

2 cups yellow corn flour (not cornmeal)

1 cup self-rising white flour

1 tablespoon Cajun spice

1. Combine mayonnaise, sour cream, horseradish and mustard in a small serving bowl. Refrigerate until needed.

2. In medium mixing bowl, combine hot sauce and lemon juice. Add crayfish and stir to coat well. Let the mixture sit for two minutes, then place crawfish in a colander to drain.

3. Place a large frying pan over medium-high heat and add peanut oil to a depth of at least one inch. Heat oil to 375 degrees. In a large mixing bowl, combine corn flour, self-rising flour and Cajun spice.

4. Dip marinated, drained crayfish into flour mixture, coating well. Place in peanut oil and fry until golden brown and floating in the oil. Use skimmer to remove crayfish. Drain on paper towels. Serve immediately with horseradish dipping sauce.

Yield: 4 servings
(Gail and Ken Troncoso Caterers,
Lafayette, La.)

CRAYFISH ÉTOUFFÉE

Time: 45 minutes

This full-bodied classic Cajun recipe can be prepared in advance until just before the crayfish tails are added, then set aside and reheated so the crayfish can be added and the dish readied for serving. The mixture of browned butter and flour makes what is called a roux, a cornerstone of Cajun cookery.

5 tablespoons plus ½ pound (2 sticks) butter

⅓ cup flour

¾ cup diced onions

½ cup diced celery

⅓ cup diced seeded red bell pepper

½ cup chopped scallions

⅓ cup chopped parsley

3 tablespoons chicken bouillon granules

1 tablespoon paprika

1 teaspoon cayenne pepper

½ teaspoon garlic powder

½ teaspoon black pepper

3 pounds cooked crayfish tailmeat, thawed if frozen

½ cup sliced green scallion tops

8 cups steamed long-grain rice

1. In a small saucepan over low heat, combine 5 tablespoons butter with the flour. Cook, stirring constantly for about 20 minutes, or until the mixture, a roux, is golden brown. Do not allow to burn. Remove the pan from the heat. Reserve.

2. In a large saucepan, heat remaining butter, and add onions, celery, bell pepper and chopped scallions. Sauté until tender, about 5 minutes. Add ¼ cup of the parsley, chicken bouillon granules, paprika, cayenne pepper, garlic powder and black pepper. Sauté, stirring, for 2 minutes.

3. Add 4 cups water to the saucepan and bring to a boil. Add roux, and stir until thickened, about 1 minute. Add crayfish and scallion tops. Heat. Garnish with remaining chopped parsley. Serve over rice.

Yield: 8 servings
(James Graham, Prejean's,
Lafayette, La.)

CRAYFISH FRICASSEE WITH WHITE WINE

Time: 1½ hours

1 cup coarsely chopped onions

1¾ cups coarsely chopped carrots

1½ cups chopped celery

¼ cup coarsely chopped shallots

1 sprig each thyme and parsley, 1 bay leaf, 12 black peppercorns all wrapped in cheesecloth

¼ cup white vinegar

Salt

4 pounds fresh crayfish in the shell

7 tablespoons unsalted butter

⅓ cup coarsely chopped leeks

½ cup peeled, seeded and coarsely chopped tomato

1½ cups dry white wine

1 tablespoon chopped red bell pepper

4 tablespoons fresh shelled peas, blanched (¼ pound unshelled)

4 tablespoons fava beans, blanched and skinned (4 pods)

Salt and freshly ground pepper to taste

4 sprigs fresh tarragon

An elegant, buttery crayfish dish will keep the cook at the stove for quite a while. But the payoff is delectably praiseworthy. The peas and fava beans add a nice touch but are not absolutely essential.

1. In a large pot, place the onions, 1 cup carrots, ½ cup celery, shallots, seasonings in cheesecloth, vinegar, salt and 12 cups water. Bring to a boil and simmer about 5 minutes.

2. Meanwhile, to prepare crayfish, take them, one by one, in the palm of your hand, belly up. With the thumb and forefinger of the other hand, remove the middle, fanlike appendage at the end of the tail, which is connected to the intestines. Pulling it out gently will remove the bitter, black intestine.

3. Add cleaned crayfish to the simmering court bouillon. Cover, and bring liquid back to a boil. Remove crayfish immediately. Allow to cool briefly so that they can be handled for shelling.

4. Reserve 4 whole crayfish with shells for decoration. Shell the rest, gently separating the head section from the tail section. Reserve heads for sauce. Remove the tailmeat in one piece by squeezing shell gently to loosen it and then gently pulling away each ring of the tail shell, one by one.

5. To make sauce, crush reserved crayfish heads with a kitchen mallet.

6. In a large saucepan melt 2 tablespoons butter, add ⅓ cup carrots, the leeks, ½ cup chopped celery and the tomato. Cook, stirring, over medium heat. Add crayfish heads, and continue to cook about 5 minutes. Add 1 cup wine and 2 cups water. Simmer 15 minutes. Strain through a fine sieve, pressing on crawfish heads, and reserve.

7. To assemble the dish, heat 1 tablespoon butter in a medium-size saucepan and add the red bell pepper and remaining carrots and celery. Cook, stirring, over medium heat, about 3 minutes. Add remaining wine, and continue cooking until the liquid is reduced by half. Add the crayfish sauce, and cook until liquid is reduced by half. Whisk in the remaining butter over medium heat, being careful not to let the sauce return to a boil.

8. Add peas and fava beans, and continue to cook only until ingredients are heated through. Season with salt and pepper.

9. Divide crayfish evenly among 4 warmed soup plates. Pour sauce over. Top each serving with a whole crayfish in the shell, and decorate with a sprig of tarragon.

Yield: 4 servings
(Michel Vignaud, Hostellerie des Clos,
Chablis, France)

Langouste (Spiny Lobster)

Langoustes, or spiny lobsters, are found in southern waters—in the Caribbean, the South Atlantic, South Pacific and the Mediterranean. They differ from regular northern lobsters in that they have proportionately more tailmeat. There is little or nothing in the claws. They are best split and grilled, but boiling is also effective. The meat may have somewhat less flavor than a regular northern lobster, but they stand up well to strong spicing. Lobster tails come frozen from South Africa and Southeast Asia.

Substitutes: lobster, king crab

SPINY LOBSTER SALAD BASQUE STYLE

Time: 2 hours

2 tablespoons duck fat, or butter

6 ounces prosciutto or serrano ham, cut in strips ¼ inch thick
by ¼ inch wide

1 red bell pepper, halved, seeded, and thinly sliced

1 green bell pepper, halved, seeded, and thinly sliced

1 Spanish onion, halved, and thinly sliced

4 garlic cloves, peeled and sliced

4 tomatoes, peeled, seeded, and thinly sliced

1 tablespoon chopped thyme leaves

½ teaspoon Espelette pepper powder (available at specialty
markets) or hot paprika

Sea salt or kosher salt and freshly ground black pepper

4 spiny lobster (langouste) tails, preferably fresh, about 1 pound
each, split

5 tablespoons extra virgin olive oil

1 teaspoon tomato paste

2 teaspoons sherry wine vinegar

4 handfuls mesclun greens

4 fresh basil leaves, torn in pieces

Regular Maine or Nova Scotia lobsters can be used if spiny lobster tails are not available.

1. In a large sauté pan over medium-low heat, heat the duck fat or butter and add the ham. Sauté until lightly browned, 3 to 4 minutes. Add the red bell pepper, green bell pepper, onion, and garlic, and sauté until slightly softened, about 5 minutes. Add the tomatoes and thyme. Cover and cook for 30 minutes, stirring occasionally, adding a little water if the mixture becomes dry. There should be a few tablespoons of liquid. Add the Espelette powder or paprika and salt and pepper to taste. Sauté for 1 minute, then remove from heat. Allow to cool completely, then cover and refrigerate until chilled, at least 1 hour.

2. About 30 minutes before serving time, preheat broiler. Split lobster tails. Brush cut sides with 2 tablespoons of the olive oil. Broil until meat is cooked and barely beginning to color, about 8 minutes. Allow to cool completely. Remove meat from the shells and cut in large chunks. Set aside.

3. To make the dressing, in a small bowl combine 2 tablespoons of the pepper stewing liquid, tomato paste, vinegar, and salt and pepper to taste. Slowly whisk in the remaining oil. Adjust seasoning. In a large bowl, combine

the mesclun greens and basil. Add 2 tablespoons of the dressing, and toss to coat the leaves. Brush lobster meat with remaining dressing.

4. To serve, spoon about ⅓ cup of the stewed peppers in the center of each of four plates. Mound the lobster on one side of the peppers and place a handful of greens opposite it.

Yield: 4 servings
(Laurent Manrique, Campton Place,
San Francisco, Calif.)

Langoustines

The Shrimp and the Lobster Get Competition
By MOLLY O'NEILL

Langoustines, also called lobsterettes, are smaller lobster cousins with hard shells, succulent tailmeat and long, narrow claws. Most of the meat, which tastes a little like lobster and a little like shrimp, is in the tails. Indeed, when only the tails are sold, they're often called Dublin Bay prawns or scampi. (Though Italian restaurants routinely refer to shrimp as scampi, the true scampi is a langoustine tail.) The langoustines sold here come mostly from Iceland, Norway, Brittany and New Zealand. Depending on the source and freshness, or, if frozen, how well they were stored, the meat can be mushy. Unlike shrimp or lobster, langoustine meat begins to deteriorate immediately after the creatures die because of bacteria under the shells that breaks down the flesh. Whole langoustines are excellent to split and broil, or to be boiled like crayfish or quickly sautéed with lots of garlic.

Substitutes: large shrimp

GINGERED LANGOUSTINES
AND SNOW PEAS

Time: 15 minutes, plus 2 hours marinating

1-inch piece of ginger, peeled and minced
2 cloves garlic, minced
1 teaspoon minced fresh green chili
2 tablespoons Asian, or toasted sesame oil
4 tablespoons vegetable oil
1 pound langoustine tails, shelled
2 cups snow peas
2 teaspoons soy sauce
2 teaspoons dry sherry
Salt and pepper to taste
Juice of two limes
1 bunch basil, leaves only
1 bunch mint, leaves only
2 cups shredded iceberg lettuce, plus 8 large leaves

Tiger shrimp are a fine substitute for this fragrant stir-fry.

1. Combine ginger, garlic, chili pepper, sesame oil and 2 tablespoons vegetable oil in a large bowl. Add langoustines, toss well and refrigerate for 2 hours.

2. Heat remaining vegetable oil in a large skillet or wok over high heat until nearly smoking. Using a slotted spoon, remove langoustines from marinade, place in wok and stir, cooking for 2 minutes. Add snow peas, toss and cook for another 2 minutes. Add soy sauce, sherry and one tablespoon water. Stir, cook for one more minute and remove from heat. Add salt and pepper to taste.

3. Using a slotted spoon, remove langoustines and snow peas from wok, reserving cooking liquid. Strain 1 tablespoon of cooking liquid into a large salad bowl. Whisk lime juice into this mixture. Add basil, mint and shredded lettuce, and toss.

4. To serve, place a portion of shredded lettuce and some langoustines and snow peas on each large lettuce leaf. Roll leaves up, and eat with fingers.

Yield: 4 servings
(Molly O'Neill)

GRILLED LANGOUSTINES WITH
WILTED ARUGULA AND GAZPACHO SAUCE

Time: 35 minutes

Butterflied jumbo shrimp, or even small lobsters, one per person, can substitute for the langoustines.

2 ripe plum tomatoes, cut in quarters
2 stalks celery, chopped
1 red onion, chopped
1 fennel bulb, trimmed and chopped
1 tablespoon prepared horseradish
Tabasco to taste
3 tablespoons extra virgin olive oil plus more for grilling
3 cloves garlic
Salt and freshly ground black pepper to taste
1 pound arugula, rinsed and patted dry
12 medium-large langoustines
¼ cup flat-leaf parsley leaves

1. Preheat a stove-top or charcoal grill or oven broiler.

2. To make the sauce, place the tomatoes, celery, onion, fennel, horse-radish, Tabasco, 1 tablespoon olive oil and 1 clove garlic in a food processor, and process for 2 minutes. Pass through a fine sieve and season to taste with salt and pepper.

3. In large skillet over medium high heat, warm 2 tablespoons olive oil and 2 crushed garlic cloves. Add arugula and toss for one minute, until wilted.

4. Cut langoustines lengthwise, brush with olive oil and grill or broil for 2 minutes. To serve, place arugula and parsley at center of 4 plates, set grilled langoustines on top and drizzle sauce around.

Yield: 4 servings
(Molly O'Neill)

LANGOUSTINE CAKES

Time: 25 minutes

> 2 tablespoons unsalted butter
> 1 clove minced garlic
> 1 pound langoustine tails, shelled and diced
> 1 scallion, minced
> 1 egg, lightly beaten
> ¼ cup mayonnaise
> 2 teaspoons Dijon mustard
> ½ teaspoon kosher salt
> ¼ teaspoon freshly ground black pepper
> ⅛ teaspoon cayenne pepper
> ¼ cup minced flat-leaf parsley
> 4 tablespoons fresh toasted bread crumbs
> 1 cup cracker crumbs
> ½ cup unsalted butter or extra virgin olive oil for frying
> Lemon wedges, for garnish

1. In a skillet over medium-high heat, melt butter. Add garlic, and cook for about a minute. Add langoustine meat, and toss for 2 minutes. Add scallion, toss and remove skillet from heat.

2. Transfer langoustine mixture to a large mixing bowl. Use two forks to shred the meat. Add egg and toss, then add mayonnaise and toss. Add mustard, salt, black and cayenne pepper, and toss. Add parsley and bread crumbs, and gently toss.

3. Form mixture into 8 small cakes, and dust each in cracker crumbs.

4. In a skillet over medium heat, melt ½ cup butter or add oil. Fry cakes 3 to 4 minutes on each side, moving them to prevent burning. Serve immediately with lemon wedges.

Yield: 4 servings
(Molly O'Neill)

Almost any seafood–shrimp, lobster, chunks of crabmeat, or scallops–can be used instead of langoustines and would probably diminish the cost of this dish.

Lobster

If lobsters have a season, it's summer. Better fishing conditions make them easier to trap and more abundant. This brings prices down, especially for smaller sizes. Lobsters in the 1½-to-3-pound range fetch the highest prices. Larger specimens sell for less. When properly cooked, very large lobsters can be as succulent and delectable as small ones, and they have chunks of meat in places that are not worth exploring in smaller ones. Just be sure to have a hammer on hand for cracking the claws.

Some people prefer female lobsters because of the dense, briny-sweet coral, or roe, which can be used to enrich a sauce. They can be distinguished from the males by their tail shell, which is broader, and also by looking at the two small appendages just behind the legs, where the body joins the tail; these are soft in the female and rigid in the male.

Lobsters do not have claws of equal size, so if you buy culls, or one-claw lobsters, look for those with the heavier, more meaty "crusher" claw with the large rounded teeth rather than lobsters that have kept the more slender "biting" claw with its row of sharp teeth.

Lobsters can vary in color from brownish to deep green to nearly blue-black. Some experts consider the most flavorful lobsters to be those from the coldest waters–northern Maine and Nova Scotia. Others swear by the phenomenally expensive blue lobsters from Brittany in France.

The key to preparing lobsters is to avoid overcooking. Lobsters can be boiled, steamed and broiled. Boiling is a quicker method than steaming. A one-pound lobster will be cooked in five minutes. Chefs often parboil lobsters for about a minute, which allows them to extract the meat easily to use in various recipes. Before serving lobsters that have been steamed or boiled, slit the tail and crack the claws and allow the excess fluid to drain out. Raw, cut-up lobsters are often used in stews, dishes like paella and in stir-fries.

GUIDE TO COOKING

Weight of Lobster (pounds)	Steaming (minutes)	Boiling (minutes)
1–1¼	10	6
1½–2	15–18	10–12
2½–5	20–25	15–20
6–10	25–40	20–30

Substitutes: langouste, shrimp, king crab

ROSEMARY-SCENTED ASIAN LOBSTER SALAD

Time: 15 minutes

2 tablespoons honey

6 tablespoons sherry vinegar

2 tablespoons soy sauce

1 half-inch piece ginger, peeled and chopped

1 stalk rosemary, leaves only

1 mild fresh chili, seeded, deveined and coarsely chopped

1¼ cups grape-seed or other light, mild-tasting vegetable oil

4 1-pound lobsters, cooked and shelled

¼ cup pickled ginger slices, patted dry and julienned

8 radishes, sliced wafer thin

4 cups watercress, arugula or other bitter greens, leaves only,
   rinsed, dried and coarsely chopped

1 cup daikon or other radish sprouts

1. To make the vinaigrette, place honey, vinegar, soy sauce, fresh ginger, rosemary and chili in a blender or food processor and puree. With machine running, slowly drizzle a steady stream of oil into the mixture to make a thick vinaigrette.

2. Cut the lobster meat into 1-inch chunks. In a large bowl, toss the lobster with pickled ginger and radishes and enough vinaigrette to barely moisten the mixture (½ to ¾ cup).

3. Divide greens among 4 plates, place the lobster mixture on top and garnish with sprouts. Drizzle a little additional vinaigrette over the greens and around them on the plate and serve.

Yield: 4 servings
(Jean-Georges Vongerichten, Vong,
New York City)

CORN AND LOBSTER CHOWDER

Time: 1 hour

Other seafood, especially crabmeat, can be used in this chowder with the lobster or in place of it. It's a summer dish, best made when fresh sweet corn is in season.

6 ears corn

4 cups heavy cream

2 tablespoons extra virgin olive oil

2 ounces lean slab bacon, finely diced

1 cup finely diced onion

2 medium leeks, white part only, finely diced

1 stalk celery, finely diced

2 Idaho potatoes, peeled and finely diced

4 tablespoons unsalted butter

2 cups small chanterelles, about 5 ounces, stems scraped

¾ teaspoon caraway seeds

6 sprigs thyme

Salt and freshly ground black pepper

½ to 1 cup chicken stock (optional)

1 pound diced cooked lobster meat

1. Strip kernels from cobs, and reserve. Place cobs in a saucepan with cream, bring to a boil, and set aside to cool.

2. Heat oil in a large, heavy saucepan. Add bacon, and sauté over medium heat until it barely begins to brown. Stir in onion, leeks and celery. Sauté until translucent. Add potatoes and stir. Remove cobs from cream, strain cream, and add to saucepan. Bring to a simmer. Add corn kernels. Cook until potatoes are tender, about 15 minutes.

3. Melt 2 tablespoons butter in a skillet. Add chanterelles, and sauté over medium-low heat until tender but not browned. Add to soup. Add caraway seeds, thyme, salt and pepper to taste. Thin soup with chicken stock if desired.

4. Just before serving, melt remaining butter in a small skillet, add lobster, and warm in butter. Put in soup plates. Bring soup to a simmer, check seasonings, and ladle over lobster.

Yield: 6 to 8 servings
(Tom Colicchio, Craft,
New York City)

CALDO VERDE WITH LOBSTER

Time: 1 hour

5 tablespoons extra virgin olive oil
1 large onion, sliced
2 ounces garlic sausage or ham, diced (optional)
1 pound Yukon gold potatoes, peeled and sliced ½ inch thick
Salt and freshly ground black pepper to taste
4 cups, packed, finely shredded kale, Swiss chard or spinach
10 ounces cooked lobster meat, diced

1. Heat 2 tablespoons olive oil in a heavy 3-to-4-quart saucepan. Add onion and sauté over medium heat until the onion is tender but not brown. Add the optional sausage or ham and sauté until the sausage or ham is cooked through. Remove the onion and sausage or ham from the pan.

2. Add potatoes and 6 cups of water to the saucepan. Bring to a boil, season with salt and cook gently until the potatoes are tender, about 15 minutes. Remove potatoes with a slotted spoon, leaving the liquid in the pan. Coarsely mash potatoes.

3. Return potatoes to the pot and stir to dissolve them in the cooking liquid, to thicken it. Season to taste with salt and pepper. Add the onion and sausage or ham and greens. Bring to a simmer and taste for seasoning. Add the lobster meat and remaining olive oil. When ready to serve, gently reheat.

Yield: 4 to 6 servings
(Florence Fabricant)

Caldo verde is a rustic peasant soup that can stand on its own without the lobster, but which takes on a touch of elegance with it. The combination of seafood and sausage is a classic one, especially in Spain and Portugal.

LOBSTER ROLLS

Time: 20 minutes

Ordinary hot dog buns would also be appropriate and, some might say, even better than the baguette.

A 12-inch loaf Italian or French baguette bread, not too crusty
2 cooked lobsters, each 1 to 1¼ pounds, or ¾ pound cooked
   shelled lobster meat
Juice of ½ lemon
½ cup finely minced celery
2 tablespoons finely minced scallions
Salt and pepper to taste
½ cup mayonnaise, homemade or commercial
2 tablespoons Dijon mustard

1. Split the bread in half lengthwise and pull out most of the soft insides and discard.

2. Shell cooked lobsters if you are using them. Cut lobster meat in small pieces and mix in a bowl with the lemon juice, celery and scallions. Season to taste with salt and pepper.

3. Mix mayonnaise with mustard. Fold into the lobster salad mixture. Spoon lobster salad into half the baguette and top with the other half. Using a sharp knife, cut the filled baguette in four portions and serve.

Yield: 4 servings
(Florence Fabricant)

SAFFRON LASAGNETTA WITH LOBSTER SAUCE

Time: 1 hour

Chefs frequently parcook lobsters by boiling them for a minute or sautéing them, cut up, in their shells

1 poblano chili
6 tablespoons extra virgin olive oil
6 1-pound lobsters, cut up
3 cups lobster stock or fish broth (recipes pages 322 and 321)
½ teaspoon saffron threads, optional
1 clove garlic, minced
Kernels stripped from 1 ear yellow corn
⅓ cup cooked black beans

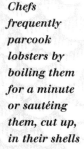

2 ripe tomatoes, peeled, seeded and pureed

Juice of 3 limes

6 tablespoons soft unsalted butter

Salt

1 tablespoon chopped cilantro leaves, plus 6 sprigs cilantro for garnish

12 sheets saffron pasta (recipe follows) or 12 ounces pappardelle noodles

1. Roast chili over open flame or under broiler until softened and blackened. Scrape off skin. Core, seed and cut in slivers. Set aside.

2. In a 12-inch sauté pan, heat 2 tablespoons of the oil. Add lobster claws and cook over high heat about 2 minutes, turning once. Remove. Add tail pieces and cook over high heat about 2 minutes, turning once. Remove. Add knuckles, cook one minute and remove. Add lobster bodies, cook two minutes and add stock. Bring to a simmer and cook 10 minutes.

3. While bodies are cooking, remove meat from claws, tails and knuckles. It will not be fully cooked. Dice lobster meat and set aside.

4. When bodies are cooked, remove and discard them. Strain lobster stock through a fine strainer or a coffee filter. If not using homemade saffron pasta, add saffron and allow to steep several minutes. Meanwhile, wash and dry pan and return it to stove over medium heat. Add 3 tablespoons olive oil.

5. Add garlic and one or more tablespoons of the slivered chili, to taste, and cook, stirring, about 30 seconds. Add corn and beans and cook one minute. Add tomatoes, cook another 30 seconds, then add lobster stock with saffron. Bring to a boil and cook until thickened and reduced to about 2 cups. Turn heat to low. Stir in lime juice and add lobster to pan. Simmer 2 minutes. Whisk in butter about a tablespoon at a time. Check seasoning. Scatter with cilantro and keep warm over very low heat.

6. Bring a pot of salted water to a boil for the pasta. If using lasagna, cook sheets in boiling water about 30 seconds, drain, rinse to prevent sticking and drain on paper towel. Brush with remaining tablespoon of oil to prevent sticking. With pappardelle, cook about 3 minutes, drain and toss with remaining oil.

7. To serve, place a sheet of pasta or about one-sixth of the pappardelle on each of 6 warm plates, reserving about 12 strands of pappardelle. Spoon some of the lobster sauce on top of pasta. Cover with another sheet of pasta or garnish with reserved pappardelle. Garnish with cilantro sprigs and serve.

Yield: 6 servings

(Mark Militello, Mark's Las Olas, Fort Lauderdale, Fla.)

for about two minutes, as in this recipe. Though the lobster is still nearly raw, the brief cooking permits the meat to be removed from the shell more easily than if uncooked. Then the recipe can be continued without overcooking the lobster.

SAFFRON PASTA

Time: 1½ hours

> 1 tablespoon dry white wine
> ½ teaspoon saffron threads
> 2 eggs, beaten
> 2 cups all-purpose flour, plus flour for dusting
> Salt to taste

    1. Heat wine to a boil in a small saucepan, add saffron and remove from heat. When cool, whisk in eggs.

    2. Place flour on work surface and make well in center. Add egg mixture and gradually work flour into center, adding a little water if mixture is dry, and kneading once ingredients are incorporated to make a firm, smooth dough. Dough can be made in food processor. Cover and let rest 45 minutes.

    3. Use pasta machine to roll pasta gradually to finest setting. Cut pasta sheets in 12-inch lengths, then cut each in half. Place pasta on lightly floured parchment paper and cover with a towel until ready to cook.

Yield: 6 servings

LOBSTER RISOTTO

Time: 1 hour

> 2 1-pound lobsters
> 2 tablespoons extra virgin olive oil or butter
> 4 large cloves garlic, chopped
> 1 tablespoon finely slivered fresh ginger
> 1½ cups Italian arborio rice
> ⅔ cup finely chopped fresh or canned tomato pulp,
>   well drained, juice reserved
> ½ cup dry white wine
> 4 to 5 cups hot fish broth or lobster stock (recipes pages 321
>   and 322)
> Salt and freshy ground black pepper
> 1 tablespoon finely minced chives

Omit the ginger in this recipe and it no longer has an Asian touch. But then, a little cream added at the end, or some fresh minced basil, will enhance it.

1. Boil lobsters until cooked through, about 6 minutes. Set aside about 10 minutes, until just cool enough to handle, then remove all the meat and dice it. If there is any roe, cut it up too. Discard the green tomalley. Keep the lobster pieces covered so they do not dry out.

2. Heat oil or butter in a heavy saucepan over medium heat. Add garlic and half the ginger, stir, then add the rice. Stir and cook gently 2 to 3 minutes, then stir in the tomato pulp. Bring to a simmer.

3. Stir in the white wine and the juice from the tomatoes, bring to a simmer and cook, stirring gently, until the liquid has been nearly absorbed, 3 to 5 minutes.

4. Add the stock about a half cup at a time, stirring it in and adding more every 3 minutes or so, as it is absorbed. Continue until the rice is just tender, about 20 minutes total cooking time. Season with salt and pepper.

5. Fold in the lobster, the remaining ginger and the chives. Cook another couple of minutes, then serve.

Yield: 4 servings
(Florence Fabricant)

CHINESE LOBSTER WITH NOODLES
Time: 30 minutes

2 1-pound lobsters, cooked
½ pound fresh Chinese egg noodles or other thin, fresh egg pasta
3 tablespoons peanut oil
½ cup thinly sliced onions
¼ pound shiitake mushrooms, stems discarded, sliced thin
3 garlic cloves, minced
1 tablespoon minced fresh ginger
½ cup chopped scallions
1 teaspoon soy sauce
1 tablespoon Chinese oyster sauce
1 tablespoon rice vinegar
Salt, freshly ground black pepper and red chili flakes to taste
1 tablespoon minced cilantro

1. Remove lobster from shells and dice it.

2. Bring a large pot of water to a boil. Add noodles and cook 3 minutes, stirring to keep the noodles separate. Drain noodles, rinse under cold water and drain again. Place in a colander lined with a paper towel to remove excess moisture.

3. Heat peanut oil in a wok or a large skillet. Add onions and sauté until they are tender. Stir in the mushrooms and sauté until they have wilted. Add the garlic, ginger and all but 1 tablespoon of the scallions and sauté briefly.

4. Add the lobster, then add the noodles to the pan and mix well. Add the soy sauce, oyster sauce and vinegar and toss to combine all the ingredients. Season to taste with salt, pepper and red chili flakes.

5. Sprinkle with cilantro, toss again, then transfer to a warm serving bowl, sprinkle with the remaining scallions and serve.

Yield: 3 to 4 servings
(Florence Fabricant)

LOBSTER FRA DIAVOLO
Time: 1 hour

The origin of this dish is in doubt. Some say it's an Italian-American invention, perhaps even from New York's Little Italy, while others insist that it came from Naples.

5 tablespoons extra virgin olive oil
¾ cup finely chopped red onion
½ cup finely chopped red bell pepper
½ cup finely chopped green bell pepper
2 1½-pound live lobsters, cut up
1½ cups fish broth (recipe page 321), white wine or water, or a
    mixture
1 tablespoon finely chopped garlic
1 teaspoon red chili flakes or to taste
14-ounce can plum tomatoes, chopped
2 tablespoons tomato paste
1 teaspoon dried oregano
Salt and freshly ground black pepper
12 ounces spaghettini or linguine
1 tablespoon finely chopped flat-leaf parsley

1. Heat 2 tablespoons of the oil in a large, shallow saucepan or a deep skillet with a cover. Add the onion and red and green bell pepper and sauté over medium heat until the vegetables are tender and begin to brown. Remove from the pan.

2. Add another 2 tablespoons of oil to the skillet, add the lobster pieces and sauté over medium heat, stirring, until the shells start to redden, about 5 minutes. Remove all the lobster tail and claw pieces, leaving the bodies and legs in the pan. Add the fish broth, wine or water. A mixture of broth and wine is best, but it does not make a huge difference which you use. Bring to a simmer, cover and cook until the remaining lobster pieces are thoroughly cooked, about 6 minutes. Remove the lobster from the pan, strain the liquid and reserve it. You should have a cup or so. Discard the cooked lobster bodies and legs or set them aside, if you prefer, to garnish the dish.

3. Add the remaining tablespoon of oil to the pan, return the vegetables, along with the garlic and chili flakes. Cook over medium heat for a minute or so, then add the tomatoes, tomato paste and oregano. Stir in the reserved liquid. Bring to a simmer, cook uncovered about 5 minutes, then add the reserved pieces of lobster claw and tail. Cover and simmer about 10 minutes, until the lobster is cooked. Season the sauce to taste with salt and pepper. Remove from heat.

4. Spoon out 1½ cups of the sauce from the pan and set aside.

5. Bring a large pot of salted water to a boil, add the spaghettini and cook until al dente, about 6 minutes. Drain and return to cooking pot. Toss with reserved sauce and transfer to a platter or a serving dish. Arrange the lobster and its sauce over or around the spaghettini, dust with parsley and serve.

Yield: 4 servings
(The Blue Grotto, New York City)

LOBSTER THERMIDOR

Time: 1 hour

4 tablespoons finely chopped shallots
2 tablespoons chopped fresh tarragon leaves or
  1 teaspoon dried
2 tablespoons chopped chervil or parsley
¾ cup dry white wine
3 tablespoons butter
3 tablespoons flour
½ cup heavy cream
1¼ cups milk
¼ teaspoon cayenne pepper
Salt and freshly ground black pepper to taste
1 egg yolk, lightly beaten
1 tablespoon Dijon mustard
4 lobsters, 1¼ pounds each, uncooked and split lengthwise
3 tablespoons vegetable oil
4 tablespoons freshly grated Parmesan cheese

1. Preheat the oven to 425 degrees.

2. Place the shallots, tarragon, chervil or parsley and wine in a small saucepan and bring to a boil. Simmer until most of the liquid has evaporated.

3. Melt 2 tablespoons of the butter in another small saucepan and whisk in flour. Gradually whisk in cream and milk. Add cayenne, salt and pepper. Bring to a boil and simmer for 1 minute. Add herb mixture, whisk and remove from heat. Cool slightly. Whisk in the egg yolk and mustard. Set aside.

4. Place the lobster halves, split side up, on one or two baking dishes along with the claws. Sprinkle each half with salt and pepper and brush with the oil. Bake for seven minutes.

5. Remove the meat from the shells and cut into bite-size pieces. Crack the claws and cut the meat into similar pieces.

6. Melt the remaining butter in a small saucepan and toss the meat quickly to coat. Fold in half the cream sauce. Spoon the mixture into the lobster shells and spread the remaining sauce evenly over it. Sprinkle with cheese and bake for 10 minutes or until brown. Serve immediately.

Yield: 4 servings

(Pierre Franey)

ROAST LOBSTER WITH VANILLA SAUCE

Time: 1 hour

2 lobsters, 1¼ to 1½ pounds each

1 tablespoon extra-virgin olive oil

7 tablespoons plus 2 teaspoons unsalted butter

3 shallots, peeled and finely chopped

½ cup dry white wine

1½ tablespoons white wine vinegar

½ vanilla bean, split lengthwise

½ teaspoon kosher salt

Freshly ground pepper to taste

¾ pound baby spinach

1 pound watercress, stemmed

1. Place a roasting pan large enough to hold the lobsters in the oven, and preheat oven to 450 degrees. With the tip of a sharp knife pierce the lobsters between the eyes to sever the spinal cord. Crack the claws using the blunt edge of a cleaver or a hammer. Place the lobsters in the hot roasting pan, drizzle with oil and roast until red, about 15 minutes. Remove from the oven, and set aside.

2. Melt 2 teaspoons butter in a small saucepan, add shallots and sauté over low heat until soft and translucent, about 3 minutes. Add wine and vinegar, raise heat and cook at a moderate boil until the liquid is reduced to 1 tablespoon, about 5 minutes. Remove pan from the heat, and whisk in 6 tablespoons butter, about 1 tablespoon at a time, until all is incorporated. Scrape the seeds from the vanilla bean into the sauce, stir to combine and strain into a clean saucepan. Season with ¼ teaspoon salt, and pepper to taste, and set aside.

3. When the lobsters are cool enough to handle, remove the meat from the claws. Detach the tails, and discard the heads. With a pair of scissors, cut the shell on the underside of each tail in half lengthwise, remove the meat and cut into ¼-inch-thick slices. Loosely cover the meat with aluminum foil, and keep warm.

4. Melt 1 tablespoon butter in a large pot, and add spinach and watercress. Stir until greens have wilted, and continue to cook, stirring occasionally, until greens are tender, about 5 minutes. Season with ¼ teaspoon salt, and pepper to taste.

Many chefs have tried to prepare lobster with vanilla sauce, but few achieve the balance of flavors found in Michelin three-star chef Alain Senderens's nouvelle cuisine creation. The secret is in not making the sauce sweet, but merely allowing the vanilla to perfume the lobster, which has a sweetness all its own.

5. To serve, reheat sauce over low heat until warm, whisking constantly. Place a bed of greens on each plate, arrange lobster meat on top and spoon the sauce over the lobster. Serve immediately.

Yield: 2 servings
(Alain Senderens, Lucas Carton,
Paris, France)

Mussels

Belle of the Bivalves: The New Mussel; After a makeover, the wallflower of shellfish gets to dance
By AMANDA HESSER

At the Fulton Fish Market in New York, forklifts are buzzing from stall to stall, many of them piled high with sacks of mussels. At one stall, a fishmonger is already inspecting the stacks that have arrived that day. He has mounds of cultivated mussels from Prince Edward Island, all evenly sized, their shells clamped tight. They are so clean they sparkle. There's a small pile of New Zealand mussels, their shocking green shells gleaming through holes in the boxes.

In the back cooler is what may be the greatest prize of all, the Mediterranean mussel, cultivated on the West Coast and making its way for the first time to some major cities in the United States. It is arguably the plumpest and sweetest mussel there is.

The stir at the Fulton market is a frenetic demonstration of how large the demand for this bivalve has become and how varied and, yes, even beautiful the once lowly and homely mussel is now. Today's mussels are a different animal, one that, through farming, has been tamed for the kitchen. These mussels are user-friendly—meatier, grit-free and in need of only a light rinse before cooking. And the nuisance of debearding—removing the wiry thread that the mussel uses to attach itself to a perch—is almost gone. Increasingly, producers mechanically trim the beard. And when it's so small, more goatee than beard, the cook can forget about it.

Mussels are positioned in the water so that they are one of the first sea creatures to feel the effects of toxins or red tide. Like clams, they are filter feeders, meaning they suck in water and draw out plankton and whatever else they can for food. Contaminated water enters their system as easily as plankton. In some areas, marine biologists actually use mussels to track water quality.

Today there are several aquaculture techniques, but in all of them the mussels are bred under controlled conditions that either suspend them above the seafloor or seed them in selected beds. Unlike fish, which are farmed in ponds, mussels are cultivated in the ocean, but in water that is routinely tested for contamination. ❧

Substitutes: littleneck, Manila or mahogany clams

BELGIAN MUSSELS
Time: 25 minutes

> 8 pounds mussels, scrubbed and debearded
> 2 tablespoons chopped shallots
> 1 tablespoon chopped garlic
> ½ tablespoon chopped rosemary
> ½ tablespoon chopped thyme
> ½ tablespoon chopped flat-leaf parsley
> ¾ cup Chimay or other dry Belgian ale
> ¼ cup vegetable stock
> 1½ tablespoons unsalted butter
> Salt and freshly ground black pepper, to taste

1. In a 10-quart or larger stock pot, combine mussels, shallots, garlic, rosemary, thyme, parsley, beer and vegetable stock. Cover, and place over medium-high heat. Bring to a boil, and steam until mussels open, about 5 minutes. Leave any unopened mussels in pot and steam a few minutes longer. Discard any that remain unopened.

2. Remove mussels to serving plates or a large serving bowl. Add butter to pot, and stir. Season to taste with salt and pepper. Pour sauce over mussels and serve immediately.

Add French fries and you have the classic moules-frites. But be sure to serve mayonnaise with the potatoes.

Yield: 8 servings
(Allen Zakarin, Steak Frites,
New York City)

CURRIED MUSSELS

Time: 40 minutes

For this and the other recipes in this book, small mussels are preferred. But big, green-lipped mussels from New Zealand would also work in this dish, and the following one, for mussels with cilantro, which have strong flavor and can be made with mussels that are less delicate.

1 cup heavy cream
1 tablespoon curry powder
1 tablespoon lemon juice
3 tablespoons unsalted butter
¼ cup shallots sliced thin
4 sprigs thyme
1 bay leaf
1 cup dry white wine
3 pounds mussels, cleaned and debearded
2 tablespoons flour
Salt to taste

1. Combine cream, curry powder and lemon juice in a small bowl, and mix well.

2. Melt 1 tablespoon of the butter in a large pot over high heat, and add shallots, thyme and bay leaf. Stir until wilted. Add white wine and bring to a simmer. Add mussels, cover and cook for 5 minutes, or just until the mussels open. Stir from time to time to assure even cooking. As soon as mussels have opened, remove from heat. Strain cooking liquid through a fine sieve into bowl. Reserve 2 cups.

3. Remove the top shell from each mussel and discard it, leaving the mussel meat attached to its bottom shell. Discard any unopened mussels. Arrange decoratively on a serving platter. Cover with foil to keep warm.

4. In a large saucepan, melt remaining butter over medium heat, and whisk in the flour, stirring until the mixture is smooth. Cook a minute longer. Slowly add 2 cups of reserved cooking liquid, whisking constantly. Bring to a rolling boil. Whisk in the cream-and-curry mixture, and combine well. Strain sauce through a fine sieve. Add salt, and check for seasoning. Ladle the sauce over mussels, and serve immediately.

Yield: 4 servings
(Richard Coutanceau,
La Rochelle, France)

MUSSELS WITH CILANTRO

Time: 45 minutes

1 bunch cilantro, about 20 stems
1 tablespoon extra virgin olive oil
¼ cup finely chopped scallions
1 large clove garlic, finely slivered
3 serrano chilies, seeded and cut in fine slivers
1 cup dry white wine
Juice of 1 lime
2 pounds mussels, scrubbed and debearded
½ cup heavy cream

1. Reserve 4 small sprigs of cilantro for garnish. Remove the leaves from the stems of the rest, and discard the stems. Rinse and dry leaves, and set aside. You should have about 1½ cups loosely packed cilantro leaves.

2. Heat oil in a heavy 3-quart saucepan. Add the scallions, garlic and chilies, and sauté a few minutes over medium heat until soft but not brown. Add wine and lime juice, bring to a boil, then add mussels.

3. Cover, and cook until the mussels open, 6 to 8 minutes. Using a slotted spoon, remove mussels from pan and place in a bowl. Cover to keep warm.

4. Return saucepan to the heat, add cilantro and simmer a few minutes, until it wilts. Place the contents of the saucepan in a blender, and puree. Pour back into the saucepan, add the cream and bring to a simmer. Return the mussels to the saucepan, cover and reheat briefly.

5. To serve, spoon the mussels in 4 soup plates and spoon the sauce over each portion. Garnish with the reserved sprigs of cilantro.

Yield: 4 first-course servings
(Monica Patiño, La Galvia and Taberna de León,
Mexico City, Mexico)

MUSSEL AND POTATO SALAD

Time: 1 hour

Adding steamed mussels to almost any potato salad will dress it up to serve as a first course or luncheon dish. Be sure to add a little of the mussel steaming broth to the dressing.

5 pounds mussels, scrubbed and debearded
¾ cup dry white wine
1½ pounds medium-size Yukon gold potatoes
5 scallions, peeled and minced
3 cloves garlic, peeled, crushed and finely chopped
¾ teaspoon salt
1 teaspoon finely ground black pepper
1½ tablespoons Dijon-style mustard
1½ tablespoons red wine vinegar
⅓ cup extra virgin olive oil
2 cups mixed salad greens, rinsed and thoroughly dried

1. Place mussels in a large pot and add wine and 1 cup water. Cover and bring to a boil over high heat. Toss the mussels lightly in pan and cook 5 minutes until opened. Remove those that are open and place in a bowl. Cook unopened mussels 1 to 2 minutes longer to give them another chance to open. Discard any that have not opened at this point.

2. When mussels are cool enough to handle, shuck them into a large bowl.

3. Meanwhile, wash potatoes, place in a large saucepan, cover with cold water, and bring to a boil. Reduce the heat to low, and simmer potatoes uncovered, until tender, 20 minutes or longer. Drain, and set aside until they are cool enough to handle. Peel potatoes, and slice ¼ inch thick. Add to the mussels along with the scallions and garlic.

4. In a small bowl, mix together the salt, pepper, mustard, vinegar and oil. Add to the potatoes and mussels. Toss gently.

5. Arrange salad greens on six plates and spoon potato and mussel salad onto the greens. Serve at room temperature.

Yield: 6 servings
(Jacques Pépin)

STEAMED MUSSELS IN SAFFRON BROTH

Time: 1¾ hours

1 tablespoon extra virgin olive oil
1 medium onion, finely chopped
1 bulb fennel, chopped
3 cloves garlic, crushed
1 generous pinch saffron threads
3 tablespoons fresh or canned tomato puree
1 cup dry white wine
4 cups fish broth (recipe page 321) or chicken stock
2 to 3 sprigs fresh thyme
2 bay leaves
2 pounds mussels, preferably small ones, scrubbed and
    debearded
Red chili flakes to taste

Add other seafood and some fish and you have what amounts to a bouillabaisse. (Additional recipes for seafood stews appear on pages 297 to 308.)

1. Heat oil in a heavy, three-quart saucepan. Add onion, fennel and garlic, cover and sweat over low heat until vegetables are tender, about 15 minutes. Add saffron, tomato puree, wine, broth, thyme and bay leaves. Simmer uncovered for one hour. Strain.

2. Just before serving, reheat tomato mixture to a simmer. Add the mussels, cover and steam until the mussels open, about 10 minutes.

3. Using a slotted spoon, divide the mussels among four soup plates. Season broth to taste with chili flakes and pour over the mussels. Serve at once.

Yield: 4 servings
(Florence Fabricant)

Octopus

Embracing the Octopus, Tenderly
By MARK BITTMAN

Octopus is an ancient denizen of the deep whose ancestors lived at least 200 million years ago. It has adapted well to warm and temperate waters all over the world, feeding on crustaceans and fellow mollusks. It's a graceful creature in its native habitat, but at the seafood store, a raw octopus resting on the ice couldn't be uglier. And then, once the octopus is cooked, its beauty returns, snowy flesh tinged royal purple, with a flavor that is tender and mild, with just a touch of pleasant resistance, like lobster.

An octopus is a sac (the head) with eight legs. In the head are two eyes, a mouth, two beaks and a filelike organ for drilling through the shells of its prey. Frozen octopus is cleaned before freezing, which is probably how you will buy it. The quality of octopus, like that of squid, does not suffer noticeably when it is frozen.

The main stumbling block for the cook, hideous appearance aside, is the often deserved reputation of the octopus for being so tough that extraordinary measures must be taken to tenderize it. Methods that hint of superstition are applied to this beast, none of which are likely to work any better than slow cooking in water. Which takes a lot less fuss.

There are no hard-and-fast rules for timing your simmering pot of octopus. Some people say octopus should cook for about 30 minutes for two pounds, but the timing can be significantly longer or shorter depending on the specimen. The safest approach is to check with the sharp point of a thin-bladed knife; with a two-pound octopus, you would begin testing after about 30 minutes. When the knife meets little resistance, as in a baked potato, the octopus is done.

Do not cook further, or else it will begin to dry out and toughen again.

Three pounds of octopus is about right for four people—octopus shrinks startlingly. It doesn't matter much whether you buy one larger specimen or several smaller ones, though it affects the cooking time. But size can be an issue. Deliciously succulent tiny octopuses, less than six ounces, may be difficult to find and tend to be expensive. But they're great cooked for a couple of minutes and then served with little more than olive oil, lemon and salt, but they are really tidbits, mostly suitable for appetizers.

Once tenderized by simmering, the octopus can be served with little further preparation. It can be tossed in olive oil and lemon juice, with or without other seafood and vegetables, to make a salad. It can be incorporated into a risotto or pasta sauce. Or of course, it can be grilled briefly after the simmering, making it both crisp and tender. This ultimately appealing combination is easily achieved, as long as the fire is hot enough to crisp the exterior before drying out the interior.

Finally, there is the issue of octopus skin, ugly when raw, but which becomes a lovely gelatinous, almost fatty substance once cooked. It's worth noting that this gelatin is so powerful that cooked octopus can be made into a terrine simply by weighting it. 🐚

OCTOPUS CONFIT
Time: 1½ to 2 hours

> **2 pounds cleaned octopus, approximately**
> **12 whole cloves garlic, peeled**
> **2 dried red chilies**
> **5 branches thyme**
> **Salt**
> **3 cups extra virgin olive oil, approximately**
> **2 tablespoons soy sauce**
> **2 tablespoons lime juice**

1. Wash octopus well. Combine with garlic, chilies, thyme and large pinch of salt in saucepan, add 3 cups olive oil, or enough so that oil completely covers octopus.

2. Place the saucepan over medium-high heat; bring to a slow simmer (if you have a thermometer, the ideal temperature is about 190 degrees). Adjust heat to maintain this slow simmer, and cook until octopus is tender, an hour or more. Check with point of a sharp knife.

3. Remove garlic and octopus to a platter; discard thyme and oil, or reserve oil for another use. Cut up octopus. Serve warm or cool, drizzled with soy sauce and lime juice.

Yield: 4 to 8 servings
(Tadashi Ono, Sono, New York City)

Techinques for tenderizing octopus vary from country to country. A Greek cook might beat octopus against some rocks or, less primitively, against the kitchen sink; a Spanish cook will dip it in boiling water three times and then cook it in a copper pot (only copper will do); an Italian might cook it with two wine corks, and a Japanese might rub it all over with salt, or knead it with grated daikon, then slice the meat at different angles, with varying strokes.

OCTOPUS SALAD WITH CRISPY VEGETABLES

Time: 1½ to 2 hours, plus 3 to 4 hours marinating and cooling

> 6 medium carrots, peeled
> 4 small red onions, peeled
> 2 medium celeriac, trimmed and peeled
> 1 bay leaf
> 1 tablespoon black peppercorns
> 1 cup white vinegar
> 2 pounds cleaned octopus
> ½ cup extra virgin olive oil, or more to taste
> Juice of 1 lemon, or more to taste
> Salt and freshly ground black pepper to taste
> Red chili flakes
> 1 cup chopped basil, plus more for garnish
> 5 red-skinned potatoes, about ¾ pound

1. Roughly chop half the carrots, onions and celeriac, and combine in saucepan with bay leaf, peppercorns and white vinegar. Bring to boil and add octopus and water to cover. Cook at least 1 hour, or until octopus is tender (check with point of sharp knife). Let octopus cool in cooking water.

2. Discard cooked vegetables. Cut octopus into small pieces, and toss with olive oil, lemon juice, salt, pepper, chili flakes and basil. Marinate, refrigerated, for 3 to 4 hours. Simmer potatoes in salted water until tender. Chop remaining raw vegetables.

3. Blanch carrots for about 5 minutes and onions for about 2 minutes, just to remove some of the crunch; plunge in ice water to chill. Mix octopus with raw celeriac, cooked potatoes and blanched carrots and onions. Adjust seasoning, and then drizzle with fresh olive oil and lemon juice. Garnish with minced basil, and serve.

Yield: 4 to 6 servings
(Alessandro Giuntoli, Osteria del Circo,
New York City)

OCTOPUS AND POTATOES

Time: about 1½ hours, plus cooling time

> **3 pounds cleaned octopus**
> **2 pounds small waxy potatoes, peeled and cut into ¼-inch-thick slices**
> **1 teaspoon Spanish paprika, or to taste**
> **⅓ cup extra virgin olive oil, or to taste**
> **Coarse salt to taste**

1. Simmer octopus in water to cover until nearly tender, for 1 hour or more (check with point of sharp knife). Add potatoes, and cook 10 to 15 minutes longer or until tender.

2. With slotted spoon, remove potatoes to platter or a shallow bowl, and octopus to cutting board. Cool octopus for a couple minutes; then cut into bite-size pieces. Combine with potatoes. Sprinkle with paprika, drizzle with plenty of olive oil and toss gently. Fold in salt, and serve.

Yield: 4 to 6 servings

(Ignacio Blanco, Meson Galicia, Norwalk, Conn.)

To make a terrine, follow cooking instructions, but omit potatoes. Layer cooked octopus, cut into bite-size pieces, in small terrine lined with plastic wrap. Cover it, and weight it with cans or a bag of beans or rice; refrigerate for 24 hours. (It will be a solid block.) To serve, cut into ½-inch-thick slices, serve cold or warm slightly in oven or microwave, and sprinkle with olive oil, salt and paprika.

GRILLED OCTOPUS

Time: 2 hours

> **3 pounds cleaned octopus**
> **1 bay leaf**
> **4 thyme branches**
> **20 peppercorns**
> **Salt**
> **1 head garlic, cut in half along its equator**
> **3 lemons**
> **3 tablespoons extra virgin olive oil**
> **Freshly ground black pepper to taste**
> **Minced parsley for garnish**

1. Combine octopus, bay leaf, thyme, peppercorns, 1 teaspoon salt, garlic and 1 lemon, cut in half, in a saucepan. Add water to cover. Turn heat to

medium, cover, and bring to boil. Adjust heat so that liquid simmers slowly, and cook until octopus is tender, for 30 to 90 minutes, depending on whether you're using 2 smaller octopuses or 1 larger one (check for doneness with point of sharp knife). Drain, discarding everything but octopus. Set aside.

2. Start charcoal or wood fire, or preheat gas grill; fire should be quite hot. Place grill rack about 4 inches from heat source. Cut octopus into large serving pieces, brush it with half the olive oil, and sprinkle with salt and pepper. Grill quickly until outside browns but inside is not dried out. Cut remaining lemons into wedges.

3. Brush octopus with remaining olive oil. Serve with lemon wedges, hot or at room temperature, garnished with parsley.

Yield: 4 to 6 servings
(Mark Bittman)

You can prepare the octopus 24 hours in advance before grilling it. Refrigerate the octopus and bring it to room temperature before grilling.

SPAGHETTI WITH OCTOPUS BRAISED IN RED WINE

Time: 1½ to 2 hours

The octopus can be cooked in advance and refrigerated in its wine bath. Quickly reheat it to toss with the freshly cooked pasta and serve.

6 tablespoons extra virgin olive oil

1 carrot, peeled and chopped

1 medium onion, peeled and chopped

1 celery stalk, chopped

Salt to taste

2 medium octopuses, about 12 ounces each, cleaned and halved vertically

Freshly ground black pepper to taste

2 cups dry red wine

1 bay leaf

1 clove garlic, minced

1 pound spaghetti or linguine

2 tablespoons unsalted butter

16 cherry tomatoes, cut in half

½ cup roughly chopped basil

1. Place 2 tablespoons olive oil in large skillet or sauté pan and turn heat to medium high. Add carrot, onion and celery. Sprinkle with pinch of

salt, and cook, stirring occasionally, until onion becomes translucent, about 5 minutes.

2. Add octopus, some pepper and a little more salt. Cook, stirring, for 1 minute, and then add wine, bay leaf and garlic. Bring to a simmer, lower heat and cook, covered, until octopus is tender, for about 1 hour (check with point of sharp knife). Remove octopus and cut into bite-size pieces. Return octopus to skillet and keep at a slow simmer.

3. Meanwhile, bring large pot of salted water to boil. Fifteen minutes before serving, begin cooking pasta. When it is not quite al dente, drain it, reserving about 1 cup cooking liquid. Add pasta to octopus mixture, with half the reserved liquid. Cook until pasta is tender but not mushy. Add remaining liquid if needed to keep mixture from drying out.

4. Add remaining olive oil, the butter, cherry tomatoes and basil. Stir until butter melts, adjust salt and pepper as needed, then serve.

Yield: 4 to 6 servings
(Alessandro Giuntoli, Osteria del Circo,
New York City)

Oysters

When It Comes to Oysters, Some People Can't Play Favorites
By MARK BITTMAN

Though oysters are sold year-round, connoisseurs will still contend that cold weather (those legendary *r* months) is when oysters are best. Cold water means peak flavor, and in winter the waters in the best beds are as cold as they get.

The many varieties of oysters sold in this country are from five species, each markedly different from the others. The form is the same, but the gustatory experience is hardly so.

Even the differences within each species are nothing short of amazing. When Atlantic oysters, for example, are tasted side by side, you can readily distinguish not only between a Florida Apalachicola and a Prince Edward Island, but also between a Blue Point and a Fishers Island, or a Cuttyhunk and a

Martha's Vineyard, each of which may be grown just a few miles from the other.

That's because much of the distinctive flavor of a given oyster comes not only from its species but also from its home. All of which makes it easy to like several types and difficult for true oyster lovers to have a favorite.

Once, Wellfleet and Blue Point were the oysters of choice in New York; they were from clean, local waters and were plentiful and easily transported. Now, however, Wellfleets are in short supply and Blue Points, technically speaking, don't even exist: The company that owned the Blue Point name went out of business about 50 years ago. Today, *Blue Point* is used to refer to many Long Island Sound oysters. Now, the relatively new Fishers Island oyster, from the island in the eastern sound, is rapidly being adopted as a local favorite by many New Yorkers, especially chefs.

The species: Until recently, four major species of oysters were seen in the United States: the familiar Atlantic (Crassostrea virginica), known for its brininess and grown along the East and Gulf Coasts; the European (Ostrea edulis), a round, metallic-tasting, flat-shelled oyster, grown in the Northwest and in a few spots in Maine; the Olympia (Ostrea lurida), the half-dollar-size oyster indigenous to the Northwest and grown only there; and the Pacific (Crassostrea gigas), known for its wildly scalloped shell and fruity flavors.

Geneticists now say that Kumomoto (Crassostrea sikamea) is a fifth species. It is a small Pacific oyster with a deeply cupped shell that has become the sweetheart of the Northwest half-shell trade.

And most of the species are known by other names. The Atlantic is called the Eastern, but is also referred to by its place names, especially Blue Point, Wellfleet and Apalachicola. The European is known as the flat and also as the Belon, the name of a small region in France; and the Pacific, which is also grown in Europe, is sometimes called a Portuguese, from a species that is now extinct and that once made up the majority of oysters grown in Europe.

How to open an oyster: Place a bowl on a work surface to catch the juices (often called the liquor). Cover the palm of your hand with a folded kitchen towel, and place an oyster in the center. Take an oyster knife and scrape away any barnacles. Wipe the knife and, with your hands over the bowl, thrust the knife into the hinge of the shell. Run the knife around the oyster and flip it open. Discard the top shell. Cut the muscle that holds the meat to the shell. Never rinse the oysters.

Substitutes: for roasting: littleneck clams; for stewing: mussels

ROASTED OYSTERS WITH SPINACH, PERNOD AND ORANGE MAYONNAISE

Time: 30 minutes

½ cup orange juice

1 large egg yolk

1 teaspoon lemon juice

½ cup extra virgin olive oil

Salt and freshly ground pepper to taste

2 tablespoons vegetable oil

2 cups spinach leaves, washed, dried and chopped

1 teaspoon minced garlic

2 teaspoons Pernod or other anise liqueur

1 dozen oysters on the half shell, bottom muscle severed

This recipe was inspired by Oysters Rockefeller. A large madeleine pan is perfect for baking oysters.

1. Heat oven to 500 degrees. To make the mayonnaise, in a medium sauté pan bring the orange juice to a boil over high heat. Reduce heat to medium high, and continue to boil, 10 minutes or so, until juice is reduced to about 2 tablespoons. Meanwhile, combine the egg yolk, lemon juice, 2 tablespoons of the olive oil and salt and pepper in the bowl of a food processor or blender, and pulse to blend. With the motor still running, add the remaining olive oil in a slow, steady stream. It should form a thick, creamy emulsion. Stir in the reduced orange juice, and set aside.

2. In a large sauté pan, heat the vegetable oil over high heat until it is hot but not smoking. Add the spinach, and sauté, stirring briskly, until spinach is just wilted, about 1 minute. Remove from heat, drain well and stir in the garlic and Pernod.

3. Remove the oysters from their shells. Divide the sautéed spinach equally among the 12 shells, place the oysters back in the shells on top of the spinach, and spoon the mayonnaise on the oysters.

4. Place the oysters on a baking sheet, put in oven, and roast until the mayonnaise is slightly browned, about 10 minutes. Remove from the oven, and serve at once.

Yield: 4 servings

(John Willoughby and Chris Schlesinger)

BUCKWHEAT-FRIED OYSTERS

Time: 15 minutes

> **1 cup flour**
> **1 cup finely ground buckwheat groats (kasha) or**
> **buckwheat flour**
> **2 tablespoons white cornmeal**
> **Oil for deep frying**
> **30 oysters, scrubbed and freshly shucked, shells**
> **reserved**
> **Rémoulade (recipe page 327)**

1. Combine flour, buckwheat and cornmeal in a shallow dish. Arrange 5 reserved shells on each of 6 serving plates.

2. Pour oil to a depth of 3 inches in a large, heavy skillet or Dutch oven, and heat to 350 degrees. Dredge oysters in flour mixture, shaking off excess, and gently place in hot oil in batches. Fry about 2 minutes, or until crispy. Drain on paper towels.

3. Place oysters on shells on plates, and top with generous dollops of lemon rémoulade. Serve at once.

Yield: 6 servings
(Anne Rosenzweig, Inside,
New York City)

SIMPLE GRILLED OYSTERS IN THEIR SHELLS

Time: 15 minutes

½ cup unsalted butter

1 tablespoon minced garlic

2 tablespoons lemon juice

2 to 3 teaspoons Tabasco sauce

¼ cup Worcestershire sauce

Salt and freshly ground black pepper to taste

2 dozen oysters, well washed to remove sand and grit

3 tablespoons roughly chopped flat-leaf parsley

2 lemons, quartered

1. Build a medium-hot fire in a grill.

2. In a shallow baking pan, combine butter and garlic, and place the pan at the edge of the fire to melt the butter. When butter has melted, add lemon juice, Tabasco, Worcestershire and salt and pepper to taste, and stir to combine.

3. Place the oysters on the grill directly over the fire and cook for 2 to 3 minutes. At this point you can pull them off and open them with an oyster knife, or you can leave them on the fire for another 2 to 3 minutes until they open completely.

4. Remove the oysters from the fire, pull off the top shell, and sever the bottom muscle. Sprinkle the oysters with parsley, douse them with the butter sauce, and then serve them in their shells with lemon quarters for spritzing.

Yield: 8 appetizer servings

(John Willoughby and Chris Schlesinger)

OYSTERS WITH BACON AND HORSERADISH

Time: 30 minutes

> **4 ounces finely diced slab bacon**
> **2 tablespoons minced onion**
> **1 tablespoon flour**
> **1 teaspoon thyme leaves**
> **1 cup dry white wine**
> **1½ teaspoons prepared white horseradish**
> **Salt and freshly ground pepper to taste**
> **12 oysters on the half shell**
> **2 teaspoons dry bread crumbs**

1. Put bacon in a skillet and cook over medium heat until crisp and browned. Remove bacon, leaving the fat in the pan. Drain bacon on paper towels and reserve.

2. Add onion to the skillet and sauté in bacon fat until tender and golden. Stir in flour and thyme, then whisk in the wine. Cook, whisking constantly, until the mixture is smooth and thick. Stir in horseradish and bacon and season to taste with salt and pepper.

3. Spread mixture on top of each oyster. Sprinkle with bread crumbs. The recipe can be prepared in advance up to this point and refrigerated until just before serving.

4. Preheat broiler. Line a baking sheet with crumpled foil to hold oysters steady. Arrange oysters on baking sheet. Broil until lightly browned and bubbling, three to five minutes. Serve at once.

Yield: 4 servings
(Florence Fabricant)

OYSTERS WITH SEAWEED
AND CUCUMBER MIGNONETTE

Time: 1 hour

2 tablespoons hijiki seaweed

6 tablespoons rice vinegar

¼ cup sake

2 tablespoons mirin

1 tablespoon fresh ginger, peeled and minced

½ teaspoon freshly cracked pepper

24 oysters on the half shell

2 tablespoons cucumber, peeled and minced

3 tablespoons flying-fish roe (tobiko)

1. Soak hijiki in warm water for 30 minutes or until it is soft. Drain and chop coarsely. Mix with vinegar, sake, mirin, ginger and pepper. Refrigerate for 20 minutes, or until ready to serve.

2. Arrange oysters on ice on four plates. Add the cucumber to the sauce. Top oysters with sauce and a small dollop of flying-fish roe.

Yield: 4 servings

(Brad Steelman, The Water Club, New York City)

If small Kumomoto or Olympia oysters are available, they can be used, but plan on serving 8 per person.

OYSTER-OYSTER STEW

Time: 45 minutes

⅔ cup finely diced firm white bread

3 tablespoons unsalted butter

⅔ cup finely chopped onion

⅔ cup finely chopped fresh fennel

6 ounces oyster mushrooms

¼ cup Pernod or Ricard

30 shucked oysters with their liquor

1 cup (approximately) clam juice or fish broth (recipe page 321)

1 cup heavy cream

Salt and freshly ground black pepper

1 tablespoon finely chopped fresh fennel tops

The small croutons are replaced with toasted brioche rounds two inches in diameter, which can then be floated on the stew with a dollop of sturgeon caviar on top.

1. Lightly brown bread cubes in toaster oven or dry skillet. Set aside.

2. Melt butter in saucepan, add onion and fennel and sauté over medium heat until tender and golden. Add mushrooms and sauté two to three minutes longer. Stir in the Pernod.

3. Drain the oysters, reserving the liquor. Measure the liquor and add enough clam juice, broth or water to make two cups of liquid. Add the liquid to the mixture in the saucepan.

4. Add the cream to the saucepan and bring to a boil. Season to taste with salt and pepper.

5. Add the oysters to the saucepan and simmer just until they begin to curl around the edges. Remove from the heat and divide among four shallow soup plates.

6. Sprinkle with the croutons and fennel tops and serve at once.

Yield: 4 servings
(Florence Fabricant)

Scallops (Bay)

Winter's Vanishing Feast
By MARK BITTMAN

NANTUCKET, MASS.: It isn't hard to understand why the Argopecten irradians—sometimes called the Cape or Nantucket scallop—is nothing short of a local treasure.

Bay scallops once grew wild from Cape Cod to North Carolina, wherever the eelgrass in which they reproduce was plentiful, the temperature moderate and the water shallow. But a shrinking and often polluted habitat now limits commercial scalloping to Peconic Bay off Long Island, the inshore waters of Nantucket and Martha's Vineyard, the sheltered harbors and bays of a few Cape Cod towns and a few isolated areas in southeastern Massachusetts.

In each of those locations, the catch is diminishing. On Long Island, the culprit is brown tide, a phytoplankton that has hit hard. Brown tide turns the sea brown, kills eelgrass, and the result is tiny harvests.

Nantucket is in slightly better shape. In Nantucket's five-mile-long main harbor, where most of the scallopers spend their days, the enemy is fertilizer runoff. Used mostly for recently established lawns, the fertilizer spurs the growth of plants other than eelgrass; it also may contain weed killers.

Other bay scallops, farm-raised ones, are an amazing success story. About 15 years ago, 26 bay scallops were brought from Nantucket to China; their descendants now produce millions of tons of scallops each year. These are a decent product, but do not compare favorably with wild bay scallops, except in price: They are relatively cheap.

The scarcity of bay scallops only seems to intensify the craving for them among aficionados. Bay scallops are best prepared as simply as possible. In fact, many of the people who deal with them daily eat them raw. One of the best recipes is to sear them lightly on two sides, then sprinkle with lemon juice–a simple feast that can be enjoyed only a few months a year. 🐚

Substitutes: sea scallops, quartered

BAY SCALLOPS WITH FENNEL, ENDIVE AND ROSEMARY-ORANGE CARAMEL GLAZE
Time: 20 minutes

> 2 tablespoons sugar
> 1 sprig rosemary, broken in half
> 2 tablespoons sherry vinegar
> ½ cup freshly squeezed blood-orange juice (or ½ cup orange juice plus 1 tablespoon lemon juice)
> Salt and freshly ground white pepper
> 1 pound bay scallops
> 2 tablespoons all-purpose flour
> 1 tablespoon extra virgin olive oil
> 1½ tablespoons unsalted butter
> 1 fennel bulb, trimmed, cored and thinly sliced
> 1 endive, trimmed, cored and cut crosswise into ½-inch rounds

1. Melt sugar in medium sauté pan over high heat. When sugar colors around edges, add a piece of rosemary, and stir until sugar is light golden brown.

When buying bay scallops, be sure to avoid tiny scallops calle Calicos, which are sometimes sold as bays. Calicos are scallops that have been dredged from the sea and steamed open, and they have little flavor.

2. Stand back and stir in vinegar; caramel will spatter. When vinegar evaporates, stir in juice and simmer. Reduce by half; sauce should lightly coat a spoon. Season with salt and pepper, and set aside.

3. Toss scallops with salt, pepper and flour. Heat olive oil in a large non-stick sauté pan over high heat until pan starts to smoke. Shake off excess flour from scallops and put them in pan with remaining rosemary. Brown 1 minute, turn scallops over, add ½ tablespoon butter, and brown 1 to 2 minutes more; transfer to a warm plate.

4. Return pan to medium heat, and add remaining butter along with fennel and endive. Season with salt and pepper, cover, and cook, stirring and scraping bottom of pan, until vegetables soften, 3 to 4 minutes. Return scallops to pan and add orange sauce. Stir everything together for just a minute, taste for salt and pepper, and discard rosemary. Divide among 4 warm shallow soup plates and serve immediately.

Yield: 4 servings
(Daniel Boulud, Daniel, New York City)

BAY SCALLOPS WITH SCALLIONS AND SESAME SEEDS

Time: 15 minutes

8 tablespoons (¼ pound) unsalted butter
½ cup thinly sliced scallions
Freshly squeezed lemon juice
Salt and freshly ground black pepper
20 bay scallops, about ½ pound
2 tablespoons lightly toasted sesame seeds

1. Bring 2 tablespoons water to a boil in a small nonreactive saucepan, lower heat and whisk in butter a little at a time until the mixture becomes syrupy.

2. Add scallions, then lemon juice, salt and pepper to taste. Keep warm over low heat.

3. Preheat a large nonstick skillet over medium heat for 2 minutes. Add scallops; do not crowd. Cook without stirring until they brown lightly on one side, about 2 minutes. Turn with a spatula and brown the other side.

4. Serve scallops drizzled with reserved sauce and sprinkled with sesame seeds.

Yield: 4 appetizer or 2 small main-course servings
(David Paulstich, The Mark, New York City)

BAY SCALLOPS WITH TOMATO AND CHIVES
Time: 15 minutes

3 ripe tomatoes, peeled and seeded
1 shallot, chopped
½ garlic clove, minced
⅓ cup heavy cream
Salt and freshly ground black pepper
¼ cup chopped flat-leaf parsley
20 bay scallops, about ½ pound
3 tablespoons soft, unsalted butter, cut into bits
¼ cup chives, minced
1 tablespoon fish broth, optional (recipe page 321)
1 tablespoon lemon juice

1. Preheat the oven to 400 degrees.

2. Puree tomatoes in a food mill, blender or food processor. Combine in a small nonreactive saucepan with shallot, garlic and cream. Bring to a boil, turn the heat to low and cook for 2 minutes. Season to taste with salt and pepper. Stir in parsley, and keep warm.

3. Place scallops on a nonstick or lightly greased baking sheet, and bake 3 minutes.

4. Reheat sauce over minimum heat and whisk in butter a little at a time until sauce thickens slightly. Add chives. Adjust texture of sauce by reducing it a little further or by stirring in a little fish broth. Taste sauce, and add a little lemon juice if it is bland. Serve the scallops with a bit of the sauce.

Yield: 4 appetizer or 2 small main-course servings
(Eberhard Müller, Bayard's, New York City)

TAGLIATELLE WITH
BAY SCALLOPS AND PANCETTA

Time: 30 minutes

Salt
2 tablespoons extra virgin olive oil
2 ounces finely minced pancetta
2 cloves garlic, minced
1 cup finely chopped well-drained fresh or canned plum
    tomatoes
¾ pound bay scallops
Freshly ground black pepper
12 ounces fresh spinach tagliatelle
1 tablespoon basil leaves, slivered

1. Bring a large pot of salted water to a boil for the pasta.

2. Meanwhile, heat oil in a heavy skillet. Add pancetta and sauté a few minutes, until it begins to brown. Stir in garlic, then add tomatoes. Cook a few minutes, until the tomatoes start to thicken.

3. Stir in scallops and cook till they start to show signs of cracking. Add salt and pepper. Remove from heat.

4. Add tagliatelle to the pot of boiling water and cook about 3 minutes. Drain thoroughly, then add tagliatelle to the skillet with scallops. Add basil. Toss ingredients and serve.

Yield: 4 servings
(Florence Fabricant)

SALAD OF BAY SCALLOPS AND POTATOES
WITH BOUILLABAISSE VINAIGRETTE

Time: 30 minutes

1 small head Bibb lettuce, cored, leaves rinsed and dried
1 small bulb fennel, trimmed, cored and thinly sliced
4 fingerling potatoes, about 1 pound
1 cup dry white wine

1 clove garlic, minced

1 teaspoon saffron threads

¼ teaspoon red chili flakes

½ pound bay scallops

Salt and freshly ground black pepper

5 tablespoons extra virgin olive oil

3 ripe plum tomatoes, chopped

¼ cup Champagne or white wine vinegar

1. Arrange lettuce on 4 plates, and set aside. Place fennel in a large bowl.

2. Place potatoes in a small saucepan with hot water to cover. Bring to a boil, then simmer for 10 minutes or until a sharp knife easily slides through one potato. Drain and keep warm.

3. While potatoes are cooking, bring wine, garlic, saffron and chili flakes to a boil in a small saucepan. Simmer over medium-low heat for 2 minutes, and set aside.

4. Season scallops with salt and pepper. Place a large nonstick skillet over high heat. When very hot, add 2 tablespoons oil. Add scallops and sauté until almost cooked through, about 30 seconds. Stir in chopped tomatoes and continue cooking until warmed through. Slide contents of skillet into bowl with fennel. Slice warm potatoes and add to salad.

5. Place skillet used to cook scallops back over high heat. Add saffron-wine mixture and vinegar. Let mixture boil until reduced to approximately ⅓ cup. Whisk in remaining 3 tablespoons oil, and season dressing with salt and pepper. Pour half the dressing over scallop-fennel mixture, and toss gently to combine. Mound salad in center of plates; drizzle with more dressing as necessary. Season with salt and pepper to taste.

Yield: 4 servings
(Chris Gesualdi, Montrachet,
New York City)

Scallops (Sea)

Sweet Bounty Returns: Sea Scallops
By JOHN WILLOUGHBY AND CHRIS SCHLESINGER

NEW BEDFORD, Mass.: In the mid-19th century, this was one of the most prosperous cities in the country. Merchants and ladies with parasols strolled its elm-lined avenues, successful ship captains vied to build the most magnificent Greek Revival–style homes and from the all-important Customs Tower whaling ships could be seen sailing in and out of the harbor, one of the most beautiful in New England.

"Nowhere in all America," Herman Melville wrote in *Moby Dick,* "will you find more patrician-like houses, parks and gardens more opulent, than in New Bedford."

That era of prosperity reached its height in 1857, when the New Bedford whaling fleet, employing some 10,000 sailors, outranked the fleets of all other whaling ports in the world combined. But shortly, as petroleum supplanted whale oil as a fuel, New Bedford went into an economic decline that has plagued it ever since. Even its scallop industry, once the city's lifeblood, withered.

Now, however, an abundance of sweet, extraplump sea scallops should be flowing out of this port city again, to markets and restaurants all over the country. The reopening of 6,000 square miles, or about 30 percent, of Georges Bank, home to the world's greatest scallop beds, just about guarantees it. Scallops are perhaps the most ethereal of all seafoods–delicately translucent, creamy, tender, with a nutty, sweet flavor.

The New Bedford scallop industry centers on sea scallops, the large variety gathered year-round from the ocean floor off New England. Their much smaller cousins, bay scallops, are harvested from the shallow waters between Cape Cod and Long Island in a season that lasts only four months, November through February. Not surprisingly, the bay scallops are much more expensive.

It takes a full day to reach the scalloping grounds on Georges Bank, about 180 miles out, so scallopers typically go for 9 to 12 days at a stretch. Some go out for as long as three weeks. Once the boat has arrived at the beds, two 13-foot dredges, basically bags fashioned from heavy metal rings fastened to a reinforced metal frame, are lowered to the ocean floor by winches amidships, then dragged along until full.

When hauled up, the dredges resemble nothing so much as dump trucks full of rocks. But as soon as they are poured out on deck, the riches are obvious.

Working by hand, the crew quickly separates the scallops from the stones and other debris. Because the shells never entirely close, scallops are particularly perishable and are usually processed almost immediately.

The scallops come off the boats in bags of 40 to 50 pounds and are sold to local processors. The best—ultrafresh scallops caught the last day out—are sold to top restaurants and seafood purveyors. These are sometimes designated day boat scallops, but this term technically refers to scallops harvested from shoal areas off the Maine coast by scallopers who go out and back the same day. They share a certain élan with "diver scallops," expensive scallops harvested one at a time from ocean shelves off Maine by divers.

Fortunately, sea scallops are prolific. Like other mollusks they are hermaphroditic and shed eggs and sperm, which unite in the water to become embryos. During the first month or so after fertilization, the incipient scallops go through three stages while still moving around in the water. They then settle on the bottom, begin to form their shells, and in three to four years reach the adult stage. What is eaten is the adductor, the large muscle that opens and closes the shell.

We have long been fans of bigger scallops for the same reason we like thick steaks: they are harder to overcook. Only sea scallops are large enough to roast, for example, since bays tend to overcook in the oven. Larger scallops also let you get a good, hard sear on the outside when sautéing or grilling, while the inside stays perfectly tender.

Whether large or small, the best scallops are "dry" scallops, which have not been chemically treated in any way. "Wet" scallops have been soaked in phosphates at the processing plants, preserving them about four days longer. Unfortunately, the process also adds weight by plumping up the scallops with water. When cooked, these scallops exude quite a bit of liquid, which can play havoc with recipe proportions and make it difficult to brown them properly.

Dry scallops tend to be ivory, pinkish gray, tan, light coral or even grayish, usually a mixture of several colors in the same package. They are sticky and rather flabby. Wet scallops, by contrast, are uniformly bright white with a slippery feeling and often sit in a telltale pool of milky liquid. The best bet is to buy from a fishmonger you trust, and ask for unsoaked scallops. 🐚

Substitute: bay scallops can be used in recipes that do not require whole, seared sea scallops.

SOUTHEAST ASIAN-STYLE
SEARED SCALLOP SALAD

Time: 30 minutes

The small protrusion on the side of the scallop is the tendon, which should always be pared off.

1 pound medium sea scallops (about 10 to 12), tough
 tendon removed
¼ cup crushed coriander seeds
Salt and freshly cracked white pepper
2 tablespoons Asian, or toasted sesame oil
1 cup loosely packed mint leaves, washed and dried
1 cup loosely packed cilantro leaves, washed and dried
1 cup loosely packed basil leaves, washed and dried
2 cups arugula, washed and dried, heavy stems removed
1 red bell pepper, seeded, cored and cut into ½-inch strips
¼ cup soy sauce
⅓ cup lime juice
2 tablespoons minced ginger
1 teaspoon minced garlic
1 to 2 tablespoons minced fresh serrano chili
2 tablespoons Thai fish sauce, optional

1. Rub scallops thoroughly with coriander seeds and sprinkle with salt and white pepper to taste.

2. In a large sauté pan, heat sesame oil over medium-high heat until hot but not smoking. Add scallops in a single layer, and cook about 2 to 3 minutes, or until they just begin to brown. Flip them over, and cook 2 to 3 minutes on the other side. Remove from heat and set aside.

3. In a large bowl, combine mint, cilantro, basil, arugula and bell pepper. Set aside.

4. In a small bowl, combine soy sauce, lime juice, ginger, garlic, chili pepper and the fish sauce, if using. Whisk together. Pour over the greens to moisten. Toss gently, top with scallops and serve.

Yield: 4 appetizer servings
(John Willoughby and
Chris Schlesinger)

BUFFALO SCALLOPS WITH BASIL AND LIME

Time: 20 minutes

Juice of 2 limes
8 to 10 dashes Tabasco
1 teaspoon minced garlic
⅓ cup roughly chopped fresh basil
¼ cup extra virgin olive oil
Salt and freshly ground black pepper to taste
2 tablespoons vegetable oil
1 pound large sea scallops, tough tendon removed

1. In a large bowl, combine lime juice, Tabasco, garlic, basil, olive oil, salt and pepper. Mix well and set aside.

2. Place vegetable oil in a medium-large sauté pan, and heat over medium-high heat until hot but not smoking. Sprinkle scallops generously with salt and pepper. Add them to pan, in batches if necessary, to avoid crowding. Sauté, turning occasionally, until they are just browned on both sides, about 3 minutes total.

3. Remove scallops from heat, add to bowl with other ingredients, toss well and serve hot.

Yield: 4 servings
(John Willoughby and
Chris Schlesinger)

The creamy blue cheese sauce that's usually served with Buffalo chicken wings would also complement this scallop dish. Simply mash blue cheese with mayonnaise and/or sour cream to make a smooth dressing.

SAUTÉED SCALLOPS WITH SPICY BACON-CORN RELISH

Time: 35 minutes

3 tablespoons vegetable oil
1 pound large sea scallops, tough tendon removed
5 slices bacon, diced small
½ red bell pepper, diced small
½ green bell pepper, diced small
½ red onion, diced small
4 ears sweet corn, blanched in boiling water 1 minute
   and kernels sliced off
1 tablespoon minced garlic
1 tablespoon chili powder
1 tablespoon ground cumin
¼ cup roughly chopped cilantro leaves
2 tablespoons lime juice
Salt and freshly ground black pepper to taste

1. In a large sauté pan, heat oil over medium-high heat until hot but not smoking. Add scallops, in batches if necessary to avoid crowding, and cook, turning occasionally, until lightly browned on both sides, 3 to 4 minutes total. Remove scallops from pan and set aside.

2. In same pan, cook bacon over medium-high heat until crispy, 4 to 5 minutes. Remove from pan. Drain almost all bacon fat from pan, add peppers and onion and cook 2 minutes longer, stirring occasionally. Add corn and cook 2 minutes more, stirring occasionally. Add garlic, chili powder and cumin, and cook 2 minutes more, stirring occasionally. Stir in bacon.

3. Remove mixture from heat. Add cilantro, lime juice and salt and freshly ground black pepper and mix well.

4. Place a generous helping of relish on each plate, top with a quarter of the scallops and serve at once.

Yield: 4 servings
(John Willoughby and
Chris Schlesinger)

ROSEMARY-GRILLED SCALLOPS

Time: 45 minutes

About 20 rosemary sprigs, each 3 to 4 inches long
3 ounces prosciutto in paper-thin slices
1½ pounds sea scallops, tough tendon removed
3 tablespoons extra virgin olive oil
3 tablespoons lemon juice
Coarse salt and freshly ground black pepper

1. Strip leaves off bottom 2 inches of rosemary sprigs and reserve. Set sprigs aside. Cut prosciutto into strips just large enough to wrap around scallops (about 1 by 3 inches).

2. Lay a scallop flat on a work surface. Wrap a piece of prosciutto around it. Skewer a rosemary sprig through prosciutto and scallop to other side. Repeat with remaining scallops. Arrange scallops in a baking dish. Drizzle olive oil and lemon juice on both sides, sprinkle with rosemary leaves and season with salt and pepper. Marinate for 15 minutes.

3. Preheat grill to very hot.

4. Oil grate. Arrange scallops on grate and grill until just cooked, about 2 minutes a side. Serve at once.

Yield: 6 appetizer servings or
4 main-course servings
(Steven Raichlen)

Use bay scallops instead of sea scallops and serve these skewered scallop kabobs with drinks.

SPAGHETTI WITH SCALLOPS, LEMON AND BREAD CRUMBS

Time: 30 minutes

Salt

2 cups stale bread cut into ½-inch cubes

1 pound spaghetti

Salt

6 tablespoons extra virgin olive oil

3 medium garlic cloves, minced

2 tablespoons lemon juice

2 tablespoons flat-leaf parsley leaves, minced

½ teaspoon red chili flakes or to taste

1 pound sea scallops, tough tendon removed, scallops cut
into ¾-inch cubes

1. Bring 4 quarts salted water to a boil in a large pot.

2. Place bread cubes in a food processor fitted with metal blade and grind into coarse crumbs, about 1 minute. Place crumbs in a large skillet set over medium heat. Toast, shaking the pan often, until crumbs are golden brown. Remove crumbs from the pan, and set aside.

3. Add spaghetti to boiling water.

4. While pasta is cooking, briefly heat oil in the skillet. Add garlic and cook until golden, about 1 minute. Stir in lemon juice, parsley, red chili flakes and salt to taste. Cook 30 seconds. Add scallops and cook, stirring, until they are opaque and cooked through, 3 to 4 minutes. Do not overcook. Adjust seasonings. Keep warm.

5. Drain spaghetti when al dente, but do not shake bone-dry. Transfer spaghetti, still dripping with a little cooking water, to a large bowl, and toss with scallop sauce. Sprinkle with bread crumbs and toss well. Divide pasta into individual bowls, and serve immediately.

Yield: 4 servings

(Jack Bishop)

SCALLOP PANCAKE WITH CHINESE GREENS

Time: 45 minutes

1 pound sea scallops, coarsely chopped

1 tablespoon rice flour

1 shallot, finely chopped

1 tablespoon finely chopped chives

3 ounces mustard greens

3 ounces baby spinach

3 ounces sugar snap peas

1 ounce enoki mushrooms

4 slender scallions

1 tablespoon extra virgin olive oil

2 teaspoons soy sauce

1 teaspoon minced fresh ginger

2 teaspoons lemon juice

1½ teaspoons rice vinegar

½ tablespoon minced cilantro leaves

Other seafood, including shrimp, crabmeat and lobster, can be substituted for the scallops.

1. Mix scallops with rice flour, shallot and chives. Shape into 8 patties. Set aside.

2. Cut mustard greens, spinach and sugar snap peas into slivers and blanch 1 minute in boiling water. Drain and place in bowl of ice water. Drain and set aside in a bowl. Add enoki mushrooms to the bowl.

3. Brown scallions lightly in a nonstick pan. Mix with the other vegetables.

4. Lightly sauté scallop cakes on both sides in a nonstick pan, 1 to 2 minutes on each side. Set aside.

5. Add olive oil to pan and quickly stir in vegetables. Add soy sauce, ginger, lemon juice and rice vinegar and toss well. Divide warm vegetables among 4 plates, place 2 scallop cakes on top of each, sprinkle with cilantro and serve.

Yield: 4 servings

(Joachim Splichal, Canyon Ranch, Tucson, Auz.)

SCALLOPS AND MÂCHE WITH PUMPKINSEED OIL

Time: 15 minutes

> 2 tablespoons canola oil
> 16 large sea scallops, tough tendon removed
> Salt and freshly ground black pepper to taste
> 1 clove garlic, cut in half
> 4 ounces mâche, rinsed and drained
> 4 tablespoons pumpkinseed oil
> 5 teaspoons white wine vinegar

1. Warm canola oil in a large sauté pan over high heat. Add scallops, reduce to medium high, season lightly with salt and pepper and cook for 3 minutes. Turn, season lightly again and cook for an additional 2 minutes or until scallops feel almost firm to the touch. Set the scallops aside, discarding oil.

2. Rub the insides of a salad bowl with the garlic halves and discard the garlic. Add the mâche and 2 tablespoons of the pumpkinseed oil, and toss gently.

3. Sprinkle vinegar over greens, season lightly with salt and pepper, and toss. Divide the salad among four plates. Top each with four scallops, drizzle the remaining pumpkinseed oil over the scallops and serve.

Yield: 4 servings
(Ulli Stachi, Ulli's Heavenly Recipes,
New York City)

SCALLOPS WITH ARTICHOKES AND JERUSALEM ARTICHOKES

Time: 1½ hours

> 1 pound Jerusalem artichokes, scrubbed
> Salt
> 1 tablespoon honey
> ¼ cup sherry vinegar
> 2 tablespoons sherry
> 2 cups peanut oil

3 large fresh artichoke bottoms, thinly sliced

2 tablespoons extra virgin olive oil

12 large sea scallops, tough tendon removed

Freshly ground black pepper to taste

3 tablespoons butter

2 teaspoons minced shallots

2 thyme sprigs, chopped

½ bunch fresh sage, leaves only, julienned

1. Boil Jerusalem artichokes in salted water until tender. Drain well, peel and puree in blender. Set aside and keep warm.

2. In a small saucepan, heat honey over medium heat until darkened. Add vinegar and cook until thickened. Add sherry, set aside and keep warm.

3. In a deep, heavy saucepan, heat peanut oil over medium-high heat. Cook sliced artichoke bottoms in batches until crisp and lightly browned. Drain on paper towels and keep warm.

4. In a large sauté pan, heat olive oil over high heat. Season scallops with salt and pepper and cook until browned on one side, then turn and cook a few seconds longer. Stir in butter, shallots and thyme. Remove scallops and add honey mixture to pan. Bring to a boil.

5. Reheat puree and spoon onto 4 serving plates. Divide scallops among the plates, spoon sauce over and around, then top with artichoke slices and sage.

Yield: 4 servings
(Cyril Renaud, Fleur de Sel,
New York City)

Sea Urchin

Maine Sea Urchin Is a Star in Japan
by DENA KLEIMAN

PORTLAND, ME.: The sea urchin—a creature once cursed as a pest to fisher-men and routinely destroyed—is prized as uni in the most sophisticated eating salons of Japan, where it is a sushi delicacy regarded by some as an aphro-disiac. Sea urchins are abundant along the remote island reefs that stretch up and down the Maine coast and gave rise to a new industry that was started in the late 1980's. It's a daring underwater treasure hunt in which divers brave wintry waters as cold as 34 degrees to satisfy a passion for a food that until recently most Americans would never think of putting in their mouths.

In taste the sea urchin seems a cross between an oyster and sweetbreads, though hints of chocolate and cinnamon are not uncommon in the flavor. Like sturgeon caviar, each one has a slightly different taste.

These spiny echinoderms, which look like green rubber balls encased in pine thistles, steal bait out of lobster traps and send sharp thorns into swim-mers' fingers and feet. In other waters they might be black or purple. But they are valued for their soft reproductive organs, which are euphemistically referred to as "roe" and range in color from yellow to orange. There are five sections, like tangerine sections, in each sea urchin.

Increasingly, instead of being shipped to Japan, the urchins from Maine and also from California are being kept at home to be served in fine sushi bars and in seafood restaurants. And they are also sold in some retail markets, with the top half of the shell taken off at the equator—shears do the job nicely—and with the roe ready to serve raw, on a seafood platter or a plate of three per per-son, with a squeeze of lemon. The French also like them broiled briefly in the shell with a little cream sauce on top. The meat can also be removed and baked in a soufflé. ❧

Shrimp

Savor the Charms of the Mighty Shrimp
By MARK BITTMAN

Americans eat more shrimp than any other fresh or frozen seafood; only canned tuna is more popular. Along with Japan, whose smaller population works its way through as much shrimp as Americans do, the United States is the world's leading shrimp-eating nation. Yet most Americans know little about shrimp except that they come small, medium, large or, in the proverbial oxymoron, jumbo.

Small, medium, large, extra large, jumbo and other size classifications are subjective and relative. Small shrimp of 70 or so to the pound are frequently labeled medium, as are those that are twice that size and even larger. Nor are shrimp graded like eggs or meat; you are really on your own.

Some shrimp are wild, some are farmed, and they come from all over the world, from the Gulf of Mexico to the estuaries, bays and ponds of China, India and Ecuador. In short, all shrimp are not alike. There are 300 species of shrimp worldwide, but six are most commonly found in American markets.

Shrimp varieties:

GULF WHITE (Penaeus setiferus): Certainly the most expensive shrimp and frequently the best. With good flavor and firm texture, they may be wild or farm-raised. Usually grayish-white in color, these are similar in appearance to the less desirable Gulf Brown shrimp, so be careful. Ask to see the box, which may help.

ECUADOREAN or MEXICAN WHITE (P. vannamei): Similar to Gulf whites, these may be wild, as are most Mexican shrimp, or farm-raised. The United States imports more shrimp from Ecuador than from any other country.

BLACK TIGER (P. monodon): These are huge, widely farmed shrimp from Asia. They may be dark gray with black stripes and red feelers, or bluish with yellow feelers; when cooked, they turn pink. Inconsistent but frequently quite flavorful and firm.

GULF PINK (P. duorarum): Another high-quality shrimp, wild or farm-raised. The shell is usually redder than that of whites, but may be light brown.

GULF BROWN (P. aztecus): The wild shrimp most likely to taste of iodine, these tend to be reddish brown, but can easily be confused with whites or pinks.

Consumption of shrimp in the United States has more than doubled in the last 20 years. Americans ate 640 million pounds last year, as compared with 300 million pounds in 1972. Caterers say that when shrimp is one of the hors d'oeuvres, they have to have a double quantity on hand. Shrimp cocktail, with red cocktail sauce, is probably the favorite preparation.

CHINESE WHITE (P. chinensis): Asian farm-raised shrimp with grayish white color, soft, sometimes watery texture and mild flavor. Usually relatively inexpensive. Benefits greatly from brining treatment before cooking.

Some other varieties of shrimp that show up in American markets from time to time are fresh Maine shrimp, which are often quite small, and rock shrimp, also small and always sold shelled. With few exceptions, shrimp arrive in American fish markets frozen and are sold thawed. 🐚

Such a Pleasure, So Brief a Stay: Maine Shrimp
By FLORENCE FABRICANT

Maine shrimp, a tiny variety of shellfish from deep waters, are rarely available fresh. But when they are, usually in winter, they are worth scooping up. These shrimp are so tender and sweetly flavorful that they can be eaten raw. Fresh Maine shrimp are often sold with their heads on. Usually the season starts December 1 and runs until the end of March.

With shrimp, bigger is generally considered better. But Maine, or northern, shrimp–Pandalus borealis and Pandalus jordani–are a modest delicacy, with about 40 whole, unshelled shrimp in a pound, as against 15 or so cocktail shrimp from southern waters without the heads.

Northern shrimp are also found off Canada, Greenland, Iceland, Scandinavia, the Aleutians and Japan. In Maine, their southernmost habitat, the waters are relatively warm, so the shrimp tend to grow faster and larger. In Scandinavia, where they are usually sold peeled and cooked, a pound may comprise as many as 300 shrimp. The Japanese call these northern shellfish amaebi, or sweet shrimp.

In their complex life cycle, the shrimp start out as males, and after a year of growth near the coast they migrate 50 or 60 miles out, where the Gulf of Maine is about 500 feet deep. Then for two years the creatures–which are protandric, or progressive, hermaphrodites–undergo a natural sex change.

In summer the new females mate with newly arriving males, and by December they return closer to shore, where the water may be 300 feet deep, to lay their eggs. The larvae hatch in January. In a good season, the mature females fill the trawlers' traps.

It's best to buy Maine shrimp the day they will be cooked, and to rinse them well. If the heads are starting to turn dark or black, the shrimp are not fresh enough.

Peeling uncooked Maine shrimp takes work, because they are so small and sticky. So the home cook is probably wise to poach or steam them in the shell, then serve them warm or cold to peel and eat with a dip. Once they are cooked, peeling is fairly easy. Brining for an hour before cooking tends to firm them up and even enrich the flavor. 🐚

Substitutes: langoustines, crayfish tails

SHRIMP COCKTAIL
Time: 1 hour

> **1½ pounds jumbo shrimp (16 to 20 per pound),**
>   **peeled and deveined, shells reserved**
> **5 tablespoons kosher salt**
> **3 cups white wine**
> **1 tablespoon black peppercorns**
> **1 tablespoon coriander seeds**
> **2 bay leaves**
> **1 cup flat-leaf parsley leaves**
> **4 sprigs fresh tarragon**
> **2 lemons, halved**
> **Cocktail sauce (page 323), green sauce (page 329) or rouille**
>   **(page 326)**

1. In a large pot, combine shrimp shells, 2 quarts water and 3 tablespoons salt. Bring to a boil over high heat, reduce heat to low and simmer 20 minutes. Remove pot from heat and steep until cool.

2. Strain shrimp broth into another large pot, and bring to a boil over high heat. Add wine, peppercorns, coriander seeds, bay leaves, parsley, tarragon and lemons. Boil 2 minutes. Add shrimp and remove pot from heat. Steep shrimp until they are opaque, about 3 minutes. Fill a large bowl with water, ice and the 2 remaining tablespoons salt. Transfer shrimp to bowl. Let shrimp cool 3 minutes, then drain well. Refrigerate with a bag of ice on top until ready to serve.

3. To serve, divide shrimp among four plates. Place sauces in individual ramekins on each plate, or in three small bowls to pass at the table.

Yield: 4 servings

(Rick Moonen, Oceana, New York City)

THAI DAIKON AND SHRIMP SOUP

Time: 30 minutes, plus chilling

5 cups defatted, salt-free chicken stock
½ pound daikon radish, peeled and sliced paper thin
1 slender green chili, about 3 inches, or 1 jalapeño chili, seeded and minced
3 tablespoons rice vinegar
1 teaspoon salt
½ pound medium shrimp, peeled, deveined and split in half
2 tablespoons Thai fish sauce
1 tablespoon lime juice
Pinch of sugar
1 tablespoon cilantro leaves

1. Place chicken stock in a saucepan, bring to a simmer and add daikon. Simmer about five minutes, until daikon becomes translucent.

2. While daikon is cooking, place chili, vinegar and salt in a blender or mini food processor. Process to make a pale green liquid. Stir this into soup.

3. Stir in shrimp, fish sauce, lime juice and sugar. Simmer about 2 minutes longer, until shrimp are cooked.

4. Serve at once or transfer soup to a bowl, cover and refrigerate until cold. To serve, float cilantro leaves on top of each portion.

Yield: 6 servings

(Oriental Hotel, Bangkok, Thailand)

HOT AND SOUR SHRIMP SOUP (TOM YUM GOONG)

Time: 35 minutes

2 stalks fresh lemon grass (bulb only), or 1 teaspoon dried
    lemon grass

4 fresh Kaffir lime leaves, or substitute 4 dried leaves soaked for
    15 minutes in hot water, or use the zest of ¼ lemon

1½ quarts rich chicken stock

5 ⅛-inch-thick slices galingale, or substitute the same amount
    of fresh ginger or 2½ teaspoons Laos powder

3 tablespoons Thai fish sauce

4 tablespoons lime juice

5 small fresh Thai chilies or 3 or 4 serrano chilies, seeded and
    minced, or to taste

½ teaspoon light brown sugar

1 cup bamboo shoots, fresh or canned

1 15-ounce can straw mushrooms, drained and halved

1 pound medium shrimp, peeled and deveined

1 cup chopped cilantro

2 scallions, minced

1. Slice fresh lemon grass into ¼-inch pieces. Leave dried pieces whole. Remove the ribs of fresh or dried lime leaves, crush and cut into large pieces. Place lemon grass and lime leaves in piece of cheesecloth and tie.

2. In a medium saucepan, bring chicken stock to a simmer. Add galingale and bag of lemon grass and lime leaves and simmer 5 minutes.

3. Add fish sauce and lime juice and bring to a simmer again. Add chilies and sugar, stirring to dissolve sugar. Add bamboo shoots and mushrooms and bring to a boil. Add shrimp and cook until opaque, 1 minute. Add cilantro and remove from the heat.

4. Discard lime leaves and lemon grass. Serve immediately, or chill and serve cold. Garnish with scallions.

Yield: 4 servings
(Mick Vann)

FRESH MAINE SHRIMP

Time: 15 minutes, plus 1 hour refrigeration

You can
improve the
flavor and
texture of
almost any
species of
shrimp by
brining them
slightly, as in
this recipe.
Another way
is to stir one
cup of salt
and one-half
cup of sugar
into two cups
of boiling
water until
dissolved;
pour the
mixture into
a large bowl
filled with ice
and water,
and add up to
two pounds of
shrimp. Let
the shrimp sit
in the brine,
refrigerated
(or adding ice
occasionally),
for two hours
or so. Rinse
the shrimp
well.

3 tablespoons kosher salt or sea salt
2 pounds fresh Maine shrimp with heads
½ lemon
1 bay leaf
1 teaspoon black peppercorns
Melted butter or rémoulade sauce (page 327)

1. Mix salt with 3 cups ice water in a bowl large enough to hold shrimp. Rinse shrimp, add to salt water, cover and refrigerate 1 hour.

2. Bring 2 quarts water to a boil in a saucepan. Squeeze lemon juice into water, then add the lemon to the pot along with bay leaf and peppercorns. Simmer 10 minutes. Rinse shrimp, add to simmering water and cook no more than 1 minute, until the water barely returns to a simmer. Drain shrimp.

3. Serve shrimp hot, to peel and eat with melted butter, or cold with rémoulade sauce. Or peel to use in other recipes.

Yield: 4 servings
(Florence Fabricant)

SMOKED FRESH MAINE SHRIMP

Time: 30 minutes, plus 1 hour marinating

3 tablespoons light brown sugar
3 tablespoons rice vinegar
2 tablespoons Chinese cooking wine or dry sherry
1 tablespoon Chinese oyster sauce
1½ teaspoons salt
½ teaspoon Chinese five-spice powder
¼ teaspoon Chinese chili oil
60 fresh Maine shrimp, unpeeled, heads removed
   (about 1½ pounds with heads)
2 tablespoons long-grain rice
2 tablespoons black tea leaves, preferably Lapsang souchong

1. Dissolve 1 tablespoon sugar in vinegar in a bowl large enough to hold shrimp. Stir in wine, oyster sauce, salt, five-spice powder and hot oil. Rinse shrimp, add them and toss to coat. Cover, and marinate at room temperature for 1 hour. Drain shrimp.

2. Line a wok and its cover completely with aluminum foil. Mix remaining sugar with rice and tea, and spread in bottom of wok.

3. Place wok over high heat. Cover. Fragrant smoke should start to rise after about 5 minutes. Place shrimp on steaming rack that will fit into wok, either a bamboo steamer or a collapsible vegetable steamer on legs. Place in wok, cover tightly, reduce heat to medium and smoke 10 minutes.

4. Remove shrimp from wok, cool to room temperature and serve to peel and eat.

Yield: 4 servings
(Florence Fabricant)

This is a Chinese technique, called tea smoking, that adds a lovely haunting whiff of flavor but requires no special equipment. Though Lapsang souchong is the best tea to use because it has a naturally smoky flavor, any black tea is suitable.

SHRIMP BAKED WITH FETA CHEESE
Time: 45 minutes

3 cups canned Italian plum tomatoes, crushed
¼ cup extra virgin olive oil
1 teaspoon finely chopped garlic
¼ cup fish broth or shrimp stock (recipes, pages 321, 322), or clam juice
1 teaspoon dried oregano, preferably Greek
1 teaspoon red chili flakes
2 tablespoons drained capers
Salt and freshly ground black pepper
3 tablespoons unsalted butter
24 large shrimp (about 1 pound), shelled and deveined
¼ pound feta cheese, crumbled
¼ cup ouzo, optional

1. Place tomatoes in a saucepan and simmer, stirring occasionally, until reduced to 2 cups.

2. Heat oil in a 3-quart saucepan. Stir in garlic, cook 30 seconds, and add tomatoes, fish broth, oregano, chili flakes, capers and salt and pepper to taste.

3. Melt butter in a skillet. Add shrimp, toss briefly over medium heat just until they turn pink, then remove from heat.

4. Preheat oven to 350 degrees.

5. Spread half the sauce among 4 6-inch ramekins. Arrange 6 shrimp in each on the sauce, top with remaining sauce and scatter feta over sauce. Bake about 10 minutes, until sauce is bubbling. If desired, sprinkle 1 tablespoon ouzo on each and ignite, then serve.

Yield: 4 servings
(Craig Claiborne and Pierre Franey)

STEAMED SHRIMP ROLLS WITH TARRAGON

Time: 30 minutes

This recipe will also work with scallops and with smoked fish.

1 pound large shrimp, shelled and deveined
3 tablespoons fresh tarragon leaves, finely chopped
Sea salt
60 small rounds of toasted brioche or slices of peeled cucumber
Lemon wedges, for garnish

1. Place shrimp in a food processor, and pulse until finely chopped but not pureed. Mix in tarragon and salt to taste.

2. Lay out four pieces both of foil and of plastic wrap, each about 8 inches square. Put foil on top of plastic and spoon ¼ of mixture into center of each. Shape each mound into a roll about 1-inch thick. Roll up tightly in foil, then in plastic, twisting ends to seal. Rolls may be refrigerated for up to 12 hours.

3. To cook rolls, place 2 inches of water in bottom of a steamer and bring to a boil. Place plastic-wrapped rolls in top half of steamer. Cover, and reduce heat to medium low. Steam until shrimp rolls are opaque and firm, about 10 minutes. Remove from heat, and cool to room temperature.

4. To serve, unwrap rolls and slice ¼ to ⅜ inch thick. Arrange slices on a platter, overlapping in a spiral pattern, or to make canapés, place slices on rounds of toasted brioche or cucumber slices. Garnish with lemon wedges.

Yield: 60 canapés (10 to 12 servings)
(Wayne Nish, March, New York City)

SHRIMP IN GARLIC SAUCE

Time: 15 minutes

⅓ **cup extra virgin olive oil**
2 **cloves garlic, peeled and sliced**
1 **dried hot red chili**
1 **pound large shrimp, about 20, peeled and deveined**
Salt to taste
1 **tablespoon dry white wine**
1 **teaspoon minced curly parsley for garnish**

1. Warm olive oil in a 10-inch skillet over medium-low heat. Add garlic and chili. When garlic begins to color, raise the heat to medium high and add shrimp and salt. Cook for about 2 minutes on each side, turning once, or until shrimp are pink.

2. Add wine, remove chili, garnish with parsley and serve.

Yield: 4 small servings
(Ignacio Blanco, Meson Galicia,
Norwalk, Conn.)

Learn to judge shrimp size by the number it takes to make a pound, as retailers do. If the shrimp aren't labeled, ask to have them weighed. Shrimp marked "16/20," for example, require 16 to 20 of them to make a pound. Those labeled "U-20" require fewer (the U stands for "under") than 20 to make a pound.

RISOTTO WITH ORACHE AND ROCK SHRIMP

Time: 45 minutes

*Orache,
sometimes
called
mountain
spinach, was
widely used in
Europe before
spinach
arrived from
Persia. Now
grown as a
specialty crop,
it has meaty
leaves that are
deep red on
one side and
greenish on
the other and
bleed when
cooked. This
risotto, if
made with
orache, will
be almost
magenta. The
radicchio
accomplishes
the same
purpose.*

2 tablespoons extra virgin olive oil
¾ cup finely chopped red onion
2 cloves garlic, minced
1½ cups arborio rice
½ cup chardonnay
2 cups seafood stock (recipe page 322)
2 cups vegetable stock or water
1 cup packed, finely chopped orache (about 2 ounces);
    red radicchio leaves can be used instead
Salt and freshly ground black pepper
Pinch sugar
1 pound peeled rock shrimp or peeled medium shrimp
½ cup finely slivered orache; red radicchio leaves can be used
1 tablespoon minced fresh dill
2 tablespoons crumbled feta cheese

1. Heat oil in a heavy 3-quart saucepan. Add onion and garlic. Sauté over medium-low heat until translucent. Increase heat to medium, stir in rice and cook, stirring, until rice is opaque. Stir in wine and cook until it evaporates. In a separate pot, combine stocks and bring to a simmer.

2. Fold chopped orache into rice and cook, stirring, until rice turns pink. Season with salt, pepper and sugar. Add hot stock in ¾-cup portions, stirring each time, adding more as stock is absorbed. Continue until rice is al dente.

3. Fold in shrimp and cook 2 minutes until fully cooked. Fold in slivered orache and dill. Season to taste with salt and pepper. Serve with a little feta sprinkled on each portion.

Yield: 6 servings
(Florence Fabricant)

SCRAMBLED EGGS WITH SHRIMP AND GARLIC SHOOTS

Time: 10 minutes

> ½ pound peeled rock shrimp or other small shrimp, cut into
> ½-inch pieces
> Sea salt
> 4 large eggs
> 2 tablespoons extra virgin olive oil
> ⅔ cup garlic shoots (available at farmer's markets and specialty
> stores), cut into 1-inch lengths, or 2 cloves garlic, crushed
> to a paste plus ¼ cup sliced chives

1. Spread shrimp on a plate and season generously with salt. Let sit 5 minutes. Crack eggs into a bowl and set near stove.

2. Place a 12-inch nonstick skillet over medium-high heat. Add olive oil. When it shimmers, add garlic shoots and sauté 1 minute. If using garlic cloves and chives, add at same time as shrimp. Add shrimp and cook for another minute, just until they are opaque on edges.

3. Working quickly, pour eggs into pan and stir vigorously with a wooden spoon or spatula. Eggs should just set but not become stiff or brown. Transfer to a serving dish.

*Yield: **2 generous servings***
(Amanda Hesser)

SHRIMP AND GRITS

Time: 1½ hours

1 pound unpeeled medium shrimp
Bouquet garni or 3 bay leaves
1 cup stone-ground grits or polenta
1 cup milk
Salt
2 medium tomatoes or 4 small green tomatoes
    or 4 large tomatillos or any combination
    of the three
1 teaspoon minced, seeded jalapeño chili
4 tablespoons unsalted butter
¼ cup chopped green bell pepper
¼ cup chopped onion
2 teaspoons flour
Salt and pepper to taste

1. Peel shrimp and reserve. Place shells and bouquet garni in 2½ cups water and boil 20 minutes. Strain and reserve to cool.

2. While stock is cooking, stir grits into a bowl of cold water and allow to settle. Corn hulls will float to the surface. Skim off hulls and drain grits. This step is not necessary if using polenta.

3. In a pot, bring milk and 2 cups water to a boil. Spoon in grits or polenta, stirring with a wooden spoon. Add salt and simmer, stirring occasionally. Once grits thicken, lower heat and stir frequently, adding water if grits become too stiff. Cook at least 25 minutes, until grits are fluffy. Set aside.

4. While grits cook, broil tomatoes until skins blacken, 5 to 10 minutes. Press tomatoes through a sieve. Measure ½ cup sieved tomatoes and set aside. Stir in jalapeño.

5. In a large pan, melt butter and sauté green pepper and onion until softened, about 2 minutes. Add shrimp and sauté 5 minutes total, turning to cook both sides. Remove shrimp and set aside.

6. Whisk flour into 1 cup cooled shrimp stock. Place in saucepan with peppers and onions and simmer 5 minutes. Add sieved tomatoes, stirring. Simmer until sauce thickens, about 5 to 10 more minutes. Add shrimp back to pan and continue cooking for another 2 minutes.

7. Reheat grits and spoon onto each of 4 plates. Ladle shrimp and gravy on top. Season to taste with salt and pepper.

Yield: 4 servings
(Matt Lee and Ted Lee)

BAKED SHRIMP

Time: 30 minutes

2 tablespoons unsalted butter
½ cup finely diced onion
½ cup finely diced green bell pepper
½ jalapeño chili, seeded and finely slivered
3 cloves garlic, crushed and minced
1 pound medium shrimp, peeled and deveined
1 cup finely chopped peeled fresh tomato
3 tablespoons chopped flat-leaf parsley
Salt and freshly ground black pepper to taste
1 tablespoon extra virgin olive oil

1. Preheat oven to 400 degrees.

2. Heat butter in large skillet. Add onion, green pepper, jalapeño and garlic and cook until softened. Stir in shrimp, cook 1 or 2 minutes until just opaque, and add tomato and parsley. Season with salt and pepper.

3. Transfer to a shallow baking dish, preferably earthenware. Drizzle with oil and bake for 10 to 15 minutes, until bubbling. Serve at once.

Yield: 4 servings
(Balikci Sabahattin, Istanbul)

Istanbul is a city of fish markets with pristinely fresh wares. This is a typical recipe from a seafood restaurant, or balikci, near the Hagia Sofia.

Squid

Squid may prove to be the most valuable seafood of all. This variety of cephalopod, actually a kind of mollusk, is abundant in the world's oceans, highly nutritious with more than three-quarters of the creature edible and rich in protein, and, from a culinary standpoint, as good frozen as fresh.

The meat has a mild flavor and a pleasant chewiness that can be minimized by proper cooking. Long a favorite in ethnic markets, especially Mediterranean and Asian, squid has become a popular menu item, even in fast-food outlets. For many people, the most appealing way to eat squid (or calamari, as it is frequently called) is deep-fried to a crisp golden turn, with some rich mayonnaise or a tomato sauce for dipping. But for the home cook, that is not the easiest preparation.

In restaurants special equipment for deep-frying is always ready for that batch of squid, potatoes, onions or whatever. The oil or shortening is hot. The home cook who does not have an electric deep-fryer must empty a quart or two of oil into a deep pan or a wok, often for onetime use, be prepared to serve whatever is fried within minutes, then deal with all the grease and spatters on the stove—cookery at its least enjoyable.

But that does not remove squid from the menu. Squid can be stewed, as long cooking will tenderize it. But it can also be flash-grilled over a hot fire, because quick-cooking also keeps it tender. The briefest simmering, then chilling, readies squid for salad.

A fish similar to squid is cuttlefish, or sepia. It is found in European waters and is imported into American markets. The cuttlefish has a rounder, thicker body than squid, making it somewhat meatier. But cuttlefish are prized in Europe because they have much larger ink sacs than squid.

How to clean squid: Most of the squid in the market is already cleaned. In fact, unless it is a local catch, it was probably frozen and thawed. To clean fresh squid, first reach into the long, slender body and pull out everything that's inside, including the clear, slender, cartilaginous quill. Slice off and reserve the tentacles at the top of the head, discarding everything else from inside the squid. Peel or scrape off the grayish film that may cover the body, then rinse the squid.

BEAN AND CALAMARI SOUP

Time: 1 hour, 10 minutes, plus soaking and cooling

1¼ cups dried cranberry beans
8 cloves garlic
2 sprigs rosemary
2 sprigs sage
Salt to taste
2 medium red onions, roughly chopped
½ cup peeled and diced butternut squash
¼ teaspoon or more red chili flakes, or to taste
2 tablespoons tomato paste
¼ cup extra virgin olive oil, plus additional for flavoring
½ cup white wine
1 pound calamari, cleaned and cut into ¼-inch strips
Freshly ground black pepper

1. Rinse beans, removing pebbles or dirt. Soak overnight in 8 cups cold water. Drain and rinse beans and place in 3-quart saucepan with 8 cups fresh water. Wrap 2 garlic cloves, 1 sprig rosemary and 1 sprig sage in cheesecloth and add to pot. Bring to boil, then simmer 20 minutes. Add salt. Continue to cook 25 to 30 minutes, or until beans are tender. Add water as needed to keep beans covered. Let beans cool in water.

2. In a food processor, place onions, 6 cloves garlic, 1 sprig rosemary, 1 sprig sage, butternut squash, chili flakes and tomato paste. Puree. In a soup pot, heat ¼ cup olive oil and the puree. Cook 5 minutes. Add white wine. Let wine reduce by half.

3. Drain beans, reserving liquid. Add beans to soup pot with up to 4 cups of the cooking liquid and simmer 25 minutes. Add calamari in last 2 to 3 minutes. Thin with cooking liquid as needed. Drizzle with pepper and olive oil. Serve.

Yield: 4 servings
(Cesare Casella, Beppe,
New York City)

The beans in this recipe take long, slow cooking, as constrasted to the squid, which is quickly simmered. Instead of dried beans, fresh shell beans like cranberry beans in season, shucked from their pods, can be used. With shell beans the soaking is not necessary and the cooking time is reduced to about 30 minutes.

CALAMARI, WATERMELON AND AVOCADO SALAD

Time: 30 minutes

4 cups cilantro, coarsely chopped, plus ½ cup leaves
    for garnish
¼ cup rice vinegar
1 tablespoon grape-seed oil
Salt and freshly ground black pepper to taste
12 ounces cleaned squid, cut into rings, including
    tentacles
1 egg white, beaten
1½ teaspoons ground coriander
1¾ tablespoons extra virgin olive oil
1½ teaspoons unsalted butter
1½ tablespoons finely chopped shallots
1 tablespoon chopped fines herbes (mixed chervil,
    tarragon, chives and parsley)
1 tablespoon lemon juice
1 lemon
2 ounces mesclun, rinsed and dried
16 thin slices of watermelon, rind and seeds removed,
    cut into 1-inch squares
8 slices of avocado, ¼-inch-thick

1. Fill a saucepan half full of water, and bring to boil. Set aside a bowl of ice water. Place 4 cups chopped cilantro in boiling water and immediately lift out with slotted spoon and transfer to ice water. Squeeze cilantro dry. In a blender, combine cilantro, rice vinegar and grape-seed oil. Puree until smooth. Transfer to a bowl and season with salt and pepper to taste.

2. In a medium bowl, combine squid, egg white and ground coriander; mix well. In large sauté pan over medium-high heat, heat 1 tablespoon olive oil until it is smoking. Add squid mixture and sauté until translucent, about 2 minutes. Add butter and stir until melted. Add 1 tablespoon shallots, stir, and remove pan from heat. Add fines herbes and salt and pepper to taste. Toss to mix well.

3. In small bowl, combine lemon juice, remaining olive oil, and salt and pepper to taste. Set aside.

4. Grate zest from lemon and reserve. Remove white pith and seeds and cut lemon into segments. In mixing bowl, combine lemon zest, lemon segments, salad greens, remaining shallots, squid and juice mixture. Toss quickly to blend well.

5. To serve, spread squid mixture in center of large serving platter. Arrange watermelon and avocado on top. Drizzle cilantro mixture over salad and around edge of plate. Garnish with cilantro leaves.

Yield: 4 servings
(Rocco DiSpirito, Union Pacific,
New York City)

CEVICHE VERDE

Time: 50 minutes

1 pound cleaned squid, in ½-inch rings
1 chopped jalapeño chili
3 cloves garlic
1 teaspoon dry oregano, preferably Mexican
¼ cup red wine vinegar
1 cup loosely packed flat-leaf parsley leaves, finely chopped
1 cup loosely packed cilantro leaves, finely chopped
½ cup extra virgin olive oil
¼ cup lime juice
Salt and freshly ground black pepper to taste

1. Bring a pot of water to a boil, add squid and cook 30 seconds. Drain and place in ice water.

2. Place jalapeño pepper, garlic, oregano, vinegar and ¼ cup water in a blender, and puree. Transfer to a bowl and add parsley, cilantro, olive oil and lime juice. Season to taste with salt and pepper. Drain squid and add to bowl. Marinate 15 minutes and serve.

Yield: 4 servings
(Aarón Sánchez, Isla,
New York City)

This recipe provides another example of flash-cooking squid to keep it tender.

FRIED CALAMARI

Time: 30 minutes

A tempura batter, as in the recipe for soft-shell crabs, page 202, also works well with squid.

1 pound fresh cleaned squid

1 cup milk

Vegetable oil for deep-frying

½ cup flour

Salt, freshly ground black pepper and cayenne pepper
 to taste

1 lemon, quartered

½ cup tartar sauce (recipe page 328)

1. Cut the tentacles off squid and set aside. Cut squid bodies in thin slices crosswise, making rings. Place milk in a bowl and place squid in milk, separating the rings and adding the tentacles.

2. Pour oil to a depth of about 2 inches in a wok. Heat oil over medium-high heat.

3. Place flour in a shallow bowl and season to taste with salt and both black and cayenne pepper. It should taste spicy.

4. Test to see if oil is hot. It should register 375 degrees on a deep-frying thermometer or be hot enough to start browning a small cube of white bread as soon as it is dropped in.

5. Remove about ¼ of squid from milk, draining well. Place in flour, separating the pieces and tossing lightly in flour to coat. Transfer squid pieces to the wok and fry until golden, turning once. Remove and drain on paper towels as they are done. Continue to coat squid with flour and fry pieces until all are cooked. Season with salt and pepper to taste.

6. Pile the fried calamari on a platter lined with a napkin and serve with lemon wedges and tartar sauce on the side.

Yield: 4 servings
(Florence Fabricant)

THAI SQUID SALAD

Time: 30 minutes

3 tablespoons long-grain rice

1 pound cleaned squid, sliced into rings

2 tablespoons Thai fish sauce

¼ cup lime juice

1 teaspoon red chili flakes

2 tablespoons sliced peeled shallots

2 tablespoons sliced scallions

1 tablespoon thinly sliced seeded fresh green chili

1 tablespoon chopped fresh mint leaves

2 limes, cut in wedges

The toasted ground rice adds texture to the squid. Rice flour toasted in a skillet can be used instead.

1. Place rice in a small, dry skillet and cook over medium heat, stirring gently about 3 minutes, until it turns nut brown. Pulverize rice to a powder in blender or spice mill. Set aside.

2. Bring a saucepan of water to a boil; add squid, separating the rings, and cook 30 seconds. Drain well and place in a mixing bowl. Combine fish sauce and lime juice in a small bowl. Add chili flakes, shallots and scallions. Pour over squid and mix well. Fold in pulverized toasted rice.

3. Transfer salad to a serving dish, scatter chili slices and mint leaves on top and arrange lime wedges around it.

Yield: 6 servings
(Oriental Hotel, Bangkok,
Thailand)

CUTTLEFISH WITH SHAVED FENNEL
AND BROKEN VINAIGRETTE

Time: 50 minutes

> 2 small heads fennel, trimmed
> 6 tablespoons Dijon mustard
> ½ cup lemon juice
> 2 large cloves garlic, peeled and lightly crushed
> Coarse salt
> ¾ cup extra virgin olive oil, more for oiling pan
> 8 whole cleaned cuttlefish, thawed if frozen, or 16 cleaned
>   calamari
> Coarsely ground black pepper
> 3 handfuls haricots verts, trimmed
> 4 tablespoons chopped parsley

1. Using a mandoline or a sharp knife, thinly shave fennel crosswise and set aside. In a small bowl, combine mustard and lemon juice. Add the garlic cloves and salt to taste. Stir the mixture while gradually adding ½ cup olive oil until it is somewhat mixed but not fully incorporated; there should be large beads of oil flecking the liquid. Taste and adjust seasoning, and set aside.

2. Preheat the broiler, placing the rack 6 inches below the heat. Over high heat, bring a medium pot of lightly salted water to a boil. Lightly oil the broiling pan and arrange cuttlefish in a single layer. Sprinkle with remaining ¼ cup olive oil, and season to taste with salt and pepper.

3. Add the haricots verts to boiling water and blanch until tender, 3 to 4 minutes. Drain well and cut into thirds. Place cuttlefish under the broiler and cook, turning once, until puffed and opaque, about 2 minutes for each side.

4. To serve, make a pile of fennel on each of 4 plates. Sprinkle a handful of haricots verts over each and spoon 1 or 2 tablespoons of vinaigrette over them. Place cuttlefish on top and pour some cooking juices over them. Add a touch more of vinaigrette, and sprinkle with parsley. Serve immediately.

Yield: 4 servings
(Gabrielle Hamilton, Prune,
New York City)

BLACK PASTA WITH SPICY TOMATOES

Time: 30 minutes

4 tablespoons extra virgin olive oil

4 large cloves garlic

½ teaspoon red chili flakes, or to taste

1 pound ripe plum tomatoes, chopped

**1 14-ounce can Italian plum tomatoes, well drained and
   chopped**

Salt

**1 pound fresh black linguine, purchased or homemade (recipe
   follows)**

2 tablespoons finely chopped flat-leaf parsley leaves

1. Heat 3 tablespoons oil in a large skillet. Add garlic and chili flakes, sauté for a few seconds, then add fresh and canned tomatoes. Adjust heat to medium and simmer about 15 minutes, until the sauce has somewhat thickened. Season to taste with salt. Remove from heat and add remaining tablespoon of olive oil.

2. While the sauce is simmering, bring a large pot of salted water to a boil for the linguine. As soon as the sauce has finished cooking, add linguine to the water and cook about 5 minutes, until al dente. Drain thoroughly.

3. Place pasta in skillet, toss with the sauce, adjust salt and chili flakes, sprinkle with parsley and serve.

Yield: 4 servings
(Francesco Antonucci, Remi,
New York City)

BLACK PASTA

Time: 40 minutes

*What is sold
as squid ink is
actually
cuttlefish ink.
The ink is
available
fresh or
frozen in
some fish
markets. A
little goes a
very long way.*

2 cups all-purpose flour
Pinch of salt
2 large eggs
1 teaspoon extra virgin olive oil
1 ounce (2 tablespoons) squid or cuttlefish ink
1 to 3 teaspoons water
Cornmeal

1. Combine flour and salt in the work bowl of a food processor. Mix the eggs, oil and squid ink together. With the machine running, add them through the feed tube. Add as much of the water as needed to form a ball of dough.

2. Pass the dough through increasingly fine settings of a pasta maker to form thin, smooth sheets of dough. For linguine, cut the sheets into thin strands by hand or using the cutting blade of the pasta machine. For fettuccine cut the pasta in ½-inch widths.

3. If not using at once, toss with cornmeal and refrigerate or allow to dry completely at room temperature.

Yield: 1 pound
(Francesco Antonucci, Remi,
New York City)

CHAPTER THREE

Fish Roes and Smoked Fish

Bottarga

Bottarga is the pressed and salted roe of tuna, mullet, ling, hake and herring, and is important on the Mediterranean table. In Sicily it is eaten in slices on ripe tomatoes. Each kind tastes different and has a different texture, but they're all salty and fairly intense, so a little goes a long way. Hake bottarga is the mildest.

SPAGHETTI ALLA CHITARRA WITH BOTTARGA AND BREAD CRUMBS

Time: 30 minutes, plus one hour if needed for drying bread

Spaghetti alla chitarra, or guitar spaghetti, is a kind of fresh pasta cut on a device strung with narrowly spaced wires that looks a little like a guitar.

3 ounces bottarga (sold in some fish markets and fancy food shops)
2 thick slices crusty Italian white bread, preferably stale, in chunks
7 tablespoons extra virgin olive oil
¼ teaspoon minced garlic
1 teaspoon finely grated lemon zest
4½ tablespoons minced flat-leaf parsley leaves
Salt and freshly ground black pepper to taste
1 pound chitarra spaghetti or regular spaghetti
1 dried red chili
2 large cloves garlic, thinly sliced

1. Place bottarga, wrapped in plastic, in the freezer.

2. If bread is not stale, spread it on a baking sheet and dry it for an hour in a 250-degree oven. Lightly toast stale or dried bread under broiler. Process to fine crumbs in food processor or blender. You should have about ½ cup of crumbs.

3. Heat 1 teaspoon olive oil in small skillet. Add minced garlic and brown lightly. Add lemon zest, cook 30 seconds and add bread crumbs and 1 teaspoon parsley. Season with salt and pepper. Set aside.

4. Bring large pot of water to a boil for the pasta. When water boils, season generously with salt, add pasta and cook until barely al dente, about a minute less than the manufacturer recommends.

5. While pasta is cooking, heat 2 tablespoons olive oil in large skillet. Add chili and sliced garlic and cook until garlic is just beginning to color. Remove pan from heat. Remove bottarga from freezer and, using a mandoline or a sharp knife, slice paper thin.

6. Drain pasta, reserving 1 cup cooking water. Pour water into skillet with chili and garlic, add drained pasta, return to medium heat and simmer about a minute. Add remaining parsley and half the bread crumbs. Toss to combine. Season with salt and pepper. Drizzle with remaining olive oil. Transfer to 4 warm shallow bowls, top each with remaining bread crumbs and scatter with slices of bottarga. Serve at once.

Yield: 4 servings
(Dave Pasternack, Esca, New York City)

TARAMOSALATA

Time: 15 minutes

1 English muffin, preferably onion-flavored
10 tablespoons cured grey mullet or carp roe (tarama)
1 clove garlic, finely minced
5 tablespoons lemon juice, or more, to taste
⅔ cup extra virgin olive oil
½ cup finely chopped scallions

1. Place English muffin in a small bowl and add warm water to cover. Let stand until thoroughly saturated. Squeeze muffin to extract all excess moisture. Crumble muffin in bowl of food processor.

2. Add tarama, garlic, lemon juice and 2 tablespoons water. Pulse. With machine running pour in olive oil in a thin stream until mixture is the consistency of mayonnaise.

3. Transfer to a bowl and fold in scallions. Serve with toasted pita triangles or raw vegetables for dipping.

Yield: about 12 hors d'oeuvre servings
(Craig Claiborne and Pierre Franey)

Taramosalata, a Greek meze or appetizer spread, is made with tarama, the cured roe of gray mullet or carp, that's sold in jars. Sometimes the spread is made with mashed potatoes instead of bread.

Caviar

For Caviar, a New World Order
By MOLLY O'NEILL

A caviar connoisseur is someone who relishes the various. Bursting between the tongue and the roof of the mouth, caviar varies from fish to fish, region to region, season to season. That is part of its allure. Unfortunately, buying caviar is complicated, and a mistake can be costly. A significant amount of caviar is being imported from Russia, the other former Soviet republics around the Caspian Sea, Iran, China and even Bulgaria. Add the growing amount of farm-raised caviar from California, Russia and France, and you get an array of choices that can be thrilling–and confusing.

Today the Caspian Sea waters that were once regulated by the Soviet Union are worked by fishermen from two independent republics (Kazakhstan and Azerbaijan) and two Russian regions (Astrakhan and Dagestan), producing caviar whose taste and quality are completely unpredictable. Overfishing and poaching are rife, as are unskilled handling and processing of the precious roe. Fishermen along the Mississippi River are landing hackleback sturgeon, and the roe from those fish is being sold as caviar, along with that of paddlefish from the Great Lakes. Stolt Sea Farms in Sacramento, Calif., has developed some excellent caviar from farm-raised sturgeon, as have five tiny sturgeon farms in France and Russia. The country of origin should be listed on the front or back label.

Some retailers try to wedge new varieties into the three traditional classes of caviar–beluga, osetra and sevruga–thus diminishing the meaning of those terms, each of which identified a particular type of sturgeon. 🐚

Buying Techniques

Would you buy a diamond without seeing it? It's not easy to sample the caviar, but if you're buying four ounces or more, don't be intimidated–it is customary to ask for a taste. And if you don't like what you taste, don't buy it. Fresh, unpasteurized caviar should glisten; upon close inspection, the eggs should be luminous, pert-looking and consistent in size and color. If they look noticeably different, different grades of caviar may have been mixed together and the offering inaccurately labeled and overpriced. Smashed, soupy or misshapen eggs are likely to have been mishandled or frozen.

Caviar should not smell fishy. The grains should be firm, but not rubbery or tough. Hard grains usually mean that the caviar has been pasteurized, and should be labeled as such.

Bear in mind that the days of bargain caviar are over. Shop at a reputable retailer, and expect to pay top dollar, even for sevruga. And remember you'll probably get more for your money and better quality if you do not buy beluga, the scarcest and most fragile of the sturgeon roes.

Tasting Techniques

Use small spoons made of bone or mother-of-pearl, which do not affect the flavor of caviar. (Most metal spoons impart unpleasant metallic notes; even plastic is preferable.)

Before tasting, inhale the aroma; there should be very little. Then slip the caviar into your mouth. As it sits on your tongue, pull a little air into your mouth, close your eyes and, without hesitation or any attempt at delicacy, crush the eggs by forcing them against the roof of your mouth.

The immediate taste should be mildly oceanic. Then come earthier impressions: fruit, nuts, even truffles. The final sensation should be a slight brininess, tinged with the sort of coppery nuance of a Belon oyster, for a balance of the disparate sensations in the mouth.

The Varieties

BELUGA (Huso huso): The king of the 27 varieties of sturgeon that produce edible roe, beluga has a snub nose and the appearance of a pit bull. It can grow 20 feet long and weigh a ton. It takes 15 to 20 years to reach maturity, lives about 150 years and can contain up to 15 percent of its body weight in roe. At its best, beluga caviar is pale to steel gray; the eggs are the largest, and perhaps the most tender. The texture is buttery, and the flavor is the most delicate of all the caviars.

OSETRA (Acipenser gueldenstaedti): The fish has an elongated jawbone like a swordfish and can grow to seven feet long and about 400 pounds. It reaches maturity in 12 years, lives about 40 years and can contain nearly three pounds of roe. The egg is firmer, and the color varies from gold to dark brown. Osetra is rich and nutty tasting.

SEVRUGA (Acipenser sevru): This is the smallest of the three sturgeon that produce luxury caviars, at a little over five feet and 70 pounds. It matures in seven years. Small, glittering, nearly black eggs have a characteristically intense flavor, deep on the briny side, with a dark, dangerous sexiness, as opposed to the languid sensuality of beluga.

FARMED AMERICAN STURGEON (Acipenser transmontanus): Domestic caviar has come into its own. The bead is small and firm, with a lively pop, a subtle hint of the sea and a deep, pronounced hazelnut flavor. The color ranges from violet to a nearly cream-colored gold, to blackish gray to jet.

KALUGA (Huso dauricus): This sturgeon is harvested from the Amur River; if it is landed on the southern banks, it is Chinese; on the northern banks, Russian. The eggs are firm, large and beautiful; they seem to glow a deep olive green and tortoiseshell. Their taste is less breathtaking: lighter, fresher and younger than Caspian beluga. The Latin *kaluga* shares part of its spelling with *beluga* and is often mislabeled either beluga or osetra, depending on the size of its egg.

PRESSED CAVIAR: A jammy confection made of broken beluga, osetra and sevruga, this can be very good indeed. If you plan to cook with it-in an omelette, as a topping for potatoes, as a filling for crepes or even blini-pressed caviar is an economical option.

OTHER FISH ROES: Large red salmon roe, smaller and more delicate pinkish trout, golden whitefish roe that is sometimes flavored with wasabi or ginger, tiny grains of flying-fish roe (tobiko) and bottarga, the cured, pressed roes of mullet and tuna, are some other types of fish roe worth using in the kitchen.

CROQUE-MONSIEUR WITH SALMON AND CAVIAR
Time: 40 minutes

> 12 slices sandwich bread, ½ inch thick
> 6 ounces Gruyère cheese, sliced ⅛ inch thick
> 12 ounces sliced smoked salmon
> 1 tablespoon blanched lemon zest

1 tablespoon sliced chives

6 ounces osetra caviar

8 tablespoons soft unsalted butter

1. On 6 slices of bread, place cheese; on other 6 slices, place smoked salmon. Sprinkle salmon with lemon zest; sprinkle cheese with chives. Place an ounce of caviar on each of the slices with salmon. Form 6 sandwiches by putting the slices with salmon together with the slices with cheese.

2. Preheat a large sauté pan over medium heat. Brush butter over both sides of each sandwich, including edges. Working in batches, place sandwiches in pan with the cheese side down, and sauté until browned, about 2 minutes. Raise heat to high, turn and sauté 1 minute on salmon side.

3. Slice croque-monsieurs on diagonal, then on diagonal again, and serve.

Yield: 6 servings
(Eric Ripert, Le Bernardin, New York City)

SALMON CAVIAR, BEET AND POTATO SALAD

Time: 20 minutes

⅓ **cup extra virgin olive oil**

2 **tablespoons red wine vinegar**

½ **teaspoon coarsely ground black pepper**

¼ **teaspoon salt**

1 **teaspoon caraway seeds**

1½ **cups diced, peeled boiled yellow or red potatoes, chilled**

½ **cup chopped sweet onion**

½ **cup chopped celery**

½ **cup (loosely packed) chopped flat-leaf parsley**

1½ **cups diced cooked or canned red beets, chilled**

¾ **cup sour cream**

6 **ounces salmon caviar**

1. In a small mixing bowl combine olive oil, vinegar, pepper, salt and caraway seeds. Set aside.

Other types of caviar, including American sturgeon, can be used in place of osetra to make these elegant sandwich hors d'oeuvres less costly. And as finger food, with a glass of Champagne, the recipe will serve 8 to 12.

2. In a medium bowl combine chilled diced potatoes, onion, celery and parsley. Add the olive oil mixture, and mix gently but thoroughly. Carefully fold in beets.

3. Divide the salad among 6 serving plates or bowls. Top each with 2 tablespoons of sour cream and 1 heaping tablespoon caviar. Serve immediately.

Yield: 6 servings
(John Loring, Tiffany's)

CAVIAR NOODLES

Time: 30 minutes

Salt
6 ounces soba (buckwheat) or green-tea soba noodles
¼ cup finely julienned carrot
¼ cup finely julienned daikon radish
4 scallions, finely shredded
5 tablespoons rice vinegar
1 teaspoon freshly grated ginger
1 shallot, finely chopped
3 tablespoons canola oil
4 ounces tobiko (flying-fish roe), trout roe or sturgeon
   caviar, preferably sevruga
Generous pinch of white pepper

1. Bring a large pot of salted water to a boil. Add noodles. Cook about 10 minutes, until tender. Drain noodles, cool in ice water for 5 minutes, then drain thoroughly.

2. Toss noodles in a bowl with carrot, daikon and scallions.

3. Mix vinegar with ginger and shallot. Beat in the oil, then fold in tobiko or caviar. Pour this mixture over the noodles, and toss gently. Season with pepper, and salt if desired. Serve.

Yield: 6 servings
(Elka Gilmore, Kokachin,
New York City)

Smoked Salmon

At one time all it took to enjoy smoked salmon was a bagel. Now you need a Baedeker. At some delicacy counters you'll find as many as six or eight kinds of smoked salmon from around the globe, each with a distinctive flavor and texture.

In regions where salmon was always fished in the wild, some of the catch was always smoked. And usually consumed locally. The global smoked salmon market is a recent phenomenon, brought about in part by the intensive cultivation of the fish in Europe, North America and elsewhere. Norway, Iceland, Scotland, Denmark, Ireland, Canada and even Chile are all smoking some of their farm-raised salmon as an alternative to selling it fresh in a glutted market.

The term *nova* is shortened from *Nova Scotia*. It originally referred to the milder-cured Atlantic salmon from Canadian waters that once was about the only alternative to lox. Much lower priced than Nova Scotia salmon, lox was brine-cured, extremely salty and only lightly smoked, if at all.

Starting in the late 1940's in New York, the nation's most active smoked salmon market, the public began to turn away from the harsher lox to which the older generation of Jews of Eastern European background had been accustomed.

The major New York smokers began curing Western salmon in the lighter Nova Scotia style to sell as an alternative to lox. Then, beginning in the early 1980's, the availability of farmed Atlantic salmon permitted vastly increased production of Eastern nova as well.

Today nova is the backbone of the industry. Old-fashioned lox has all but disappeared. Consumers want a smoked salmon that is more delicate than ever, and the industry has responded. At the same time, the preference also seems to be for fish that is fatty and rich. Some of the fish are so rich that one wonders how people can bear to eat it with cream cheese, a habit from the salty-lox days.

One exception to the nova style is in the Pacific northwest, where king salmon may be hot-smoked, giving it a smokier taste and the texture of cooked fish. It might even be smoked long enough to turn it into a kind of jerky, called squaw candy.

For the nova style, the gutted, filleted fish, usually weighing at least 10 pounds and sometimes as much as 20, is rubbed with a mixture of salt and often brown sugar and left to cure for about three days.

In a few smokehouses this dry cure is followed by a wet cure, in which the fish is soaked in brine for a few days as well. The more salt used, the saltier and sometimes the drier the product.

After the cured fish is dried, it is cold-smoked at about 80 degrees, which gives the fish the flavor of smoke without its being heated enough to cook. The longer the smoking—over hardwoods such as hickory, alder or fruitwood—the smokier the taste. It's the length of smoking, not the type of wood, that most affects the flavor.

The quality of smoked salmon is also affected by its freshness, how well it is trimmed and sliced and whether or at what point in its preparation it has been frozen.

The only wild salmon regularly on the market now comes from the Pacific, not the Atlantic, and some of this fish is being shipped to European smokers.

There is also a mystique about Scottish salmon, a holdover from the days when it was the superior product on a market that consisted only of lox and nova. Although some extremely fine Scottish smoked salmon is on the market, including a small amount of wild salmon, the generalization no longer applies. Yet it is often priced higher than any other kind.

Salmon from Scotland, Ireland and from some of the new American boutique smokehouses tend to have a smokier and saltier flavor. Icelandic smoked salmon can also be fairly smoky and rich.

Because cold-smoking does not act as a preservative, smoked salmon is perishable. Once sliced, it has a shelf life, if well wrapped and under refrigeration, of no more than one week. Exposure to air at a deli counter will cause it to dry, affecting the flavor and texture; a given variety of salmon will always be better when purchased from a shop that does a brisk business and has a rapid turnover.

It should be sliced extremely thin, at a sharp angle so the slices are as large as possible. Slices from the tail end tend to be drier. Sides of presliced salmon from Europe are usually reliable, but there are exceptions. Through the plastic of the vacuum package the fish should have good color, with no browning on top, and the slices should appear close together. Hand-cut presliced salmon is more expensive because the slices are considerably larger than machine slices.

When salmon is frozen after smoking, it can deteriorate. A holiday gift of a side of smoked salmon should be kept in a home freezer no longer than one month, despite what the package might say.

QUICK SMOKED-FISH MOUSSE

Time: 10 minutes

> 1 cup smoked bluefish, mackerel or trout, skinned (about 6
>   ounces)
> ¼ cup finely chopped scallions
> ⅓ cup plain nonfat yogurt or half yogurt, half mayonnaise
> 1 teaspoon fresh lemon juice
> Salt and freshly ground black pepper to taste
> Rye crackers or thin slices of dark bread

1. Break up the fish in pieces and place it, along with the scallions, in the bowl of a food processor. Process until finely ground. Add 2 tablespoons of the yogurt and the lemon juice and process briefly. Transfer the mixture to a bowl.

2. Stir in the remaining yogurt by hand and season the mixture to taste with salt and pepper. Serve with crackers or bread for spreading.

Yield: about 1½ cups
(Florence Fabricant)

For a richer mousse, use sour cream instead of yogurt.

POTATO AND SMOKED MACKEREL SALAD WITH CREAMY MAYONNAISE

Time: 35 minutes, plus 1 hour cooling

> 1¼ pounds small red-skinned potatoes
> Sea salt
> ¼ red onion, thinly sliced
> 1 stalk celery, thinly sliced on the diagonal
> 1 smoked mackerel fillet, skin discarded
> Freshly ground grains of paradise (pink peppercorns) or
>   black pepper
> ⅓ cup mayonnaise, perferably homemade
> 1 tablespoon heavy cream, approximately

1. Place potatoes in a medium pan, cover with water and season generously with salt. Bring to a boil, reduce to a simmer and cook until tender, about 15 minutes. Drain. When cool enough to handle, slice into ¼-inch-thick rounds.

2. In a large bowl, combine potatoes, red onion and celery. By hand, shred mackerel into half-inch pieces. Add to salad. Season with salt and grains of paradise or pepper.

3. In a small bowl, whisk together the mayonnaise and cream. Fold into potato mixture. There should be just enough dressing to coat ingredients. Add a little more cream if necessary. Cover, and refrigerate for at least an hour. Adjust seasonings before serving, adding more salt or vinegar as needed.

Yield: 4 servings
(Amanda Hesser)

SALAD OF POTATOES, SMOKED SABLE AND EGG MIMOSA

Time: 45 minutes

4 cups Yukon gold potatoes, peeled and cut in ¼-inch dice
6 whole cloves
2 tablespoons olive oil
4 garlic cloves
4 thyme sprigs
3 black peppercorns
2 bay leaves
4 tablespoons finely chopped shallots
6 tablespoons finely chopped flat-leaf parsley
3 tablespoons finely chopped scallions
½ cup finely chopped celery heart
Fleur de sel and freshly ground white pepper to taste
1½ cups lemon mayonnaise (recipe page 325)
1 cup smoked sable, boneless and skinless, coarsely chopped
6 eggs, hard-cooked and pushed through a sieve

1. Place potatoes, cloves, olive oil, garlic, thyme, peppercorns and bay leaves in a saucepan with water to cover. Cook until potatoes are tender. Remove whole cloves, garlic, thyme, peppercorns and bay leaves.

2. In a large salad bowl, fold together diced potatoes with shallots, parsley, scallions and celery. Season with salt and pepper to taste. Dress with 1 cup mayonnaise and taste; if salad is dry, add more mayonnaise.

3. Spread ½ potato salad in a shallow bowl. Top with smoked sable and then with remaining potato salad. Cover completely with hard-cooked egg. Press gently but firmly. Refrigerate until ready to serve.

Yield: 6 servings as an appetizer or side dish
(Michael Otsuka, Verbena, New York City)

SMOKED FISH HASH

Time: 40 minutes

> 2 medium-to-large boiling potatoes, peeled
>   and diced
> Salt
> 3 tablespoons cooking oil
> 1 large onion, chopped
> 1½ cups diced smoked fish
> Juice of 1 lemon
> Freshly ground black pepper
> 1 tablespoon minced flat-leaf parsley
> 1 tablespoon minced scallion
> Poached eggs (optional)

1. Place potatoes in boiling salted water and cook about 10 minutes, until barely tender. Drain.

2. Heat oil in a large, heavy skillet. Add potatoes and sauté over medium-high heat until they begin to color. Add onion and continue to sauté until the onion and potato are golden. Fold in smoked fish and cook for 5 minutes. Add lemon juice and cook a minute or so longer.

3. Season to taste with salt and pepper and fold in parsley and scallion. Serve at once, topped, if desired, with poached eggs.

Yield: 4 servings
(Florence Fabricant)

Leftover chunks of meaty fish like swordfish can be combined with the smoked fish in this hash.

SMOKED TROUT CHOWDER

Time: 1 hour

> 1½ tablespoons unsalted butter
> ⅔ cup chopped leeks
> 1½ cups diced, peeled boiling potatoes
> 3 cups milk
> 2 smoked trout, about 7 ounces each, skinned and boned
> Salt and freshly ground black pepper
> ½ cup heavy cream (optional)
> 2 tablespoons minced chives

1. Heat butter in a large, heavy saucepan. Add leeks and sauté until tender but not brown.

2. Add potatoes and half the milk. Bring to a simmer, cover and cook until potatoes are tender, about 30 minutes.

3. Using a fork, roughly mash the potatoes, leaving some pieces, then add remaining milk.

4. Break the trout into 1-inch pieces and add it to the saucepan. As the soup cooks and is stirred, the pieces will become smaller.

5. Simmer 15 minutes. Taste for seasoning and season judiciously with salt and generously with pepper. Stir in the cream, if desired. Serve with chives sprinkled on top.

Yield: 4 servings
(Tadich Grill, San Francisco)

CHAPTER FOUR

Mixed Seafood

Bouillabaisse, Soups, Stews, Chowders, Paellas, Risottos, Gumbos, Noodle Dishes...

A Prime Kettle of Fish
By R. W. APPLE JR.

MARSEILLE, FRANCE: It is made from bony, spotty, spiny little fish, each one uglier than the last, creatures that cooks in many places disdain as trash. It was originally a product of peasant thriftiness, created by fishermen as a cheap way to feed themselves and their families with the fish their customers would not buy. But one man's trash is another man's treasure, and the fish have become so expensive that today a carefully fashioned bouillabaisse can cost $40 or more.

All along the corniche that follows the coast south from Marseille, and tucked into the calanques or coves beyond that, you come across small, little-heralded restaurants, some of them not much more than shacks, few of them paid great heed by gastronomic guides. At such spots, they take their bouillabaisse seriously. So, too, on the Riviera, at glossy Bacon in ritzy Cap d'Antibes and fashionable Tétou, smack on the sands in Golfe-Juan.

Nothing that you can put in a bowl or on a plate catches the magic of a summer's day on this bewitching coast quite as perfectly as bouillabaisse. Every spoonful evokes the fresh sea breezes, the clean, salt-seasoned air and the brilliant light that so captivated Cézanne when he came to the neighboring village of L'Estaque to paint.

In Marseille, the venerable, polyglot, slightly louche Mediterranean port city where bouillabaisse was invented, the real thing–the rust-brown, tomato-and-fennel-based, saffron-infused bouillon, enriched by dollops of a fiercely garlicky mayonnaise called rouille, is classically followed by a plate of fish that have been cooked in the bouillon.

Controversy clings to bouillabaisse like barnacles to a ship. Is it a soup? Perhaps not, because the broth and the solids are eaten separately. Is it a stew? Surely not, because a stew by definition is cooked slowly, and bouillabaisse must be boiled furiously to achieve an amalgamation of olive oil with water and wine. It is best described as a fish boil, which is what its name seems to imply. *Bouillir* means "to boil" in French, and *peis* means "fish" in Provençal, but inevitably that etymology is challenged, too.

Although it was once a one-pot meal, cooked in a cauldron over a wood fire on the beach, bouillabaisse is usually prepared today in two stages for greater richness. First, a stock is made using tiny fish or fish heads (often including the bulbous head of a monkfish), vegetables and seasonings. After the stock has been strained and well laced with saffron, it is used to poach larger fish and sliced potatoes.

But exactly what fish? You will not be astonished to hear that learned authorities disagree. Even the authoritative Bouillabaisse Charter of Marseille, signed by 11 restaurateurs in 1979, does little to clear up the confusion. The French version of the document specifies that at least four fish from a list of eight must be used if the bouillabaisse is to be considered authentic, and it includes monkfish, which the English version omits. The English version lists only six fish, and it includes skate, which the French version omits.

Sometimes a small crab or two or a spiny lobster goes into the pot, to the immense irritation of purists. Restaurants more interested in ostentation than culinary tradition sometimes toss in a baby lobster. And nobody in the South of France would dare attempt a bouillabaisse without rascasse (scorpion fish, a cosmetically challenged denizen of the coastal rocks) or its cousin, chapon; galinette (gurnard, another notably unpretty rockfish); conger eel, for body, and vive (weever), a small, elongated fish with poisonous spines that provides a certain mellowness of flavor.

But these fish are almost impossible to find outside an hour of the Mediterranean, which gives rise to yet another controversy. Can an acceptable version of bouillabaisse be fabricated hundreds or even thousands of miles from its homeland? Use monkfish and John Dory, two of the fish on the official list that are fairly readily available in the United States, plus American substitutes such as red snapper, halibut, porgy and, if you can find it, sea robin. Acceptable, all of them, but the result will only be an approximation. ❧

BOUILLABAISSE

Time: 4 hours

5 pounds scraps and bones from white-fleshed fish:
    halibut, red snapper, cod, monkfish

2 medium-to-large live blue crabs, chopped

½ cup extra virgin olive oil

½ cup thinly sliced fennel

2 leeks, well rinsed, white part only, thinly sliced

1 large onion, thinly sliced

3 shallots, finely chopped

1 whole head garlic, peeled and finely chopped

2 to 3 medium sea robins, skinned and filleted with
    bones reserved, or 1½ pounds monkfish fillets

¾ cup dry white wine

¼ cup pastis, preferably Ricard

1 bouquet garni (bay leaf, parsley and thyme tied in
    cheesecloth)

3 ripe tomatoes, chopped

3 tablespoons tomato paste

Pinch of cayenne pepper

Kosher salt

Large pinch of saffron

4 medium-to-large new red potatoes (about 1 pound), peeled
    and sliced ¼ inch thick

12 small mussels, scrubbed and debearded

12 littleneck clams, scrubbed

4 large sea scallops, cut in half horizontally

1 10-to-12-ounce red snapper, filleted and cut into four pieces

10 to 12 ounces monkfish, cut into medallions

Rouille (recipe page 326)

8 rounds of French bread, toasted and rubbed with garlic
    and olive oil

1. Place all fish bones and scraps, along with the crabs, in a large piece of cheesecloth and tie securely.

2. Heat the oil in a 10-to-12-quart pot. Add the fennel, leeks, onion, shallots and garlic along with sea robin or monkfish fillets and cook slowly, until

the vegetables are tender. Add wine and pastis. Place bag of fish bones and the bouquet garni in the pot and add tomatoes, tomato paste and about 3 quarts water to completely cover fish bones.

3. Season lightly with cayenne pepper and salt. Bring to a simmer and cook slowly for 2½ hours.

4. Remove bag of fish bones and bouquet garni and drain well. Pass the soup mixture through a food mill, add saffron, place in a large saucepan and simmer for 45 minutes to reduce it further. Adjust seasonings. Strain through several thicknesses of cheesecloth. There should be between 2½ and 3 quarts. This soup can be prepared in advance and frozen.

5. To make the stew, heat two cups of the fish soup in a saucepan and cook potatoes in it until they are tender. Remove the potatoes with a slotted spoon and wrap in foil to keep warm.

6. Transfer fish soup used for the potatoes to a 3-quart saucepan and place mussels and clams in it. Steam mussels and clams, covered, until they just open. Remove from the heat and keep covered.

7. Place 6 cups fish soup in a saucepan just large enough to hold scallops, red snapper and remaining monkfish cut in medallions. Heat soup to just barely simmering, add remaining seafood and cook until just done, removing each type of seafood to a warm dish as it is cooked.

8. To serve bouillabaisse, divide the potato rounds among four shallow, warmed soup plates. Arrange cooked fish over the potatoes, then divide mussels and clams, with the top shells removed, among the four plates.

9. Stir some of the soup used to poach the seafood into the rouille, then wisk the rouille back into the soup. Bring to barely simmering, then pour over the seafood in the plates and serve with croutons. Alternatively, the fish soup can be served as a first course, followed by the seafood and potatoes.

Yield: 4 servings
(Gilbert Le Coze, Le Bernardin,
New York City)

Any extra fish soup, including the soup used for mussels and clams, can be frozen for another use.

MEDITERRANEAN FISH SOUP

Time: 1¼ hours

To turn this recipe into bourride, a creamy, garlicky fish stew, stir all the garlic mayonnaise into the reheated soup in Step 5, then simmer two pounds of monkfish, in chunks, and a pound of shelled large shrimp in it until cooked, about 6 minutes, and serve with the toast on the side.

5 tablespoons extra virgin olive oil

3 pounds white-fleshed fish fillets (red snapper, grouper, monkfish, cod), cut into 1-inch squares

10 to 12 large cloves garlic, peeled

2 carrots, diced

2 small onions, peeled and diced

1 leek, white part only, diced

½ cup diced fennel bulb

½ cup Pernod or Ricard

2 tablespoons tomato paste

1 pinch saffron threads

1 bay leaf

Salt

1 6-inch piece of baguette, thinly sliced

1 cup mayonnaise

Freshly ground black pepper

Cayenne pepper

1. In a 6-quart casserole or soup pot over medium heat, warm 3 tablespoons olive oil. Add fish. Sauté until fish is opaque, transfer to a bowl, and set aside.

2. Dice 6 cloves garlic. Rinse and dry pot, and return to medium heat. Heat 1 tablespoon oil. Add diced garlic, carrots, onions, leek and fennel, and sauté until tender. Return fish to pot, and add Pernod. Take a long kitchen match, and carefully hold it to the contents (avert your face). When flames die, add 3 quarts water, tomato paste, saffron, bay leaf and salt to taste. Simmer uncovered, stirring occasionally, for 45 minutes.

3. Puree soup using a food mill or food processor. Strain mixture through a fine strainer into a clean pot, and set aside.

4. Rub baguette slices with a garlic clove, brush with remaining olive oil. and toast in oven or broiler. Mince 2 or more cloves garlic and mix with mayonnaise. Thin mayonnaise with a bit of soup.

5. To serve, reheat soup and season to taste with salt, pepper and cayenne pepper. Serve soup hot, each portion garnished with a spoonful of garlic mayonnaise and toasted baguette slices.

Yield: 6 to 8 servings

(Philippe Feret, Brasserie Julien, New York City)

CIOPPINO

Time: 2½ hours

8 tablespoons extra virgin olive oil

8 tablespoons unsalted butter

1 small onion, chopped

1 small stalk celery, chopped

1 medium carrot, chopped

1 small fennel bulb, chopped

½ red bell pepper, chopped

1 small leek, rinsed and chopped

1 28-ounce can crushed tomatoes

1 tablespoon tomato paste

1 tablespoon kosher salt

¼ teaspoon freshly ground pepper

1 tablespoon minced oregano leaves

1 tablespoon minced basil leaves

1 teaspoon minced thyme leaves

4 whole bay leaves

Dash cayenne pepper

1 teaspoon minced garlic

½ cup flour

½ pound halibut fillet, cut into 1-inch pieces

½ pound swordfish, cut into 1-inch pieces

8 large sea scallops

8 large shrimp, peeled and deveined

¼ pound bay shrimp (or other small shrimp), peeled

6 ounces lump crabmeat

1 cup dry white wine

8 littleneck or mahogany clams, scrubbed and steamed
   until opened

Minced parsley for garnish

8 slices French bread, spread with additional butter, seasoned
   with additional garlic and oregano, and toasted until golden
   brown (optional)

1. Place 4 tablespoons oil and 4 tablespoons butter in a heavy saucepan over medium heat. Add onion, and cook gently 1 minute; do not brown. Add celery, carrot, fennel, bell pepper and leek, and continue to cook gently 5 min-

utes, stirring. Add tomatoes, tomato paste, 2 cups water, salt, pepper and remaining herbs and spices. Simmer, partly covered, 2 hours, stirring occasionally.

2. In a large skillet over high heat, sauté garlic in remaining butter and oil for several seconds; do not brown. Lightly dust all seafood except clams with flour, and add to skillet. Sauté 2 minutes, until golden; then stir in white wine. Cook 1 minute, allowing wine to reduce.

3. Add tomato mixture, cover skillet and cook over low heat 7 minutes. Transfer to a large, shallow casserole. Place steamed clams on top, and garnish with minced parsley. Serve hot with toasted French bread.

Yield: 4 servings
(Tadich Grill, San Francisco, Calif.)

ASIAN SEAFOOD SOUP
Time: 45 minutes

1 cup cilantro leaves
5 cups light chicken or fish broth (recipe page 321)
1 jalapeño chili, halved and seeded
3 slices fresh ginger
Juice of 1 lime
1 stalk lemongrass, cut in 1-inch pieces
1 tablespoon soy sauce
Salt and pepper to taste
24 cleaned periwinkles, optional
24 small clams, scrubbed
12 mussels, scrubbed
8 razor clams or steamers, scrubbed
8 medium-to-large shrimp
½ pound sea scallops
2 cups pea shoots or bean sprouts
½ cup Chinese garlic chives, minced, or
    regular chives
2 limes, quartered

1. Mince half the cilantro and set aside. Simmer together the broth, jalapeño, ginger, half the lime juice, remaining cilantro, and lemon grass for 15 minutes. Strain into a deep sauté pan, large saucepan or casserole. Add soy sauce and salt and pepper; taste and correct seasoning.

2. Heat broth until it simmers, then add periwinkles. Cover and cook for five minutes. Add clams, mussels and razor clams, cover again and cook until the mollusks open, about 10 minutes. Add shrimp and scallops, and cook over medium heat, stirring, for about 2 minutes, until the shrimp turn pink.

3. Divide the pea shoots into the bottoms of 4 large bowls, then do the same with half of the garlic chives and half the remaining cilantro. Stir the remaining lime juice into the broth. Divide shellfish among the bowls and ladle in a portion of the broth. Garnish with the remaining cilantro and garlic chives, and serve with lime quarters.

Yield: 4 main-course servings
(Lynne Aronson)

RED FISH CHOWDER
Time: 30 minutes

> 2 tablespoons extra virgin olive oil
> 1 large onion, finely diced
> 6 cups fish broth (recipe page 321)
> 2 to 2½ pounds fish: monkfish, salmon and cod,
>   cut into 1-inch cubes
> 1 cup diced carrots
> 1 cup shelled peas
> 1 cup diced, peeled Yukon gold potatoes
> 2 cups diced, peeled tomatoes
> ½ teaspoon hot chili sauce, or to taste
> Salt
> 1 cup heavy cream, optional
> ¼ cup chopped fresh dill

1. In a large flameproof casserole or soup pot, warm oil over medium-low heat and add onions. Sauté until golden, about 5 minutes. Add fish broth,

and bring to a simmer. Add fish, raise the heat and bring to a boil. Immediately reduce heat to low, and simmer 5 minutes. Remove fish with slotted spoon.

2. Add tomatoes. Simmer 10 minutes. Add heavy cream, if using, and bring to a simmer. Return fish to pot.

3. Add hot chili sauce, and salt to taste. Place dill in bottom of a soup tureen. Pour soup over dill. Mix gently, and serve immediately.

Yield: 6 to 8 servings
(Richard W. Langer)

CREAMY SEAFOOD STEW
Time: 45 minutes

This recipe was adapted from an 18th-century cookbook.

1 cup medium-dry or fruity white wine
2 pounds mussels, scrubbed and debearded
1 tablespoon unsalted butter, or more to taste
1 large onion, sliced thin
1 bulb fennel, cored and sliced thin
3 shallots, sliced thin
12 jumbo shrimp, peeled and deveined
1 pound bay scallops (not calicos)
¼ cup amontillado sherry
½ cup heavy cream
Salt and freshly ground white pepper
A few drops lemon juice
1 tablespoon minced chives

1. Place ½ cup wine in a 3-quart saucepan and bring to a boil. Add mussels, cover and cook over medium heat until they open, about 10 minutes. Use a slotted spoon to remove mussels to a bowl. Strain cooking liquid through a fine sieve into a 2-cup measure. Add water to make 1½ cups, and set aside.

2. Rinse any grit out of the saucepan. Place it over medium heat to dry it. Add the butter. Add the onion, fennel and shallots, and sauté, stirring from time to time, until vegetables are tender but not brown.

3. Add remaining wine and cook over high heat until nearly all the wine evaporates. Add mussel liquid. Bring to a boil, and add shrimp. Cover, and cook about 5 minutes, until shrimp are not quite completely pink. Stir in scallops,

cover and cook about 3 minutes. Add the mussels in their shells, cover and cook 2 minutes longer, until the mussels are reheated and the other seafood is cooked.

4. Using a slotted spoon, transfer seafood, onions and fennel to a large, warmed, shallow serving bowl. Cover the bowl.

5. Bring the contents of the saucepan to a boil, add sherry and cream and cook briskly for 5 minutes or so, until the liquid has reduced and thickened somewhat. Season to taste with salt and pepper, and add the lemon juice. Swirl in a little additional butter if desired. Pour sauce over seafood, sprinkle with chives and serve.

Yield: 4 servings
(Walter Staib, City Tavern, Philadelphia, Pa.)

PEPPER POT WITH SHELLFISH AND SQUASH
Time: 2 hours

> 3 quarts chicken stock
> 3 cups dry white wine
> 4 ounces unsalted butter
> 3 cups sliced leeks (white part only)
> 2 butternut squash, peeled, seeded and cut in 1-inch cubes
> 1 cup long-grain rice
> 2 tablespoons grated fresh ginger
> 2 teaspoons minced seeded habañero chilis
> 3 heaping tablespoons tomato paste
> 1 cup heavy cream
> ½ teaspoon ground nutmeg
> 1 pound peeled shrimp
> 1 pound bay scallops
> 1 cup shucked oysters (about 12)
> Salt and pepper to taste

1. In a large stockpot, simmer chicken stock and wine for 5 minutes.

2. In a large skillet, melt butter and sauté leeks until softened. Transfer to pot with squash, rice, ginger, habañero and tomato paste, and bring to a boil. Lower heat, and simmer 40 minutes.

3. Add cream and nutmeg. Bring to a boil just to cook shellfish. Season with salt and pepper to taste, and serve.

Yield: 6 to 8 servings
(Fritz Blank, Deux Cheminées,
Philadelphia, Pa.)

SEAFOOD FRICASSEE

Time: 25 minutes

3 shallots, peeled and thinly sliced
¾ cup dry white wine
2 tablespoons minced celery
4 medium-size shrimp, peeled and deveined
8 medium-size sea scallops, tough tendon removed
6 ounces cleaned squid, sliced in rings
2 tablespoons cored, seeded and minced red bell pepper
2 ripe medium-size tomatoes, cored, seeded and chopped
4½ tablespoons unsalted butter
1 Scotch bonnet chili, seeded and minced
2 tablespoons chopped flat-leaf parsley
Salt and pepper to taste

1. In a saucepan over medium heat, cook shallots and white wine 2 minutes.

2. Add the celery and cook for 1 minute. Add shrimp, and cook for another minute. Add scallops and cook for 1 minute, stirring gently.

3. Turn heat to high. Add squid, red pepper and tomato. Cook, stirring, for 30 seconds.

4. Add butter, chili and parsley, and salt and pepper to taste. Remove from heat and set aside for 1 minute to allow flavors to meld.

5. Distribute the fricassee into 4 warm serving bowls. Serve with toasted sourdough bread.

Yield: 4 servings
(Marvin James, Chez Josephine,
New York City)

ASIAN RISOTTO

Time: 1 hour

2 tablespoons peanut oil

2 bulbs fresh lemongrass with 2 inches of leaves, chopped

1 tablespoon finely chopped ginger

2 cloves garlic, minced

½ cup finely chopped onion

1½ cups Italian arborio rice

1 cup dry white wine

2 cups fish broth (recipe page 321)

2 cups unsweetened coconut milk

1 tablespoon Vietnamese fish sauce (nuoc mam)

Juice of 2 limes

Red chili flakes to taste

1½ pounds medium shrimp, peeled and deveined

3 tablespoons chopped cilantro

Salt and freshly ground black pepper to taste

1. Heat oil in heavy saucepan. Add lemongrass, ginger, garlic and onion and sauté until tender but not brown. Add rice, cook briefly, then add half a cup of the wine. Stir and cook over medium heat until wine is absorbed.

2. In a separate saucepan, bring rest of the wine to a gentle simmer with fish broth, coconut milk, nuoc mam and lime juice. Add this mixture, about half a cup at a time, to the rice, stirring constantly. After 15 minutes or so the rice should be about al dente. Stir in chili flakes and shrimp and cook until shrimp turn pink. Then fold in cilantro and check seasonings, adding salt and pepper to taste. Serve at once.

Yield: 6 servings
(Florence Fabricant)

COCKLE AND SHRIMP PILAF

Time: 1¼ hours

> 3 tablespoons extra virgin olive oil
> 4 cups cockles or Manila clams, scrubbed
> 1 pound medium shrimp, peeled and deveined,
>   shells reserved
> 2 cloves garlic, minced
> 1 medium yellow onion, minced
> 1 medium tomato, diced
> 2 tablespoons orzo pasta
> 2 cups jasmine or basmati rice
> 1½ teaspoons kosher salt
> ¼ teaspoon freshly ground black pepper
> 10 to 12 large basil leaves, cut into fine strips, for garnish

1. Heat 1 tablespoon olive oil in a large pot over medium-high heat. Add cockles, cover and steam for 3 to 4 minutes, or until all the cockles are open. Remove cockles from the pot, and drain, reserving the broth. Set aside to cool.

2. Add another tablespoon of olive oil to the pot and set over high heat. Add shrimp shells, garlic and onion, and cook, stirring constantly, until the shells and vegetables are lightly browned, about 3 minutes. Add the reserved cockle broth, 6 cups water and the tomato. Reduce heat to a simmer and cook for 1 hour. Strain, reserve the broth and discard the solids. Measure the broth and add water to equal 4 cups. While broth is simmering, remove cockles from shells.

3. Place the remaining tablespoon of olive oil in a large saucepan set over medium heat. Add the orzo and cook, stirring constantly, until orzo is lightly browned, about 1 to 2 minutes. Add rice and stir. Add the 4 cups of broth, cover and simmer 15 minutes. Split the shrimp in half lengthwise. Add to the rice, along with shucked cockles, stir and season to taste with salt and pepper. Cook 5 minutes more, until shrimp are cooked and the rice is tender. (Add a few tablespoons water or broth if the rice looks too dry.) Set aside, covered, for 10 minutes.

4. Remove from the heat and toss gently with a fork. Garnish with the basil and serve.

Yield: 4 servings
(Molly O'Neill)

SEAFOOD PAELLA

Time: 1¼ hours

6 cups stock, half chicken and half seafood or shrimp
    (recipe page 322)

½ tablespoon saffron threads

12 monkfish medallions, about 1½ pounds total

4½ tablespoons extra virgin olive oil

Salt and freshly ground black pepper

1 onion, chopped

6 garlic cloves, chopped

¼ pound chorizo, skin removed, sliced ¼ inch thick

3 cups short-grain rice, preferably Spanish

2 cups fresh green peas

1 small red bell pepper, seared over flame to blacken skin,
    then peeled, cored and cut in strips

1 small green bell pepper, seared over flame, peeled,
    cored and cut in strips

18 large shrimp, peeled and deveined, about 1 pound

1 pound medium-size mussels

¼ cup thinly sliced scallions

1. Place stock in saucepan and bring to a simmer. Remove from heat and add saffron. Set aside. Rub monkfish with ½ tablespoon olive oil and season with salt and pepper. Set aside.

2. Preheat oven to 400 degrees. Heat remaining oil in 17-inch paella pan, placed over 2 burners if necessary, or divide between two pans. Add onion and garlic and cook over low heat until soft. Add chorizo and sauté briefly. Add rice and stir to coat.

3. Add stock and stir. Simmer 10 minutes. Check seasoning, adding salt and pepper if necessary. Stir in peas and place strips of peppers, alternating colors, around pan like spokes on a wheel. Place shrimp and monkfish around pan; add mussels, hinge-side down.

4. Place in oven and bake until shrimp and monkfish are cooked and mussels have opened, about 15 minutes. Discard any unopened mussels. Remove from oven, cover loosely with foil and set aside 10 minutes. Scatter scallions on top and serve.

Yield: 8 servings

(Eric Ripert, Le Bernardin, New York City)

Spanish short-grain rice, called bomba or calisparra rice, is similar to Italian arborio rice, which can be used in its place.

CHINESE NOODLES WITH SEAFOOD

Time: 20 minutes

> ¾ pound fresh Chinese egg noodles
> 2 tablespoons peanut oil
> 3 cloves finely chopped garlic
> 3 stalks kale, washed, ribs removed, leaves thinly
>   sliced
> 2 cups chicken stock, approximately
> 4 teaspoons black soy sauce
> 1 tablespoon light soy sauce
> 2 teaspoons oyster sauce
> 2 teaspoons rice vinegar
> Freshly ground black pepper to taste
> ½ pound medium shrimp, shelled and deveined
> ⅓ pound squid, cleaned and sliced thin
> 2 tablespoons chopped scallions

1. Blanch noodles in a pot of boiling water, and drain well. Heat oil in a skillet large enough to hold all ingredients; sauté garlic over medium heat until it begins to color.

2. Add kale, stock, soy sauces, oyster sauce, vinegar and pepper to taste.

3. Halve shrimp lengthwise. Add shrimp and squid to skillet, and stir well. Stir in noodles, and cook briefly. If dish is too dry, add more stock. To serve, sprinkle each portion with chopped scallions.

Yield: 3 or 4 servings
(Marian Burros)

FISH CHOUCROUTE

Time: 2½ hours

> 2½ pounds bulk sauerkraut
> 2 ounces salt pork, diced
> 2½ cups finely chopped onions
> 2 cloves garlic, minced

1 tart apple, peeled, cored and chopped

1½ cups fish broth (recipe page 321)

2 cups dry white still or sparkling wine

1 bay leaf

6 whole peppercorns

8 juniper berries

½ teaspoon fennel seeds

Salt and freshly ground black pepper

1 pound seafood sausage

6 medium boiling potatoes

½ pound smoked scallops

2 pounds monkfish, in 6 equal slices

2 tablespoons minced fresh dill

Dijon mustard mixed with prepared horseradish to taste

In Alsace, a number of chefs make choucroute with seafood, then serve a dry Riesling alongside.

1. Preheat oven to 325 degrees. Rinse sauerkraut and squeeze dry. Heat salt pork in a 4-quart casserole. When starting to brown, add onions, garlic and apple. Cook, stirring, over low heat until soft. Stir in sauerkraut. Add fish broth, wine, bay leaf, peppercorns, juniper berries, fennel seeds and salt and pepper to taste. Cover and place in oven 2 hours.

2. While the sauerkraut is cooking, place the seafood sausage in a pan, cover with water and simmer gently for 2 minutes. Set aside and allow to cool in the water. Place potatoes in pot of salted water, bring to a boil and simmer until tender, about 30 minutes. Drain and set aside. When cool enough to handle, slice in thick rounds, place in a bowl, cover with foil and set aside.

3. After the sauerkraut has cooked for 2 hours, taste it and add additional wine, stock and sauerkraut juice if necessary to moisten and season it. Tuck the scallops into the sauerkraut. Slice the seafood sausage into thick rounds and tuck the slices into the sauerkraut. Season the monkfish to taste with salt and pepper and place them on top. Place a sheet of foil or parchment directly on fish, cover the casserole and bake another 10 minutes. Place potatoes on foil or parchment, sprinkle with half the dill, cover casserole and bake 10 minutes longer.

5. Serve the choucroute directly from the casserole, sprinkled with remaining dill, with the potatoes and horseradish-mustard on the side, or transfer the choucroute to a platter, garnish with dill, surround with potatoes and serve with the horseradish-mustard on the side.

Yield: 6 servings

(Florence Fabricant)

QUICK GUMBO

Time: 1¼ hours

1 pound medium shrimp
2 stalks celery, chopped
3 bay leaves
4 tablespoons extra virgin olive oil
3 cups okra, sliced
4 cloves garlic, minced
1 large onion, diced
1 large green bell pepper, seeded and diced
1 28-ounce can tomatoes, drained and coarsely
   chopped
1 teaspoon salt
½ teaspoon cayenne pepper
½ teaspoon black pepper
1 teaspoon dried thyme
1 pound lump and/or backfin crabmeat
24 shucked oysters, with liquor

1. Peel and devein shrimp, place shells in a 6-quart stockpot and reserve shrimp. Add 12 cups water, 1 stalk celery and bay leaves and simmer 30 minutes over medium heat.

2. Heat 2 tablespoons olive oil in a large skillet, and sauté okra over gentle heat, stirring continuously, until dry, about 20 minutes. Remove. Add remaining oil and sauté remaining vegetables with salt, cayenne and pepper until soft.

3. Strain stock into clean pot, add sautéed vegetables and thyme and simmer 30 minutes. Add shrimp and turn off flame. Add crabmeat and oysters and fold in okra. Season with cayenne and pepper. Wait at least 5 minutes before serving over rice.

Yield: 6 to 8 servings
(Hodding Carter IV)

FRUTTI DI MARE (SEAFOOD SALAD)

Time: 3 hours

½ **pound cleaned calamari**
½ **pound sea scallops**
3 large cloves garlic, sliced paper thin
1 cup extra virgin olive oil, approximately
3 dried red chilies
3 large strands fresh seaweed (available in fish markets)
Zest of 2 lemons, finely slivered
Sea salt
¾ **pound cleaned scungilli**
1 pound large shrimp, peeled and deveined
1 pound cultivated mussels, scrubbed
12 littleneck clams, scrubbed, shucked with juice reserved
½ **cup lemon juice**
¼ **cup red wine vinegar**
1 small red onion, finely chopped
⅓ **cup minced flat-leaf parsley leaves**
⅓ **cup minced mint leaves**
1 teaspoon red chili flakes, or to taste
Freshly ground black pepper
Leaves from 6 sprigs parsley and 6 sprigs mint, for garnish

1. Remove and reserve tentacles from calamari. Slice calamari in thin rings. Remove and discard hard nugget of tendon on side of scallops. Slice scallops horizontally. Place garlic in 2 tablespoons olive oil in small dish.

2. About 2½ hours before serving time, place chilies, seaweed and half the lemon zest in a 6-quart pot. Add 4 quarts water. Bring to a boil and simmer 20 minutes. Stir in about 2 tablespoons sea salt, the water should be quite salty, almost like seawater.

3. Add scungilli and simmer about 45 minutes, until fairly tender. Remove with a slotted spoon, drain and set aside.

4. Add calamari rings and tentacles to pot, simmer 1 minute, remove with slotted spoon, drain and set aside. Add scallops to simmering water, cook about 2 minutes, until just done, remove, drain and set aside. Add shrimp to simmering water, cook about 2 minutes, until pink, remove, drain and set aside.

5. Bring liquid to a boil, add mussels and cook just until they open, about 5 minutes, remove, drain and set aside.

6. Place garlic and oil in small skillet. Cook over medium heat until softened but not colored. Place garlic and oil in large mixing bowl. Add clams and their juice, calamari, shrimp and scallops. Thinly slice scungilli and add it. Add remaining lemon zest, lemon juice, vinegar, onion, parsley, mint and ½ cup olive oil. Fold together gently. Add mussels in their shells, about 4 tablespoons olive oil, or to taste, chili flakes and black pepper. Check seasonings. Set aside, covered, about 1 hour.

7. Gently toss ingredients. Add more oil and seasonings if needed. Spoon into shallow serving bowl. Lightly bruise remaining mint and parsley between your fingers and scatter on top. Serve.

Yield: 6 generous appetizer servings
(Dave Pasternack, Esca, New York City)

ALASKAN HALIBUT AND SALMON GEFILTE FISH TERRINE

Time: 1½ hours, plus chilling

2 pounds halibut fillets, skinned and boned
1 pound salmon fillets, preferably Alaskan or Pacific, skinned and boned
3 tablespoons vegetable oil, preferably kosher for Passover, plus oil for mold
4 medium sweet onions, peeled and diced
4 large eggs
6 tablespoons matzo meal
1 tablespoon salt, or to taste
2 teaspoons ground white pepper
2 tablespoons sugar
1 tablespoon lemon juice
2 tablespoons snipped dill, plus more for garnish
2 large carrots, peeled and grated
Parsley for garnish
Prepared horseradish

1. Preheat oven to 325 degrees. Cut fish into large chunks, and place in bowl of a food processor. Pulse about 20 times to not puree, but grind fine. Transfer to bowl of electric mixer.

2. Heat oil in a large skillet, and sauté onions until soft and transparent. Let cool.

3. To the fish mixture, add the onions, eggs, 2 cups cold water, matzo meal, salt, white pepper, sugar and lemon juice. Beat in electric mixer with paddle attachment at medium speed for about 10 minutes. Add dill and carrots. Mix well.

4. Grease a 12-cup bundt mold. Spread mixture in mold, smooth the top with a spatula, and cover with foil. Place in a roasting pan filled with simmering water.

5. Bake for 1 hour, or until the center is solid. Cool until mold is cool to the touch. Run a knife around the edges. Carefully pour out any liquid and reserve. Place a flat serving plate on top of mold, then flip over, inverting onto the plate. If the mold doesn't come out easily, give the plate a shake. You should feel or hear it give. Alternatively, fish mixture can be formed into individual ovals and simmered in broth 45 minutes.

6. Refrigerate for several hours or overnight. Refrigerate liquid from mold. To serve, garnish with parsley, remaining dill, chilled fish liquid and horseradish.

Yield: 20 servings
(Joan Nathan)

INDIAN SEAFOOD SALAD

Time: 30 minutes

    2 cups cooked leftover fish or shellfish
    1 cucumber, peeled, seeded and diced
    2 medium-size ripe tomatoes, peeled, seeded and diced
    3 scallions, chopped
    ⅓ cup mayonnaise
    ⅓ cup plain yogurt
    2 tablespoons lime juice
    1 tablespoon minced fresh ginger
    ¼ cup chopped onion
    1 teaspoon ground cumin
    2 tablespoons chopped mint, plus 4 sprigs for garnish
    1 tablespoon chopped cilantro
    Salt and freshly ground black pepper
    1 tablespoon extra virgin olive oil
    1 teaspoon Dijon mustard
    2 cups baby spinach or arugula, washed and dried, heavy
       stems removed
    Mango chutney, optional

1. Break or cut seafood into chunks and put in a bowl. Gently toss with cucumber, tomatoes and scallions.

2. Mix mayonnaise, yogurt, a tablespoon of lime juice, the ginger, onion, cumin, mint and cilantro together. Reserve a tablespoon of this mixture and fold the rest into the seafood mixture. Season to taste with salt and pepper.

3. Beat reserved dressing with remaining lime juice, the olive oil and mustard. Toss the spinach or arugula with this dressing.

4. Put a bed of spinach or arugula salad on each of four plates. Divide seafood mixture among the four plates, garnish with mint sprigs and serve, with Indian mango chutney like Major Grey's, if desired, on the side.

Yield: 4 servings
(Florence Fabricant)

SUMMER FISH CAKES

Time: 40 minutes, plus chilling

> 3 tablespoons extra virgin olive oil
> ⅔ cup finely chopped onion
> ½ cup finely chopped red bell pepper
> 3 cups cooked fish fillets (flounder, fluke, whitefish, cod,
>   sole, salmon)
> ½ cup mayonnaise
> 1 tablespoon fresh lemon juice
> 1 tablespoon finely minced parsley
> Salt and cayenne pepper to taste
> 1 large egg
> ½ cup dry bread crumbs
> Tartar sauce (recipe page 328), or salsa

1. Heat 1 tablespoon of oil in a skillet, add onion and pepper and sauté until tender but not brown.

2. Break fish into small chunks in a bowl. Fold in onion and pepper, then fold in mayonnaise, lemon juice, parsley and salt and pepper to taste. Form mixture into eight cakes.

3. Beat egg in a shallow bowl. Put bread crumbs on a plate. Dip each fish cake first into the egg to coat, then into bread crumbs, spooning them over the fish cake to coat it. Handle fish cakes gently. Refrigerate fish cakes, covered, 1 hour.

4. Heat remaining oil in a nonstick skillet. Sauté the fish cakes in the oil over medium-low heat until golden, turning once. Serve with tartar sauce or salsa on the side.

Yield: 4 servings
(Florence Fabricant)

CHAPTER FIVE

Stocks and Sauces

FISH BROTH (COURT BOUILLON)
Time: 30 minutes

> **3 pounds fresh fish bones, including the heads
>   (gills removed)**
> **1½ cups dry white wine**
> **1 cup sliced celery**
> **1 cup sliced onions**
> **1 cup sliced leeks (green portion only)**
> **4 sprigs parsley**
> **1 bay leaf**
> **1 teaspoon dried thyme**
> **6 whole peppercorns**

1. Rinse bones and chop into thirds.
2. Combine all the ingredients in a kettle or saucepan. Add 6 cups water. Bring the mixture to a boil, reduce heat and simmer for 20 minutes, skimming from time to time. Strain and discard solids.

Yield: 6 cups

(Pierre Franey)

SHRIMP OR LOBSTER STOCK

Time: 1½ hours

> Shells from 24 shrimp or bodies and shells of 2
>   1-pound lobsters
> Salt
> 1 cup dry white wine
> 10 black peppercorns
> 10 coriander seeds, lightly crushed
> 2 bay leaves
> 4 sprigs parsley
> 4 sprigs tarragon
> 2 lemons, halved

1. In a large pot, combine shells, 2 quarts water and 3 tablespoons salt. Bring to a boil over high heat, reduce heat to low and simmer 20 minutes. Skim frequently.

2. Remove pot from heat and steep until cool.

3. Strain broth into another large pot, and bring to a boil over high heat. Add wine, peppercorns, coriander seeds, bay leaves, parsley, tarragon and lemons. Lower heat and simmer 15 minutes. Strain through a fine sieve, a coffee filter or a colander lined with cheesecloth.

Yield: 6 cups
(Florence Fabricant)

DASHI

Time: 20 minutes

Dashi is a basic Japanese broth that is excellent for poaching seafood or for making soups.

> 1½ strips konbu (a type of kelp)
> 1 scant cup dried bonito flakes

1. Place konbu in saucepan with 4 cups water over medium heat. Slowly heat to not quite boiling. Adjust heat so this takes about 10 minutes. Immediately remove konbu and discard. Add bonito flakes. Bring to a boil and remove

from heat. When flakes sink to bottom of pot, strain broth through fine sieve lined with coffee filter or paper towel. Transfer broth to clean saucepan.

Yield: 3 cups
(Florence Fabricant)

COCKTAIL SAUCE

Time: 15 minutes

1 cup prepared chili sauce or ketchup
1 tablespoon prepared horseradish, or more to taste
¼ teaspoon kosher salt, or to taste
1½ teaspoons Tabasco sauce, or to taste
1 tablespoon lemon juice, or to taste
1 teaspoon gin, optional
Freshly ground black pepper to taste

1. In a medium-size bowl, combine the chili sauce, horseradish, salt, Tabasco, lemon juice and gin.

2. Season to taste with additional horseradish, lemon juice, Tabasco, salt and pepper. Cover and refrigerate.

Yield: about 1 cup
(Rick Moonen, Oceana, New York City)

ASIAN DIPPING SAUCE

Time: 1 hour

1 tablespoon finely minced fresh ginger
1 tablespoon finely minced scallions
1½ teaspoons light soy sauce
4 tablespoons rice vinegar

1. Combine ginger, scallions, soy sauce and vinegar in a dish. Allow to marinate one hour.

2. Serve with fresh shellfish.

Yield: enough for 24 oysters or clams
(Florence Fabricant)

SWEET PEANUT-CHILI DIPPING SAUCE
Time: 15 minutes

> 1 cup white vinegar
> ¾ cup granulated sugar
> ¼ cup light brown sugar, loosely packed
> 1 teaspoon salt
> 2 large shallots, peeled and minced
> 1 large cucumber, peeled, seeded and diced
> 4 small, fresh green Thai chilies or 2 or 3 serrano chilies,
>   minced, or to taste
> ½ cup roasted unsalted peanuts, chopped
> 4 sprigs cilantro, chopped, to yield ⅓ cup loosely packed,
>   or to taste

1. Heat vinegar, both sugars and salt in a small saucepan just until simmering. Stir well to dissolve sugars. Let cool, or refrigerate.

2. Just before serving, add remaining ingredients and mix well.

Yield: 2 cups
(Jean-Georges Vongerichten, Vong, New York City)

CLASSIC MAYONNAISE
Time: 5 minutes

> 1 egg yolk
> 1 teaspoon Dijon or English mustard
> 2 teaspoons lemon juice

Sea salt

1 cup extra virgin olive oil, peanut oil or grape-seed oil

1. In a small bowl, whisk together egg yolk, mustard, lemon juice and a large pinch salt. Beginning a drop at a time, whisk in oil. As it emulsifies, add oil a little faster, in a slow, steady stream.

2. When mixture is thick, taste and adjust seasoning. It should be highly seasoned.

Yield: about 1¼ cups
(Amanda Hesser)

LEMON MAYONNAISE

Time: 10 minutes

1 large egg
2 teaspoons Dijon mustard
Salt to taste
⅓ cup grape-seed oil
⅓ cup fruity extra virgin olive oil
2 tablespoons Champagne vinegar
1 tablespoon lemon juice

1. Place egg, mustard, salt and ¼ cup grape-seed oil in blender. Blend at high speed until completely mixed.

2. With the blender running, slowly pour in olive oil through a cover; blend completely. Blend vinegar and lemon juice, slowly add remaining oil and blend again.

Yield: about ¾ cup
(Michael Otsuka, Verbena, New York City)

Mayonnaise is the basis of many sauces, including rémoulade. For sauce gribiche, it is not made the usual way, with raw egg yolks, but with hard-cooked eggs mixed almost to creaminess in a vinai-grette. Tartar sauce is similar, made with capers and cornichons and herbs, but without the eggs. Ravigote, also seasoned with capers, cornichons and herbs, can be made with either a mayonnaise or vinaigrette base.

AIOLI

Time: 10 minutes

> **1 large egg**
> **1 large egg yolk**
> **2 cloves garlic, minced**
> **½ teaspoon kosher salt**
> **A few grinds of white pepper**
> **1 teaspoon lemon juice**
> **¾ cup extra virgin olive oil**
> **¼ cup safflower oil**

1. Combine the egg, yolk, garlic, salt, pepper and lemon juice in a blender. Process briefly to blend.

2. With the motor running, slowly pour in the oils. Transfer to a bowl and refrigerate until ready to use.

Yield: 1 cup
(Molly O'Neill)

ROUILLE

Time: 20 minutes

> **1 small red chili pepper, seeded and minced**
> **10 strands saffron**
> **4 slices fresh white sandwich bread, crusts removed**
> **¼ cup fish soup or broth (recipe page 321)**
> **4 cloves garlic**
> **¼ cup extra virgin olive oil**

1. Crumble chili pepper and saffron in a small bowl and moisten with 1 tablespoon warm water. Set aside.

2. Break up white bread, place it in a food processor and process to make fine bread crumbs. Transfer crumbs to a small bowl and moisten with fish soup. Do not rinse food processor.

3. With processor running, drop garlic cloves in through the feed tube, then add chili and saffron mixture. Turn off processor and scrape sides of container. Add bread crumbs and process to combine.

4. With the processor running, slowly drizzle in the olive oil and continue processing several minutes, until mixture is thick and smooth, like mayonnaise.

Yield: about ⅔ cup
(Gilbert le Coze, Le Bernardin, New York City)

RÉMOULADE SAUCE
Time: 10 minutes

½ cup mayonnaise, preferably homemade
1½ teaspoons minced capers
6 drops Tabasco
1 teaspoon tomato paste
½ teaspoon minced tarragon
½ teaspoon Dijon mustard
3 grinds white pepper

1. Combine all ingredients in a small bowl and mix thoroughly.
2. Cover and refrigerate until ready to use.

Yield: ½ cup
(Molly O'Neill)

TARTAR SAUCE

Time: 5 minutes

> 1 cup mayonnaise
> 3 tablespoons capers, well drained
> 3 tablespoons finely chopped cornichons or sweet pickle relish
> 1 tablespoon minced parsley
> 1 teaspoon lemon juice
> 1 hard-cooked egg, minced (optional)

1. Stir mayonnaise and fold in capers, pickles, parsley and lemon juice.
2. Just before serving, fold in optional egg.

Yield: 1½ cups
(Florence Fabricant)

ROMESCO SAUCE

Time: 30 minutes

> ½ cup chopped blanched almonds
> 4 tablespoons extra virgin olive oil
> ½ cup finely chopped onion
> 4 cloves garlic, minced
> 2 large red bell peppers, seeded and chopped
> 2 tablespoons red wine vinegar
> 1 ripe tomato, seeded and chopped
> Salt to taste
> Red chili flakes to taste

1. Place a heavy skillet over medium-high heat, add the almonds and cook, stirring, until they are toasted. Remove them from the skillet. Place them in a food processor, grind them fine and leave them in the food processor.

2. Add the oil to the skillet, and when it is hot, add the onion. Sauté until it is golden, then stir in the garlic. Add the peppers, 1 cup water and vinegar, lower the heat and cook gently about 15 minutes, until the peppers are tender.

Stir in the tomato and season the mixture with salt and chili flakes. Remove from heat.

    3. Add the mixture to the almonds in the food processor and puree. Taste for seasoning and serve at room temperature.

Yield: 2 cups

(Florence Fabricant)

GREEN SAUCE FOR FISH
Time: 15

3 cloves garlic
1 tablespoon capers
¼ cup finely minced red onion
½ cup, packed, fresh basil leaves
½ cup, packed, flat-leaf parsley leaves
3 tablespoons extra virgin olive oil
Juice of 1 lemon
Salt and pepper to taste

    1. Turn on a food processor and drop garlic into machine through the feed tube. When garlic is finely minced, add capers, onion, basil leaves and parsley through the feed tube. Drizzle in olive oil and lemon juice.

    2. Transfer to a bowl and season to taste with salt and pepper.

Yield: 1 cup

(Florence Fabricant)

MOROCCAN CHERMOULA

Time: 10 minutes

    1 tablespoon minced cilantro leaves
    1 tablespoon minced flat-leaf parsley leaves
    2 cloves garlic, minced
    ¼ teaspoon hot Hungarian paprika
    2 teaspoons ground cumin
    1 teaspoon ground coriander
    ¼ teaspoon cinnamon
    Salt and freshly ground black pepper
    ¼ cup extra virgin olive oil
    3 tablespoons lemon juice

1. Combine cilantro, parsley, garlic, paprika, cumin, coriander, cinnamon, salt and pepper.
2. Add oil and lemon juice.

Yield: ½ cup
(Florence Fabricant)

LEMON HERB VINAIGRETTE

Time: 10 minutes

    ¼ cup lemon juice
    2 teaspoons Dijon mustard
    1 large shallot, minced
    Kosher salt and ground black pepper
    ⅔ cup olive oil
    2 tablespoons chopped tarragon
    1 tablespoon chopped parsley
    1 tablespoon chopped basil
    1 tablespoon thinly sliced chives
    3 teaspoons capers

1. In a medium bowl, combine lemon juice, mustard and shallots. Season with salt and pepper. Slowly add olive oil, whisking to emulsify. Stir

in tarragon, parsley, basil, chives and capers. Season to taste with salt and pepper.

2. Serve with poached fish.

Yield: 6 servings
(Amanda Hesser)

LEMON-BASIL BEURRE BLANC
Time: 20 minutes

1 cup loosely packed lemon basil or regular
    basil leaves
¼ cup heavy cream
¾ cup white wine
¼ cup white wine vinegar
¼ cup lemon juice
⅓ cup minced shallots
12 tablespoons cold unsalted butter
Salt to taste

1. Puree basil leaves and heavy cream in a blender and reserve. In a medium saucepan, bring wine, vinegar, lemon juice and shallots to a simmer, uncovered. When liquid has been reduced to a about one-half cup, turn off heat and whisk in the cream/basil mixture.

2. Over low heat, add butter to mixture one tablespoon at a time, whisking continuously until mixture is creamy and thickened. Strain sauce and add salt to taste. Keep warm by placing saucepan in another pan of barely simmering water. If necessary to warm the sauce, use low heat.

Yield: about 1 cup
(Florence Fabricant)

LEMON BUTTER SAUCE

Time: 15 minutes

This sauce is similar to a hollandaise and accomplishes much the same purpose with fish, but it is more stable and less tricky to prepare.

> 4 tablespoons minced shallots
> 1½ cups good-quality white wine like Riesling or chardonnay
> ¼ cup lemon juice
> 4 tablespoons unsalted butter
> ¼ cup all-purpose flour
> 6 tablespoons chilled unsalted butter, sliced thin
> ¼ teaspoon salt
> ⅛ teaspoon white pepper
> 1 clove garlic, minced
> 2 teaspoons chopped parsley

1. In a small mixing bowl, combine the shallots, wine and lemon juice. Set aside within reach of stove.

2. In a medium sauté pan over low heat, melt 4 tablespoons butter. Add flour, and stir vigorously with a whisk until well combined. Raise heat to medium high, and continue to stir until flour is nut brown but not burned, about 5 minutes. Add wine mixture, and whisk until smooth and thickened, about 1 minute. Reduce heat to medium low. Simmer until reduced to about ¼ cup, about 2 minutes.

3. Remove pan from heat and gradually whisk in chilled sliced butter, stirring constantly to keep fat from separating. Add salt and pepper. Keep warm, but do not boil. Add garlic and parsley just before serving. Serve hot over grilled or broiled trout.

Yield: 2 cups, 6 to 8 servings
(Molly O'Neill)

AVOCADO BUTTER

Time: 10 minutes

> 1 ripe Hass avocado
> 1 tablespoon fresh lime juice
> 3 tablespoons extra virgin olive oil
> Salt

1. Halve and pit avocado, remove flesh, chop and place in food processor or blender with 1 tablespoon lime juice. Process until smooth, scraping sides of container from time to time.

2. With machine running, slowly drizzle in 3 tablespoons olive oil. Scrape container and process briefly until well blended. With food processor mixture may look slightly separated. If so, transfer to a bowl and beat vigorously with a small whisk about 30 seconds or until mixture is smooth. If using a blender you may have to scrape container more often but mixture will emulsify better.

3. Season to taste with salt. If not using immediately, cover and refrigerate up to 1 hour. If mixture starts to look separated, whisk again before serving.

Yield: 1 cup

(Mark Militello, Mark's Las Olas,
Fort Lauderdale, Fla.)

GARLIC CONFIT
Time: 1 hour, 20 minutes

4 heads garlic, separated into cloves and peeled
1 cup extra virgin olive oil

1. Place garlic cloves in a 1-quart saucepan, and cover with cold water. Bring to a boil, and strain off water. Repeat this process two more times.

2. In saucepan, pour oil over garlic cloves. Place over lowest heat possible, so that the oil is barely at a simmer. Cook for about 1 hour. Allow to cool completely, then transfer to an airtight container. Garlic may be stored, refrigerated, for up to 2 weeks.

Yield: about 2½ cups, including oil
(Marian Burros)

INDEX